CITIZEN SUMMITRY

*Keeping the Peace
When It Matters Too Much
to be Left to Politicians*

Whatever you do, you need courage.
Whatever course you decide upon, there is
always someone to tell you you are wrong.
There are always difficulties arising which
tempt you to believe that your critics are
right. To map out a course of action and
follow it to an end, requires some of the same
courage which a soldier needs. Peace has its
victories, but it takes brave men to win them.

—Ralph Waldo Emerson

CITIZEN SUMMITRY

Keeping the Peace
When It Matters Too Much
to be Left to Politicians

An Ark Communications Institute book

edited by

Don Carlson and Craig Comstock

Published by Jeremy P. Tarcher, Inc.
Los Angeles

Distributed by St. Martin's Press
New York

Library of Congress Cataloging-in-Publication Data

Citizen summitry.

"An Ark Communications Institute book."
"September 1986."
1. Peace—Citizen participation. 2. United States—
Foreign relations—Soviet Union—Citizen participation.
3. Soviet Union—Foreign relations—United States—
Citizen participation. I. Carlson, Don, 1932–
II. Comstock, Craig. III. Ark Communications
Institute (U.S.)
JX1953.C55 1986   327.1'72'0973   86-14371
ISBN 0-87477-406-3

Editor-in-chief
Ark Communications Institute
250 Lafayette Circle
Lafayette, CA 94549

Produced by Schuettge & Carleton
Composition by Classic Typography
Cover Design by Norm Ung
Manufactured in the United States of America
10 9 8 7 6 5 4 3 2 1
First Edition

CONTENTS

1 Going Beyond War   8

Danger and Opportunity
Don Carlson   15

What Is It About?
Thomas Powers   29

A Longing for Something Better
Norman Cousins   34

A Better Game Than War
Robert Fuller   38

2 Getting to Know
the Other Side   58

Letter to a Russian
Larry Levinger   65

*Through the Eyes
of a Citizen Diplomat*
Joel Schatz   76

*Meeting the Soviets
Face-to-face: News Reports*
Craig Staats
Jennifer Donovan   99

Effectiveness of the New Diplomats
Michael H. Shuman
Gale Warner   112

Space-Bridge Pioneers
Jim Garrison
David Landau
Ralph Macdonald   150

3 Building a Space-Bridge: a Soviet Contribution 189

An Experience of Unity
B. V. Rauschenbach 197

A Mirror for Humanity
Joseph Goldin 203

Frame for a Mirror: an Architect's View
Alexei Gutnov 209

One Billion
Ales Adamovich 213

Citizen Tele-diplomacy
John Nicolopoulos 217

A Planetary Attraction
Alexander Lipkov 226

plus brief comments by
G. Ivanitsky, Arkady Raikin, S. Volynets

4 Transforming Our Consciousness 232

A Positive Vision in a Cynical Age
Michael Nagler 238

As in Health, So in Peace
Fritjof Capra 246

Switching on the Light
Marilyn Ferguson 254

Nuclear Weapons and the Expansion of Consciousness
Willis W. Harman 266

An Evolutionary View
Roger Walsh 285

5 Jumping Ahead and Looking Back at the Future — 297

Spinning Peace Scenarios
Mark Sommer — 302

Enlivening Our Social Imagination
Elise Boulding — 309

Against Our Will Comes Wisdom
Richard D. Lamm — 329

Acting Globally through Your Locality
Michael H. Shuman — 340

On-line with Conflict Management
Thomas Fehsenfeld — 355

The Great Turning
Craig Schindler
Toby Herzlich — 367

6 A Final Word

Dance Your Troubles Away
Craig Comstock — 383

Prevailing in Spite of It All
The Editors — 386

All introductions are by Craig Comstock

Quotations

Throughout four of the five sections in this book there are quotations from a variety of sources arranged in the margins. In every case these passages were chosen by the editors, *not* by the authors of the chapters alongside which they appear. Some of the long quotations are drawn from *Securing Our Planet*, a companion to this book, also prepared under the auspices of Ark Communications Institute (ACI). Other long quotations are taken from two radio programs, "Beyond the Boundaries" and "A Better Game Than War," which feature various contributors to the ACI books and which are available on a 60 minute audio cassette. (See ordering instructions at end of this book.) A number of other long quotations, such as those by Chellis Glendinning and LaUna Huffines, were prepared especially for this book. The many short passages are from a wide variety of sources and are favorites of Don Carlson, who proposed using a format that would allow extensive use of marginal quotations and who supervised their placement.

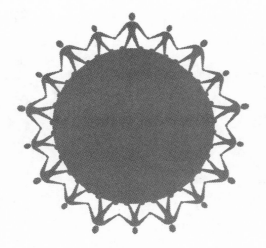

Going Beyond War

1

The crisis today in human affairs is represented not by the absence of human capacity, but by the failure to recognize that the capacity exists. . . . What gives hope its power is not the accumulation of demonstrable facts, but the release of human energies generated by the longing for something better.
—*Norman Cousins*

One place I find hope is in the growing number of people who have suddenly come to the realization that because of the failure of "experts" we must, as ordinary people, come to the rescue of our collective destiny. . . . While "experts" play out the tired old strategies, new and powerful ideas for easing planetary tensions are appearing everywhere.
—*Don Carlson*

Nothing will ruin the country if the people themselves undertake its safety. Nothing can save it if they leave it in any hands but their own.
—*Daniel Webster*

Design by Norm Ung

I like to believe that people in the long run are going to do more to promote peace than are governments. Indeed, I think that people want peace so much that one of these days governments had better get out of their way and let them have it.
—*Dwight D. Eisenhower*

I look at the arms race, and war itself, not in terms of a technical fix or some clever treaty that would reduce the number of weapons, which ultimately will be required, but rather at a different level having to do with the relationship among, and the psychologies of, people.
—*Robert Fuller*

In the field of foreign affairs, ordinary people often feel powerless, but this book describes ways in which you can help, personally, to transform the nature of our relationship with the Soviet Union, and our identity as a people. And you can enjoy doing it. The method does not necessarily involve marching with a sign or writing to Congress or to your newspaper; it does not require sending a check or attending a growth seminar. You do not need to wait for somebody else to decide, to discover, to act. Above all, though the process is crucial to our survival, its nature is not grim. It can amplify our vital energies. Along with advances in science, this transformation can fairly be called the major adventure of our time.

The basic inspiration for this book came from Don Carlson, a successful entrepreneur. Realizing that nearly all "peace books" were actually portrayals of the peril of war, or advice on how to reduce various dangers, he suggested taking a different approach. Why not a book in which readers could imagine reaching outward to the other side and, at the same time, going inside to deal with their own "shadows"? In short, why not a positive book that would show some initiatives that work? *Citizen Summitry* tells how you can get involved; a companion volume, *Securing Our Planet*, presents some of the policy alternatives in more detail.*

* *Securing Our Planet*, edited by Don Carlson and Craig Comstock (Jeremy P. Tarcher, Inc./St. Martin's Press, 1986).

Citizen summitry is the application of individual initiative to what are normally considered the hightest matters of state—relations with an adversary. As an ordinary citizen you engage in summitry not by wangling an invitation to the next meeting with Gorbachev, but by deciding that peace matters too much to be left only to politicians. Of course politicians will always be central to any decisions about war, defense, and "national security"; it is they, with the diplomats and military officers, who negotiate treaties, make alliances, take actions affecting the terms of international trade, and deploy armed forces. But in our fascination with this ruling elite, magnified as they are by the contemporary media, we may easily forget our own sources of creativity.

Fifty-four percent of our citizens agree with the statement that "when it comes to America's national security, the President has access to secret information and we should go along with what he decides." Fifty-six percent say that "the idea of nuclear war is so horrible, I try not to think about it." And what is the result of going along with the national security apparatus and of turning away from any independent thought about the nuclear danger? Thirty-eight percent of Americans believe that the "likelihood of nuclear war in the next ten years is (very or fairly) great."** This statistic staggers me. It says that, on the average, if I'm in a checkout line with four other people, or at lunch, or in a car, two of us expect to be killed by a nuclear "exchange" within the decade.

When I was born, in early 1939, the world still regarded the bombing of civilians as scandalous and monstrous, which is the point of Picasso's painting about the Fascist air attack on the Spanish village of Guernica. About the time that Hitler was defeated and Hiroshima was bombed, I started kindergarten. The year I went to college, Sputnik went up, dramatizing the potential for intercontinental ballistic missiles. Shortly after my graduation came the Cuban missile crisis, during which Jack and Bobby Kennedy had their famous chat

**The Public Agenda Foundation in collaboration with The Center for Foreign Policy Development at Brown University, *Voter Options on Nuclear Arms Policy*, 1984, page 40.

in the Rose Garden about the 50/50 odds of nuclear war. In the time it took my generation to grow up, the world went from the old distinction between civilians and combatants to the wrecking of entire cities, and then to standing threats to wreck whole countries.

Many people feel quietly hopeless about this situation. One group appears to be blinded by denial, while another group would acknowledge that if we continue on the same path we will go over the cliff and yet they have no alternative to offer. Taking these two responses together, it's as if people are saying, "It will never happen and, besides, we can't stop it." (A decade ago members of this second group would say that "if" nuclear war were to occur, such-and-such "would" be the result. Now they often say that "when" it occurs, such-and-such "will" be the result.) A third group, while sharing a sense of danger, just soberly assumes that we can muddle through— "After all, we've had no world war for 40 years," they say, and "Nobody would be so crazy."

I have sympathy with each of these responses. My mind has often wanted to deny the reality that faces us. And when I have jumped to the other extreme, to the discipline of facing the most ominous facts, it's been easy to feel fatalistic. When this internal oscillation dampens down, I, too, have come to feel, with most of my fellow citizens, that we'll somehow manage to avoid the worst. After all, what would be the sense of war? Surely leaders will behave adroitly enough to keep the peace. Yet in 1914 and 1939 the politicians failed disastrously, and these were not the most recent failures.

It's an odd feature of our age that the nuclear system remains almost completely invisible to the ordinary citizen so long as it's not activated. People grow up, go to college, get a job, marry, travel, and do business, all without ever seeing a nuclear warhead, a missile, or even a bomber, much less a bomb test. Like a hidden cancer, the nuclear system has grown without our paying attention. Until it kills us, we may hardly notice it. Even the taxes we pay for it are not especially severe, as compared with other aspects of the Pentagon budget. It remains almost wholly out of sight.

Imagine my shock when upon walking around a corner one day in Ohio I saw, at the end of a long hallway, an atomic bomb.

Going Beyond War

Since I was visiting an Air Force museum, I expected to see planes of all kinds, but I was not prepared to see a model of "Fat Boy," one of the bombs dropped on Japan in 1945. There it sat, like a heavy metal egg with fins. That day I happened to have rented a trailer, and I recall thinking that the bomb replica would fit in it. Yet the real thing had destroyed a city. And I knew that contemporary bombs were both much smaller and vastly more destructive.

As the son of an engineer, I was comforted to recall that systems designed and operated by rational, highly trained specialists are not supposed to fail. Surely the system of mutual "deterrence" would persist, without even a momentary lapse, for centuries. Yet Three Mile Island was not intended to go out of control, nor did the Soviets believe their reactor near Kiev would ever melt down.

In this book my co-editor Don Carlson and I start with what we hope is realism in analyzing the situation, combined with a hopefulness in imagining alternatives. As Carlson makes clear in his opening chapter, the danger is quite severe, but so is the opportunity to transform the system that has brought us to this point. In a sense, the bomb is a kind of stern teacher, leading us to grasp shortcomings in our customary way of thinking about our adversary, ourselves, and our future. In short, something urgently needs to change, but we have the capacity to do what's necessary.

So far this has not been a common view. As the survey already cited suggests, most people either minimize the threat of the bomb or of the Soviets, collapse into fatalism, or fall into a "pragmatic" tradition of assuming that if a system has worked—or not totally failed—in the past, it will probably continue to work. In contrast, it is one of Carlson's bracing habits, when told that something has to happen or that he has to act in a certain way, to ask, "Why?" When told that we can't do something, he often says, "Why not?" And when assured that something is the case, he likes to inquire, "What makes you think so?"

Many people will agree with our grim view of the current nuclear system, but within this group, only a slender fraction sees a way out. One way that *we* see is to appeal to the American tradition of individual action, instead of waiting for governments to alter the system that they have, in large measure, created. We are familiar, of course, with the idea that an aroused citizenry should elect leaders who embody its higher values. But we are talking about forms of action that go far beyond electoral politics, crucial as it is.

In our view, almost any government, even a democratic one, is structurally ill-adapted to transform hostility into peace. One of the primary duties of government is to identify and defend against enemies. As soon as a pair of countries begin to identify one another as enemies, as the U.S. and the Soviet Union did long ago, they generally take steps that confirm and amplify the initial fears, thus starting a familiar cycle. If a government fails to be vigilant in "threat assessment" or to procure weapons with which to threaten the enemy in return, it does not deserve to govern.

So who is left to create the conditions for peace?

The government of a large state contains many parts representing various interests, traditions, and responsibilities. While one part is reacting to what it perceives as threats, another part may be building a more constructive relation with a foreign country. However, we suggest that the main source of peaceful initiatives is ordinary citizens and voluntary associations or, as they are now often called, "nongovernmental organizations." This is citizen summitry—the application of nongovernmental energies to the highest matters of state.

In this book Carlson and I, as co-editors, present four types of citizen summitry. One is the rapidly growing phenomenon of people outside the government—call them "unofficials"—making contact with their counterparts abroad and creating a network of constructive relations. A second variety is international exchanges via "space-bridges," which are live, two-way television conversations, transmitted by space satellite and often displayed on large screens, with simultaneous translation.

A third kind of citizen summitry is internal. It takes place not in a foreign country or on a TV screen, but in the heart and mind of the participant. It consists of transforming our consciousness about who we are, and what kinds of relations are possible. Just as we talk with others, so we need to learn to converse with neglected or less developed aspects of ourselves. In the course of doing this we can reach new summits on the inside, which then allow us to act differently on the outside.

When I was a child, my mother took me into New York City to watch a performance of the popular radio program "Let's Pretend." There I learned that the thundering hoofbeats of the hero's mount were produced by a technician pounding coconut shells on pebbles, and the toasty fires were simulated by crackling cellophane. Likewise, the dashing characters who played such a role in my imagination were, in reality, actors holding scripts and clustered around a microphone. But it made me love the show even more, that ordinary people could, with such slender means, create an entire world. In a similar spirit, a fourth variety of citizen summitry is a method for overcoming fatalism by imagining the future we want, pretending that we are already there, and then writing a history of how the transition occured.

Before sketching these various methods, we sample some prevailing attitudes toward the threat of war. In an imaginary dinner party Carlson assembles warnings from some of the most experienced, best informed people of our time. Powers portrays the tragic and pointless nature of the hostility between the superpowers. Then, like a rainbow appearing after a thunderstorm, Cousins makes a sunny case for hope. And Fuller, in searching for "a better game than war," suggests the range of possibilities that opens up as soon as we go beyond denial, fatalism, and attempts to "manage" a system that urgently needs to be transformed.

This book argues that, although we are now in serious danger, our civilization does not have to perish in a nuclear war. In fact, we can have a future much better than most of us usually allow ourselves to imagine. Peace can be kept. We don't have to wait for somebody else, such as a leader, to provide the initiative; everyone can take part. Getting there will be half the fun. It will involve enriching our lives through contact with what's now alien and foreign, through inner development, and through imagining exactly what we want and working back to how we get there. In a few words, that's the message of this book.

—*Craig Comstock*

A witty entrepreneur we know was challenged to explain why a person in business would be concerned with the issue of nuclear war. "Being dead is bad for business," he replied. Don Carlson likes to add, "Being alive to the larger issues is *good* for business." After building an enterprise that now manages billions in assets, Carlson has turned his talents to the world crisis, in part by founding Ark Communications Institute, in part by supporting Business Executives for National Security and candidates who might help to break the trance of the Cold War. In this chapter, we are invited to a dinner party at which the nuclear crisis is described by a remarkable cast of speakers. Carlson's purpose, however, is not to frighten us, but to direct attention to some causes of the coming peace. Among these causes is an application of amateur spirit to questions now monopolized by "experts." It's no longer enough to "manage" the crisis. We need to shift to a new level, as when people stopped debating whether slavery *could* be abolished and began to ask how.

Danger and Opportunity

Don Carlson

EVERYBODY KNOWS WE'RE IN A CRISIS, but many of us are accustomed to regarding crisis as if it had only one side, as if it only meant trouble or danger. The present U.S. approach to national security, for example, has been strongly influenced by the thinking of a group called the Committee on the Present Danger. In its 1980 election-year pamphlet, "Countering the Soviet Threat," this committee perceived a "lunge for dominance" by the Soviets, with an "inadequate response" by the U.S. It called for "an increase in defense spending to restore the nation's capacity to deter and contain Soviet expansion." As a result of such a build-up, which has by now

15

continued into a second presidential term, the Committee foresaw "a more secure and peaceful world."

However present and real a danger is, it forms only one aspect of a crisis. As the ancient Chinese recognized in the very strokes of their written language, the other aspect of crisis is opportunity. In fact, the ideogram meaning crisis in Chinese brings together the character that promises opportunity with the one that warns of danger. With this insight in mind, isn't it now time to form the Committee on the Present Opportunity? It would be made up of those who believe that arms, however necessary, are not enough, and that the dynamics of an arms race may continue to lessen our actual security.

We can easily forgive a child who is afraid of the dark. The real tragedy of life is when men are afraid of the light.

—Plato

This book has two messages. One is the belief—supported in this chapter and then simply taken for granted—that the present danger is more severe than any of us can easily keep in mind. The other message, elaborated and illustrated in detail throughout the book, is a call to profound hope, based upon the proposition that we can turn this danger into a deeply exciting opportunity, that so far almost nothing has been tried, that the turn toward peace is the high adventure of our time, and that everyone who wants to take part can do so.

We now have a choice between two visions. One looks ahead to survivable nuclear war. As T. K. Jones put it, "dig a hole, cover it with a couple of doors and then throw three feet of dirt on top . . . it's the dirt that does it . . . if there are enough shovels to go around, everybody's going to make it." In another time these words might have appeared in a comedy routine, but T. K. Jones, as it happens, was Deputy Under Secretary of Defense for Strategic and Theatre Nuclear Forces.

The other vision, the image of our future represented in this book, looks beyond all the fear about war and imagines the causes of peace. Our contributors know, as Adlai Stevenson said in 1965, that "we travel together, passengers on a little spaceship . . . all committed for our safety to its security and peace, preserved from annihilation by the work, the care and, I will say, the love we give our fragile craft." Likewise, the poet Archibald McLeish depicted the earth as "small and blue and beautiful in that eternal silence where it floats" and mankind as "riders on the earth together, brothers on that bright loveliness."

Recognizing the fragility of our situation, we can either assume the inevitability of disaster or become bold enough to create a success. As Henry Ford put it, "there are two kinds

All truly wise thoughts have been thought already thousands of times; but to make them truly ours, we must think them over again honestly, till they take root in our personal experience.

—Goethe

The world cannot continue to wage war like physical giants and to seek peace like intellectual pygmies.

—Basil O'Connor

Man unlike any other thing organic or inorganic in the universe grows beyond his work, walks up the stairs of his concepts, emerges ahead of his accomplishments.

—John Steinbeck

17

of people, those who think they can and those who think they can't, and they're both right." This book assumes that peace has causes, and that we can be among those causes. It was the aviator and businessman Eddie Rickenbacker who said, "If you think about disaster you will get it. Brood about death and hasten your demise. Think positively and masterfully, with confidence and faith, and life becomes . . . richer in achievement and experience."

To sum up the first point, it's true that we're in awful danger. As Arnold Toynbee phrased it, "the human race's prospects of survival were considerably better when we were defenseless against tigers than they are today when we have become defenseless against ourselves." However, it's also true that we could now move beyond fear into a new era of global citizenship. In another context, Helen Keller, who had herself triumphed over a dismal set of physical disabilities, observed that "we still have it in our power to rise above the fears, imagined and real, and to shoulder the great burdens which destiny has placed upon us, not for our country alone but for the benefit of all the world." Dag Hammarskjold, former Secretary General of the United Nations, once stated that "freedom from fear could be said to sum up the whole philosophy of human rights."

In responding to the nuclear threat, many of us are momentarily caught in a trap. Unless we take the situation seriously, we are unlikely to do anything; but looking the monster in the face is so terrifying that we can't do it for long without some measure of hope.

A good idea that is not shared with others will gradually fade away and bear no fruit, but when it is shared it lives forever because it is passed on from one person to another and grows as it goes.

—Lowell Fillmore

18

Yet we're afraid to hope for fear of being disappointed, and for fear that we may have to change profoundly. We watch "The Day After" or "Threads" on television, but soon we are going on as if we'd never seen it. That's not because we can't understand or don't care. It's because fear can get our attention but it does not necessarily tell us what to do or give us the means to do it, especially when the danger is complex.

Nobody made a greater mistake than he who did nothing because he could only do a little.

—Edmund Burke

In this book we offer some ideas about how the world will increasingly look as we give up the ways that lead to war. I say "will" look instead of "would," because I believe that we have already begun to discover the causes of peace and that, as a new way of thinking spreads, our present system of terror will be abolished, as slavery was. Several writers have developed the parallel between nuclearism and slavery. Until very recently, in historical time, slavery was widely regarded as natural, necessary, and proper. In many places, it was assumed that without it the economy would collapse; there was no alternative to it. In a similar way we have been assuming that it was somehow natural for two great nations to try to assure their security by perpetually threatening one another with rapid mass destruction. With the Catholic bishops, we believe that this system is fundamentally immoral. We believe it can be replaced by something better.

Good will is the mightiest practical force in the universe.

—Talmudic saying

Franklin Roosevelt once noted that "if civilization is to survive, we must cultivate the science of human relationships—the ability of all peoples, of all kinds, to live together in the same world at peace." I recall hearing a

19

Let us have done with the past and its bickering and face the future.

—Jawaharlal Nehru

He who knows not and knows not that he knows not is a fool. Show him.
He who knows not and knows that he knows not is simple. Teach him.
He who knows and knows not that he knows, is asleep. Waken him.
He who knows and knows that he knows is wise. Follow him.

—Arabian proverb

story years ago about a senator approaching Abraham Lincoln amidst the passions of the Civil War and saying, "Mr. President, I believe that enemies should be destroyed." Lincoln replied, "I agree with you, sir, and the best way to destroy an enemy is to make him a friend." This book is about dealing with enemies according to the precepts of Lincoln, in order that we can heal this world instead of wrecking it.

First, however, I invite you to imagine that you are at a large dinner party. As coffee is served the host taps on a glass and announces a surprise—fifteen of the leading figures of our age have agreed to stop by for dessert and, in no more than a half minute each, to sum up their deepest conclusions about where we are and what we must do. These guests of honor include former presidents and other statesmen, scientists, philosophers, military officers, and spiritual leaders. Their entire presentation will take us seven minutes to hear. All of the following words have actually been said by these people, though not to a single audience.

Dwight D. Eisenhower: "War in our time has become an anachronism. Whatever the case in the past, war in the future can serve no useful purpose. A war which becomes general, as any limited action might, could only result in the virtual destruction of mankind."

McGeorge Bundy, Special Assistant for National Security to President Kennedy: "Think tank analysts can set levels of 'acceptable' damage well up in the tens of millions of lives . . . they are in an unreal world. In the

20

real world of real political leaders—whether here or in the Soviet Union—a decision that would bring even one hydrogen bomb on one city of one's own country would be recognized in advance as a catastrophic blunder; ten bombs on ten cities would be a disaster beyond history, and a hundred bombs on a hundred cities unthinkable."

Leonid Brezhnev: "Among ourselves we are saying . . . that it is dangerous madness to try to defeat each other in the arms race and to count on victory in a nuclear war. Only he who has decided to commit suicide can start a nuclear war in the hope of emerging a victor from it."

George Kennan, former U.S. Ambassador to Moscow: "Today we have achieved—we and the Russians together—in the creation of these devices and their means of delivery, levels of redundancy of such grotesque dimensions as to defy rational understanding. What a confession of intellectual poverty it would be, what a bankruptcy of intelligent statesmanship, if we had to admit that such blind, senseless acts of destruction were the best we could do!"

Henry Kissinger, Special Assistant for National Security to President Nixon: "What in the name of God is strategic superiority? What is the significance of it politically, militarily, operationally at these levels of numbers [of warheads]? What do you do with it?"

Kosta Tsipis, Professor of Physics, MIT: "The entire ecosystem will collapse if only fifty percent of the weapons in the arsenals of the two superpowers in 1985 were to be exploded

If a man take no thought about what is distant, he will find sorrow near at hand.

—Confucius

21

within a few days in a nuclear war.''

Herbert Scoville, former Deputy Director for Science and Technology, CIA: "The guy in the street is the smart guy. He knows you can't fight and win a nuclear war. It's only the generals who are brought up to fight who think you can survive. The answer is that the generals might live, but everybody else would be dead.''

However, the host at this extraordinary dinner party has also invited some of the generals and other high officers who know better:

Lt. General A. S. Collins (ret.): "Today our military strategy no longer conforms to reality: it threatens our national security, and does little to enhance the long-term security interests of the U.S. or the Western Alliance as a whole. Preventing nuclear war should not be the goal only of peace demonstrators or activists who question any use of U.S. power. It should be an imperative for every American concerned with the security of our nation.''

When the student is ready the teacher appears.

—Hindu proverb

Lord Mountbatten, Admiral, British Navy: "As a military man with a half century of active service, I say in all sincerity that the nuclear arms race has no military purpose. Wars cannot be fought with nuclear weapons. Their existence adds to our perils because of the illusion which they have generated.''

The best soldiers are not warlike.

—Chinese proverb

Rear Admiral Gene LaRocque (ret.): "It's very important for all of us to realize that the Soviet Union is not the enemy. Nuclear war is the enemy. We're going to have to learn to live with the Russians or we and the Russians are going to die at about the same time.''

Marshall Ogarkov, former Chief of Staff,

U.S.S.R.: "With the development and dispersion of nuclear arms in the world, the defending side will always retain such a quantity of nuclear means as will be capable of inflicting unacceptable damage . . . on the aggressor in a retaliatory strike. . . . In contemporary conditions only suicides can wager a nuclear first strike."

General Douglas MacArthur: "The very triumph of scientific annihilation [nuclear weapons] has destroyed the possibility of wars being a medium for the practical settlement of international differences . . . . Global war has become a Frankenstein to destroy both sides. No longer is it a weapon of adventure— the shortcut to international power. If you lose, you are annihilated. If you win, you stand only to lose."

Admiral Eugene Carroll (ret.): "Nuclear deterrence based upon the development of nuclear war-fighting forces is a failed doctrine. There is no safety, no survival, if both sides continue to build and deploy war-fighting forces designed to prevail in nuclear conflict. Safety lies ultimately in changing our way of thinking about the role of military power in the nuclear age. Armed with new insights, rather than new weapons, we may then be able to reduce or eliminate the basic causes of conflict in a vulnerable, interdependent world."

After these warnings from leading military officers, our dinner host concludes the panel with two guests—one who speaks from a religious perspective, the other from a scientific background:

Concern for man himself and his fate must always form the chief interest of all technical endeavors... Never forget this in the midst of your diagrams and equations.

—Albert Einstein

A man should never be ashamed to own he has been in the wrong, which is but saying in other words that he is wiser today than he was yesterday.

—Alexander Pope

23

Going Beyond War

Anything we can conceive, we can achieve—the most underdeveloped territory in the world is under our scalps.

—Dorothy M. Carl

Let no man imagine that he has no influence. Whoever he may be, and wherever he may be placed, the man who thinks becomes a light and a power.

—Henry George

Pope John Paul II: "In the past, it was possible to destroy a village, a town, a region, even a country. Now it is the whole planet that has come under threat. This fact should fully compel everyone to face a basic moral consideration; from now on, it is only through a conscious choice and then deliberate policy that humanity can survive."

Carl Sagan, Professor of Planetary Studies, Cornell: "What a waste it would be after four billion tortuous years of evolution if the dominant organism contrived its own self-destruction. We are the first species to have devised the means. There is no issue more important than the avoidance of nuclear war. It is incredible for any thinking person not to be concerned with this issue. No species is guaranteed tenured life on this planet. We are privileged to be alive and to think. We have the privilege to affect our future."

I am not a politician, a diplomat, an academic expert on national security, or a military officer. I am a businessman. My knowledge of weapons, strategy, international politics, and the Soviet Union comes mainly from reading and from talking with some of the people directly involved with these matters. My own expertise is in finding opportunities, creating new kinds of products, selling them, and developing organizations to provide complex services.

In the fields covered in this book I am an amateur, and in contemplating the world produced by the experts in "national security" I am distressed. Nearly all Americans are amateurs when it comes to security and world order. Many of my fellow amateurs are highly skilled in business, the professions, and other demanding fields. I sometimes wonder what would happen if we would start asking the national security experts some hard questions.

For example, can we really not do better than a policy that exposes both the U.S. and the Soviet Union to rapid destruction in the case of an accident, a miscalculation, a rash act, adventurism, or an attack by a third party? Do we really expect to survive the present system indefinitely; and if not, how should we change it?

The problem with the experts is not lack of intelligence or dedication; it's a limited way of thinking. What amateurs can do is to expand the range of thinking. Experts are needed to work out the implications of a new course, the details, the hardware; but they should never be left permanently in charge of the overall policy. The very talents that make them effective analysts within a paradigm can easily incapacitate them for challenging and replacing that paradigm; they become identified with it. With exceptions such as the officials who spoke at the imaginary dinner party, national security experts have become addicted to nuclear weapons and to other high tech schemes in place of political imagination.

Consider an analogy from medicine. If it were discovered that cancer could be cured and even prevented by a simple medicine, the enormous establishment dedicated to dealing with cancer would be devastated. Even though individual researchers and physicians would be delighted as healers, their source of support and

"One can't believe impossible things." "I daresay you haven't had much practice," said the Queen. "When I was your age, I always did it for half an hour a day. Why, sometimes I'd believed as many as six impossible things before breakfast."

—Lewis Carroll

Going Beyond War

A man's reach should exceed his grasp, or what's a heaven for?

—Robert Browning

The power of an aroused public is unbeatable. Vietnam and Watergate proved that. It must be demonstrated again. It is not yet too late, for while there is life there is hope. There is no cause for pessimism, for already I have seen great obstacles surmounted. Nor need we be afraid, for I have seen democracy work.

—Dr. Helen Caldicott

current reason for being would vanish. Similarly, if we developed entirely new approaches to achieving national security, the elite that now operates the present system would need to turn their talents in new directions.

In the case of cancer, a cure such as I've hypothesized would probably come from highly sophisticated research. In the case of peace, however, the approach would probably derive not from a startling scientific or technological discovery, but from a new vision of how to relate and new ways of relating. It's probable that this vision would come from outside the current assumptions about what's possible and about how change happens. It might come from a field other than politics, such as the professions or business, or from a spiritual tradition, or the field of human development, or from another culture. We don't know. What we can say is that it's unlikely to come from politics or diplomacy as currently practiced.

Undoubtedly, many readers believe that events are careening out of control, that despite the best efforts of so-called experts, global stress is near the breaking point. We have all read how nuclear weapons are proliferating without control. Where, in this dizzying time, is there room for realistic hope? One place I find hope is in the growing number of people who have suddenly come to the realization that because of the failure of "experts" we must, as ordinary people, come to the rescue of our collective destiny. Not encumbered with the awesome responsibilities, rituals and reputations of "experts," ordinary people are capable of fresh perception, new goals, and wonderfully creative strategies; they are not experienced enough to dismiss daring and unprecedented actions as "unrealistic" or "impossible." While "experts" play out the tired old strategies, new and powerful ideas for easing planetary tensions are appearing everywhere among people who understand that world security can no longer be left to those who got us into the present fix.

New visions generally come from a drastic shift of viewpoint. For example, people have always looked at the world from behind borders, whether those were city walls or the boundary of a princely realm or nation or the mental borders created by a religion or political ideology. It was not many centuries ago that the curvature of the earth was noticed. In our own age a drastic shift of viewpoint occurred when representatives of humankind orbited the earth and stood on the moon looking back at this planet. Suddenly, after years of watching science fiction films about spacecraft we understood that we live on one, on a floating sphere, together. Clearly this is no cruise ship. As Marshall McLuhan put it, "There are no passengers on Spaceship Earth—everybody's crew."

As one of the crew, I recently founded Ark Communications Institute to help in the search for peace and real security. In the Judeo-Christian culture, the name *ark* first brings to mind Noah's craft, in which the diversity of life was preserved against the Biblical flood. Most wooden boats are constructed on, and held in shape by, ribs—and this recalls the Latin root, *arca*, which means "chest." Thus,

Who is wise? He who learns from all men.

—Talmud

Remember your humanity and forget the rest.

—The Russell-Einstein Manifesto

27

*Lord, make me an instrument of Thy peace.
Where there is hate, let me bring love. Where there is offense, let me bring pardon. Where there is discord, let me bring union. Where there is error, let me bring truth. Where there is doubt, let me bring faith. Where there is darkness, let me bring light. Where there is sadness, let me bring joy.*

—St. Francis of Assisi

we can think of an ark as a place enclosed by ribs, the place of the heart.

In a world of modern weapons there's no craft that could shelter life from the horrors that earth would suffer in a major nuclear war. In the words of the old black spiritual, "God gave Noah the rainbow sign—no more water, the fire next time." Instead of trying to build or find a little place where we could be sheltered against a possible holocaust, we must now think of the whole world as the new ark. Our task now is to build an imaginary vessel big enough to encompass all mankind, an ark as big as the earth itself.

In this spirit, I offer you a treasure chest of thoughts and visions about the earth-ark that we share with the Soviets and with all other peoples, and in particular, about how to keep it shipshape. This is a book not about the danger of war, but about the opportunity to leave behind some outworn ways of thinking, to discover the causes of the coming peace.

In looking for causes of the coming peace, the first step is to understand clearly the pattern that needs to be altered. A contributing editor to *The Atlantic*, Thomas Powers asks the simple-sounding but profound question, "What is the Cold War about?" We assume it's about something awfully big. The cause of it *must* be big, to justify the polemics swirling around it, the stupendous amount of money devoted to it, and the unprecedented danger created by it. But what is the nature of this overwhelming conflict of interest between the U.S. and the Soviet Union?

What Is It About?

Thomas Powers

THE UNITED STATES AND RUSSIA ARE both Great Powers of the traditional kind. Both have expanded rapidly, over the past two centuries, at the expense of weak neighbors; both are blessed with abundant natural resources; both draw their power from huge populations and economies; both are convinced that the destiny of the world is in their hands; and both are showing signs of the awful financial strain of sustaining a global conflict. For both sides the focus is Europe, where Russian and American armies face each other across the line established by the calamities of the Second World War. There the Americans are far from home but have friendly allies. The Russians are closer to home but must keep an eye on hostile clients. The question at the heart of the Cold War—the thing it is most nearly "about"—is which of these two armies will go home first. It is hard to imagine a confrontation with fewer exits.

Nothing will ever be attempted if all possible objections must be first overcome.

—Samuel Johnson

29

Going Beyond War

The problem now is that the closing stages of the traditional pattern always involve great wars, but we—Russia and the West alike—cannot hope to gain from a great war. In the past, when somebody lost, somebody won. Now, nuclear weapons make that unlikely. The side closest to losing retains the power to drag down its rival with it. Many people grasped this point right away in 1945, when atomic weapons destroyed Hiroshima and Nagasaki—but, for the most part, national leaders did not. They thought we were smart enough to conduct a Great Power conflict without sliding into war. They still think so. As a result, we behave as Great Powers have always behaved—raising armies, seeking advantage, and supporting our demands with threats of war when conflict comes to crisis. The only difference now is that we tell ourselves it will never come to war in the end. It will just go on indefinitely.

In one of his essays, E. P. Thompson wrote, "If we ask the partisans of either side what the Cold War is now about, they regard us with the glazed eyes of addicts." I have found this to be true. Over the past year, I have asked perhaps a hundred people—Russians and Americans alike—what it is about. Of course, this is a hard question. I did not expect anyone to sort out the whole matter in an afternoon. But I had in mind a story, possibly apocryphal, I once read about the composer Stravinsky. He had written a new piece with a difficult violin passage. After it had been in rehearsal for several weeks, the solo violinist came to Stravinsky and said he was sorry, he had tried his best, the passage was too difficult, no violinist could play it. Stravinsky said, "I understand that. What I am after is the sound of someone trying to play it." I asked my question in that spirit.

But none of the people I approached showed anything more than a polite interest in the question. No one offered the sort of ready answer that suggested he had been thinking about it. No one found it easy to propose the name of someone who might have been thinking about it. Their eyes were not exactly glazed, but they were certainly blank. I had figured that the Russians, at least, would be quick to propose a dialectical interpretation. They were not. The few who alluded vaguely to history said all that was behind us now. The responses, after an awkward moment, were pretty much the same: "That's a very interesting question; we ought to concentrate more on that, I agree, yes, but the really pressing matter now is the question of the Euromissiles"— or something else of the kind. It was questions about hardware that interested them, or the details of negotiating positions, or the dangers posed to the fundamentals of deterrence by new weapons technology, or the rights and wrongs of the Soviet use of Cuban proxies in Angola and Ethiopia, or the slippage of Soviet control in Eastern Europe, or the motives behind the counterforce revolution in American military thinking. It is process that absorbs the managers and publicists of the Cold War—not words but the Great Game itself, not why we act but what we do. Things can go so terribly wrong tomorrow that

I know of no safe depository of the ultimate powers of society but the people themselves, and if we think them not enlightened enough to exercise their control with a wholesome discretion, the remedy is not to take it from them, but to inform their discretion by education.

—Thomas Jefferson

Security is mostly a superstition. It does not exist in nature, nor do the children of men as a whole experience it. Avoiding danger is no safer in the long run than outright exposure. Life is either a daring adventure or nothing.

—Helen Keller

31

Going Beyond War

it is hard to concentrate on anything but the awful dilemma of what to do today.

Thompson wrote in the essay quoted above, "What is the Cold War now about? It is about itself." I think Thompson is right, with one qualification: the Cold War has always been about itself. It's about what happened last week, and what we hope—or fear—will happen next week. The military power of the two sides is in constant flux. Today's allies may falter tomorrow. Each side feels that defeat on its periphery is a threat to its center. Both sides are incapable of explaining why things have to be this way, but act as if fate offered no alternative. When we ask what this great struggle is about we betray our own helplessness. The answers are just words. For nearly forty years we have talked and talked without mitigating the danger that we will fight in the end. No single issue divides us, nothing we can settle through negotiation and compromise. It is only propagandists who insist that the history of the Cold War explains it. The problem at its heart is an elemental one. It is our nature that makes us draw lines in the earth and grimace when anyone approaches in strange garb, not some legalistic litany of rights threatened or violated. The Cold War has a new name, but it follows an old pattern. Among the things we seek or fear from this conflict there is not one on a scale even close to the scale of the war we are preparing to fight with each other. We are trapped in a tightening spiral of fear and hostility. We don't know why we have got into this situation, we don't know how to get out of it, and we have not found the humility to admit we don't know. In desperation, we simply try to manage our enmity from day to day. When Germany fell in 1945, only two Great Powers remained in the world—Russia and the United States. Only Russia has the power to threaten the United States. Only the United States has the power to threaten Russia. We fear each other. We wish each other ill. All the rest is detail.

A long dispute means that both parties are wrong.

—Voltaire

To the extent that the Cold War is fundamentally about itself, we could feel depressed by the stupidity of it or, in the spirit of Norman Cousins, feel delighted by the discovery that, in the absence of a deeper cause, the two sides might be able to agree to stop threatening one another. After a review of world challenges that call out for cooperation between the superpowers, Ted Turner once said: "As long as we're fighting, the smaller nations have very poor role models. We're acting like kids, both of us. I'm not going to say whose fault it is. Who cares? The main thing is that we stop doing it." In a similar spirit, Cousins shakes us out of the fatalistic trances that lead to a waste of the human spirit. Former editor of *Saturday Review* and author of many books, including one on how he recovered from a supposedly fatal illness, Cousins reminds us of what it is to hope.

A Longing for Something Better

Norman Cousins

THE MAIN DIVISION IN THE WORLD today is not between democracy and communism, or between any two sets of political or ideological forces. The main division is philosophical. It cuts across national and ideological boundary lines. It has to do with the way human beings define themselves. Some measure only problems and fail to measure themselves. They position themselves for defeat because they see themselves as a species dependent upon or buffeted by circumstances beyond their control. Any view of human beings as belonging to an immutable species, attempting to function under a fixed ceiling, makes despair inevitable. Progress is possible only when people believe in the possibilities of growth and change.

The uniqueness of human beings is represented by the capacity to do something for the first time.

There is no single formula for human survival, but the approach to survival has two main elements. The first is that we ought never to minimize or underestimate the nature of the problems that confront us. The second is that we ought never to minimize or underestimate our ability to deal with them.

Human beings must be judged by the challenges they define for themselves. The human species is unique because it alone can create, recognize, and exercise options. This means it can do things for the first time. We can reasonably argue, therefore, that human beings are equal to their needs, that a problem can be resolved if it can be perceived, that progress is what is left over after the seemingly impossible has been retired, and that the crisis today in human affairs is represented not by the absence of human capacity, but by the failure to recognize that the capacity exists.

Is it possible to be an optimist in a world which has turned most of its organized brain power and energy into the systematic means for debasing life or mutilating it or scorching it or obliterating it? What basis is there for hope when the human future is increasingly in the hands of men who do not comprehend the meaning of the new power and who are, some of them, puny and fretful and prone to act out of frustration or false pride or mistaken notions of grandeur?

Can anyone believe in the ability of the human species to eliminate the mass injustice

Perhaps the most important lesson the world has learned in the past fifty years is that it is not true that "human nature is unchangeable." Human nature, on the contrary, can be changed with the greatest ease and to the utmost possible extent. If in this lies huge potential danger, it also contains some of the brightest hopes that we have for the future of mankind.

—Bruce Bliven

Be not afraid of life. Believe that life is worth living, and your belief will help create the fact.

—William James

35

Going Beyond War

that leads to mass violence—or the mass violence that feeds back into mass injustice? Can anyone have confidence in the capacity of human intelligence to sustain the natural environment on which humans are absolutely dependent—at a time when the progressive despoliation and poisoning of air, land, and water are fast outrunning efforts to protect the environment?

Questions like these are producing a profound upheaval within the body of contemporary Western social philosophy. For the essence of modern social thought is its belief in the idea of human progress. With a few exceptions, the leading thinkers of the past few centuries have generally accepted Aquinas's idea that man "advances gradually from the imperfect to the perfect." Pascal underscored this notion when he said that man is a creature capable not only of undergoing experiences but of comprehending them, and that the unending accumulation of experiences is therefore bound to be reflected in his own learning, understanding, and growth. Bacon, Descartes, Kant, and Hegel, each in his own way, have attempted to break free from the medieval concept of fixed limitations on human potentiality, or the Lucretian idea of cataclysmic disaster, or the prophetic notion of doom.

The only safe assumption for human beings is that the world will be what we make it. Within broad margins, the movement of history will continue to be connected to human desires. Our dreams and not our predictions are the great energizers. Those dreams may seem at times to be murky and beyond realization. But dreams must command the respect of historians. Dreams put human beings in motion. If the dreams are good enough, they can overcome happenstance and paradox; and the end product will be far more solid than the practical designs of men with no poetry in their souls.

The basic energy of a people comes from their creative capabilities, from their ideas, from their trust in one another, and from their confidence in the integrity of the species. We can learn that a good life is possible without extravagance, and that our obligations are not just to ourselves but to all earth dwellers— and especially to those who have yet to be born. The race is not to the swift but to the sensible.

The case for hope has never rested on provable facts or rational assessment. Hope by its very nature is independent of the apparatus of logic. What gives hope its power is not the accumulation of demonstrable facts, but the release of human energies generated by the longing for something better. The capacity for hope is the most significant fact in life. It provides human beings with a sense of destination and the energy to get started. It enlarges sensitivities. It gives values to feelings as well as to facts.

We are left with a crisis in decision. The main test before us involves our will to change rather than our ability to change. Nothing about human life is more precious than that we can define our own purpose and shape our own destiny.

The whole future of the Earth, as of religion, seems to me to depend on the awakening of our faith in the future.

—Pierre Teilhard de Chardin

For out of Zion shall go forth the law, and the word of the Lord from Jerusalem. He shall judge between the nations, and shall decide for many peoples; and they shall beat their swords into plowshares, and their spears into pruning hooks; nations shall not lift up sword against nation, neither shall they learn war any more.

—Isaiah

Commenting on the origins of World War I—trivial in cause but lethal in effect—a European statesman called the situation "tragic but not serious." In the following interview, Robert Fuller, a former president of Oberlin College, gets serious by turning everything on its head, and by jumping outside of whatever framework a situation is ordinarily regarded in. He declares, for example, that peace is not a viable goal for the "Peace Movement." Then he says what, in his view, *would* be a serious goal.

A Better Game Than War

Interview with Robert Fuller

Where do you see the arms race going?

If the Russians would send a man to hell, we'd say, "we can't let them beat us to it."

—Hyman G. Rickover

I was running around the track one sunny day, and I saw right behind me, connected to my own feet, my shadow. No matter how fast I ran, my shadow kept up with me, and it occurred to me that that was the metaphor for the arms race—a race with one's own shadow. No matter how fast you go, the other guy's going to keep up with you and stay connected with you; in fact, he's a *part* of you. He is the projection of yourself—of your dark side—just as your shadow is the sun's projection of your body on the ground. No one will win the arms race, nor will anyone drop out. We can never outdistance the fear of those parts of ourselves that we have projected on others: Americans on Russians, Jews on Arabs, Protestants on Catholics, Whites on Blacks. Making the bomb the issue and disarmament the goal shields us only briefly from the realization that it is we ourselves—we human beings—that are the source of the danger.

What implications does this have for dealing with the arms race?

Since the arms race is a race with our fear, we are going to have to deal with it on a psychological as well as a technical level. A real change can't be had in human affairs by focusing exclusively on the technology, the weapons themselves. In addition, we must understand why it is we are afraid of our "shadow." What is the origin of the fear of "the other," and how can we deal with it? Why do we project on other people and societies qualities we have within ourselves, and then maintain that they are the bad guys and we the good? They are, of course, doing the same thing with us. Yet in our heart of hearts, we all know that it is only together that we constitute a whole. So I look at the arms race, and war itself, not in terms of a technical fix or some clever treaty that would reduce the number of weapons, which ultimately will be required, but rather at a different level having to do with the relationships among, and the psychologies of, people.

Could you give an example of this projection in U.S.-Soviet relations?

The Russians are our shadow. We project on them what we fear in ourselves and they project on us what they fear in themselves. The Soviets' paramount social values have to do with providing a sufficiency for everyone, with some rough ideal of material

We do not understand that life is paradise, for it suffices only to wish to understand it, and at once paradise will appear in front of us in its beauty.

—Fyodor Dostoevski

I do not minimize the complexity of the problems that need to be faced in achieving disarmament and peace. But I am convinced that we shall not have the will, the courage, and the insight to deal with such matters unless in this field we are prepared to undergo a mental and spiritual reevaluation, a change of focus which will enable us to see that the things that seem most real and powerful are indeed now unreal and have come under sentence of death.

It is not enough to say, "We must not wage war!" It is necessary to love peace and sacrifice for it. We must concentrate not merely on the eradication of war but on the affirmation of peace.

—Martin Luther King, Jr.

equality; so they guarantee housing and education and medical care and safety in the streets. Our ideals have less to do with the substance of equality and more to do with the process of individual realization—with freedom of religion, freedom of speech, freedom of assembly, freedom of the press, and so on.

Each side feels vulnerable when attacked for falling short of its principles. For example, when we were criticized for denying Blacks the vote twenty years ago, we felt embarrassed and exposed. Similarly, the Russians squirm when instances of privilege are pointed out. Neither society yet lives up to its own ideals, and each projects on the other its own failures to do so and denounces it accordingly. At the same time, however, each society struggles to incorporate as much of the other's central values as it dares (the Russians, our freedoms; and we, their equity) without compromising its own primary commitment.

But saying that we're each other's shadow doesn't mean we are any less of a real threat to each other, does it?

Certainly not. The Soviets threaten us precisely *because* they're afraid of us. The threat isn't so much that they're sitting there hoping to conquer our land: they couldn't govern it if they had it—nor we theirs. The greatest threat derives from the fear they have of us and we of them, and we're afraid of them partly because we know that they're afraid of us. There's nothing more dangerous than a scared bear—or a scared eagle, for that matter. Somehow we've got to interrupt this cy-

Most of the things worth doing in the world had been declared impossible before they were done.

—Louis Brandeis

We have grasped the mystery of the atom and rejected the Sermon on the Mount. Ours is a world of nuclear giants and ethical infants. We know more about war than we know about peace—more about killing than we know about living.

—Gen. Omar Bradley

cle of fearing each other to get at the problem, which is probably a more useful formulation than saying that we have to establish trust. Trust is one of the last things to develop, even in a personal relationship between two people. It comes only after years of intimacy, and it is never born directly out of conflict.

So how do we break this spiral?

Well, not by focusing on disarmament. There's almost no chance that nations are going to disarm willingly in the near term. We must recognize that fear of the other society is the most dangerous thing, and take conscious steps to reduce this mutual anxiety. For example, the confidence-building agreements we have with the Soviets to give each other advance notice of missile firings and troop exercises are good ways to avoid arousing certain sudden apprehensions. The only real safety lies not in getting rid of one or another type of weapon—it lies in inoculating ourselves against acting upon fear.

If a man does not know what port he is steering for, no wind is favorable to him.

—Seneca

This represents rather a major shift, historically speaking, doesn't it?

Absolutely. Throughout human history it has been thought that to be stronger was to be safer, to be feared was to be more secure. Nuclear weapons change this: henceforth, to be feared is to be in jeopardy. By instilling fear in others, you diminish your own safety.

The only viable strategy that remains, given the presence of these weapons, lies in accepting parity, and eventually in mutually scaling back. We've got to stop trying, with

You can't hold a man down without staying down with him.

—Booker T. Washington

41

one more technological thrust, to be number one again. That scares the other side more than anything, and it doesn't work. Your shadow keeps up with you.

What does this have to say about the policy of deterrence?

It suggests the existence of a hidden but deadly flaw in this policy, for deterrence is a strategy based upon fear. The subject is more subtle than we've realized. We've taken it for granted that it is the fear of retaliation that has been deterring aggression. I'm beginning to question that. Such fear does not deter my 4-year-old son from initiating fights with his 6-year-old brother—fights he knows he'll lose. Perhaps it is actually something other than fear of retaliation (or the absence of such fear) that deters (or releases) aggression. And perhaps the induced fear on which deterrent strategy is based actually constitutes a hidden threat to the safety that deterrence is supposed to provide.

Ultimately, to feel safer, we shall have to attend directly and explicitly to the safety of others. The ancient ethical prescriptions, common to all religions, become self-enforcing in a nuclear world.

Some of this is not so different in a personal relationship, is it?

No, it's not. In fact, the analogy is an instructive one. You can usually get to a place in a personal relationship where the expression of anger is permitted—it's something the human animal seems to need. You do this with

Man perfected by society is the best of all animals; he is the most terrible of all when he lives without law and without justice.

—Aristotle

One of the paradoxical lessons of the nuclear age is that at the moment when we are acquiring an unparalleled command over nature, we are forced to realize as never before that the problems of survival will have to be solved above all in the minds of men. In this task the fate of the mammoth and the dinosaur may serve as a warning that brute strength does not always supply the mechanism in the struggle for survival.

—Henry Kissinger

42

the understanding that it's just something that occurs, and then you let go of it—you don't hang on to it because to do so sours the relationship. Since apparently there is something necessary about expressing anger, we need to create within society channels for doing it which aren't lethal. Athletics, of course, is one realm where on occasion you can express a certain amount of anger and even violence and have it dissipate into the world and do negligible harm. We also need to learn which particular escalations of that impulse to violence finally get out of hand and produce uncontrolled spasms of mutual destruction. For in international relations we are now capable of the ultimate nuclear spasm; it has been called "omnicide."

So the fact of nuclear energy is forcing us to examine our tendency to violence?

Yes, and to learn which of its manifestations we can no longer permit if we want to go on living on Earth. We have in the twentieth century stolen God's fire for a second time, as it were, although this time the fire doesn't just burn your finger—it destroys your civilization. The ceiling this places over our impulse to escalate violence is going to force a transformation in the nature of the human animal. There is, therefore, a respect in which we can be thankful that God placed this extraordinary energy down there in the nucleus, and that we have teased it out. The Promethean theft, forty years ago, of God's nuclear fire is forcing us to reheed His commandments.

What is required of us is that we love the difficult, and learn to deal with it. In the difficult are the friendly forces, the hands that work on us.

—Rainer Maria Rilke

If we would guide by the light of reason we must let our minds be bold.

—Louis Brandeis

43

Going Beyond War

Nothing could have been more obvious to the people of the early twentieth century than the rapidity with which war was becoming impossible. And as certainly they did not see it. They did not see it until the atomic bombs burst in their fumbling hands.

—H.G. Wells

The problem then isn't just nuclear war. Are you saying that because of the likelihood of escalation, war itself must somehow be eliminated?

Yes, that's a necessary conclusion. In my twenties, I studied and worked with some of the physicists who first built nuclear weapons. The knowledge that these weapons work, how they work, and what they can do is lodged within me; and that secret knowledge sits side by side with the "secret" that human beings love war, as well as hate it. People fight, and when they do, things can get out of hand; but with nuclear weapons, to let things get "out of hand" is to commit suicide. This is more than a "historical dilemma"; it's the worst crunch we've ever faced. We're still prone to battle, yet horrified at where it may lead. We must find new channels for our fighting energy or we'll end up with one war too many, if only to let off steam and "get it over with."

Do you see any way out of this crunch? Will war always be with us?

It's illuminating in approaching war to look at the histories of some other human scourges such as illiteracy, slavery, and hunger. Let's deal first with illiteracy. A thousand years ago the only persons who knew how to read were priests and the very wealthy, and it was believed at the time that you could not learn to read unless you were close to God, unless you were a priest, or else you were rich enough to have a tutor. This special knowledge was hoarded and transmitted selectively from elite to elite. Gradually, though, it dawned on people that anyone who went through a certain process could learn to read. Through new institutions for literacy called "schools," and then via universal compulsory education, a great transformation occurred: from the idea that only a special privileged few could ever learn to read to the idea that anyone could learn to read, and ultimately to the idea that everyone learn to read and write.

This is a prototypical example of what I call a *psychotectonic* shift. It is not a shift in genetics or biological evolution; it is a shift of our deepest assumptions about ourselves, a shift in what we take for granted, in what we think we are capable of. A psychotectonic shift is to the realm of moral understanding and human behavior what a paradigm shift is to scientific understanding and behavior. It is a reconceptualization of what it is to be human—a transformation of our "self-model"; and it projects a shift in human destiny with a full range of legal, political, economic, social and spiritual consequences.

Could you illustrate this concept with another example?

A psychotectonic shift with profound implication for mankind was the one surrounding slavery. For thousands of years it was considered a natural thing, if you could manage it, to enslave other people. Sometime about the eighteenth century, in England and in Europe, significant numbers of people began to raise doubts about the justification of one human being owning another. By mid-nineteenth century the issue came to a head in America, and what was still a widespread prac-

The search for static security—in the law and elsewhere—is misguided. The fact is security can only be achieved through constant change, through discarding old ideas that have outlived their usefulness and adapting others to current facts.

—William O. Douglas

You are mortal men. You are capable of error. You have no right to hold in your hands—there is no one wise enough and strong enough to hold in his hands—destructive powers sufficient to put an end to civilized life on a great portion of our planet. No one should wish to hold such powers. Thrust them from you. The risks you might thereby assume are not greater—could not be greater—than those you are now incurring for us all.

—George F. Kennan

45

tice rapidly became totally unacceptable and outlawed. Abraham Lincoln presided over and came to symbolize this shift in people's mind set. As decades followed, instances of slavery around the globe were eradicated, so that now it is essentially non-existent. This does not mean, of course, that all exploitation has ceased. Some day "wage slavery" will undergo a similar transformation. . . .

What is it that causes psychotectonic shifts to occur?

Before water turns to ice, it looks just the same as before. Then a few crystals form, and suddenly the whole system undergoes cataclysmic change.

—Joanna Macy

We can transcend a condition like illiteracy or slavery when we can thoroughly imagine and know how to produce another condition that's manifestly preferable. Perhaps it's easiest to see this with regard to hunger, which is a shift we are just now creating. Hunger is a phenomenon that communicates at a very deep level between human beings, so that there is actually a direct pain one experiences when one sees a hungry person. The only way really to rid yourself of this pain is to see the other person fed. The dynamic is something like that of a yawn by another person creating a yawn in you: it happens on a psychological and physiological level; it's an imitative, direct coupling to another person—something similar to but much stronger than the "power of suggestion."

Now in the past we have mostly repressed this pain because we didn't know how to alleviate hunger systemically. But now that we do, I think nations will eventually adopt an implicit and explicit policy that human starvation and hunger are simply unacceptable.

Actions that cause them, whether foreign or domestic, will be elevated into consciousness and will no longer be tolerated.

So to generalize, conditions like slavery, hunger or illiteracy become morally repugnant when we discover ways to discontinue the practices that sustain them. As long as the only way we can see to get a job done is to force another person to do it, we inure ourselves to his or her pain, and consider this a "normal" condition. As long as we see no way to get food to hungry people, we repress our true reactions. But when we find a way of dealing with these situations, of alleviating the other person's pain and thus our own, we move quickly to do this.

We like to think of new moral ideas as preceding the technical solutions, but widespread moral acceptance may as often *follow* the technical solutions. It's pointless to speculate on which comes first; they are deeply intertwined, and both the moral and the technological shifts are necessary to move mankind and transform our practice.

Does all this suggest then that our job is partly that of the ad man, in a sense "selling" the world on ending hunger or making peace?

Yes, I think so. If we're actually going to transcend war-making and to end hunger as we've ended smallpox and slavery, we're going to have to use the skills of the best "ad men." An idea must be good *and* timely in order to strike a resonance. But the speed at which "an idea whose time has come" can go forth into the world and belong to every-

In actual life every great enterprise begins with and takes its first forward step in faith.

—Schlegel

If appeasing our enemies is not the answer, neither is hating them.... Somewhere between the extremes of appeasement and hate there is a place for courage and strength to express themselves in magnanimity and charity, and this is the place we must find.

—A. Whitney Griswold

New occasions teach new duties.

—James Russel Lowell

47

Going Beyond War

body is just dazzling—it moves like a sharp knife through soft butter, taking hold of everyone who is exposed to it. One way in which non-politicians can support political leaders is to hone ideas to the point where, when they are given public expression by a leader, they have that kind of rousing effect. If we want to see the world changed, it's our job to craft the rhetoric so that when it's spoken from a public forum, it moves people towards better goals—towards feeding the world, ending material and educational deprivation, establishing justice and equity, eliminating torture, and bypassing war-making.

Returning to your earlier point about the relationship between technology and morality, if the invention of the cotton gin helped make slavery morally unacceptable and the printing press and schools did the same for illiteracy, what will it be for war? Can we say that the invention of the atomic bomb is the technological innovation that will make war unacceptable?

Well, the existence of nuclear weapons creates a situation in which we have a sharp, compelling incentive to examine our war-making tendencies. But such an examination reveals an important difference between the three psychotectonic shifts I've mentioned—having to do with slavery, illiteracy and hunger—and that of eliminating war. The difference stems from the fact that slavery, hunger and illiteracy are conditions that people live under, and that it's possible to imagine another set of conditions that could replace each of them. This alternate set of conditions may be extremely complex and require far-reaching changes in a society, such as in the case of slavery. Nevertheless an alternative can be imagined—dimly at first, then more and more concretely.

With respect to hunger, for example, you imagine a world well-fed; you can specifically imagine loaves of bread in every culinary style on every table in the world. And in the case of illiteracy, you imagine a world where everybody reads. You see books—millions of books. You see not just priests holding books with fancy calligraphy, but you see everybody reading, the Bible at first and then other books, printed books! And you imagine schools where reading is taught to all. This is not to say that imagination, although necessary, is also *sufficient* for transformation, for it leaves the actual work still to be done. But I want to stress that thoroughly imagining an opposite state is a prerequisite for the eradication of unwanted conditions.

Now the point is that we've been dealing with *conditions*; but war is an *activity*. War differs from hunger, illiteracy and slavery because it is something we *do*, a complex societal activity that we participate in. If you imagine its absence, what you get is nothing; you get a non-activity. We call it peace, but the problem with peace, and the reason it's hard to create a desire for peace except in the immediate aftermath of a war, is that no one can imagine it, or everyone imagines it so very differently. "Peace" is not a set of activities that people do. That's why I maintain that the bypassing of war will require the delineation

There are one-story intellects, two-story intellects, and three-story intellects with skylights. All fact collectors who have no aim beyond their facts are one-story men. Two-story men compare, reason, generalize, using the labor of the fact collectors as their own. Three-story men idealize, imagine, predict; their best illumination comes from above, through the skylight.

—Oliver Wendell Holmes

Imagination has always had powers of resurrection that no science can match.

—Ingrid Bengis

It is part of the cure to wish to be cured.

—Seneca

49

Going Beyond War

In the context of the communities we live in—our neighborhoods, towns, cities, clubs and churches—we may recount times when isolation, competition, and deprivation are momentarily transformed into experiences of unity, common purpose, and group commitment. We may recall as times of peace the moments when boundaries of gender, race, and religion are transcended. While the moments of national and international peace seem rarer, we find times of national unity, pride, and common purpose usually marking the end of wars, the signing of treaties, and even the celebration of the Olympic Games. We talk about our connectedness with our world and our environment, the rich experience of other cultures and places, a oneness that is enriching and empowering. These times stand in stark contrast to passive and dull images of peace.

—Educators for Social Responsibility

of a set of activities that can serve certain of the purposes that war has served, that provide people with something to do, and can meet the real needs that wars have met in the past.

Are you suggesting that peace is actually not a viable goal for the "Peace Movement"?

Yes I am, exactly. Peace is the absence of a very exciting activity—war. And nobody ever opted for nothing in place of something, especially something exciting. Peace has the connotation of peace and quiet, of serenity, of bliss; and people aren't actually attracted to that very much. It's boring after a while. Also, if you look to see who *is* in favor of it, it's usually people who are living a privileged life, and who therefore wish to maintain the status quo. People who are experiencing hunger or injustice don't want peace; they are, in fact, willing to make revolutions and wars to secure food and justice. For people who are hungry or afraid, material well-being or security is of more immediate concern than peace. So peace isn't the best way to express the goal of the anti-war movement. And you can't express it as "anti-war" either because that's merely "against." We've got to figure out what it is we actually want, and then be for that.

Is this the meaning of the question you've posed, "Is there a better game than War?"

Yes. And it's meant to be a provocative question, suggesting that war has in fact been an activity that men and women have played and have loved. They have also hated it, but it's crucial if we're ever going to bypass or transcend war-making that we admit our own eternal fascination with the business of it, with the fact that it provides moments of individual exhilaration, camaraderie, nobility, leadership, courage and glory that other human activities seldom match. The horrible side of war is well known and usually focused on, but until we acknowledge our secret attraction to it we're likely to keep on "doing" it. In using the word "game" I do not mean to suggest that war is in any way frivolous. War is war—an immensely complex, irreducible activity of institutional character involving virtually all facets of society. In addition to provoking the recognition of our attraction to it, referring to war as a game suggests there are roles, moves, transactions, strategies, outcomes, winners and losers—and, most important, that we do have a choice as to whether to keep playing it.

I suppose one of the reasons it's difficult to invent a game that is more engaging than war is that in playing war we get to experience vicariously the ultimate sacrifice, the giving of one's life. Denis de Rougemont saw in the act of dying for the one we love the supreme expression of eros.

Yes, we have to acknowledge what genuine purposes wars have served—psychological as well as political. Then we've got to see if we can invent and design and *authorize* another game, another set of activities which meet those needs which wars have met. Incidentally, it's important to realize that the game of ending particular wars is completely different from discovering the game that replaces all war. Peacemakers who have an

With malice toward none, with charity for all, with firmness in the right, as God gives us to see the right, let us strive on to finish the work we are in...to do all which may achieve and cherish a just and lasting peace among ourselves, and with all nations.

—Abraham Lincoln

51

Going Beyond War

answer to the question, "What would I do if peace broke out?" are apt to be more effective in their work. At any rate, in my thinking I've moved past disarmament as a primary strategy and past peace as an immediate goal, and on over to the question of what the activities are which will replace the game of war and meet some of the same needs. We are beginning to design a game that is more fun to participate in than the old war games, or even the inseparably related "stop-a-war" games. The game that might be better than both these games is that of *Completion*—of completing ourselves through each other by incorporating into ourselves the empowering truths that other peoples embody and exemplify. That is really what our work in the Mo Tzu project is about.

Would you describe that project and explain what you mean by this "Mo Tzu" work?

In the fifth century B.C., during the time in Chinese history known as the Warring States period, Mo Tzu and a few of his followers would travel on foot to sites of developing conflict among the various feudal "states" and there attempt a kind of diplomatic aikido. If the opposing parties would not agree to sit down together and mediate their dispute, Mo Tzu would join the weaker side, offer training in how to withstand a siege, and then again sue for a negotiated solution. Precisely what his magic consisted of is not known, but his willingness to commit himself personally to a vision of a world without war is a source of inspiration to us. The definition of what among ourselves we call "Mo Tzu-ing" is "finding what you love in what you hate." You might admit that you sometimes hate the Russians, for example, but if you can remember what it is you love within all that and use it as a handle, you can hold your hatred in its proper, subordinate place. Until you know what you love in what you hate, your hatred can assume command over your behavior. But when you've found what you love and can maintain it as a clear vision, it becomes possible to surround your hatred and get past it. That's "Mo Tzuing." And it applies as much to personal relationships as to relationships between whole cultures, societies, or nations. The minute you find what you love in someone else, you're bigger yourself and stronger; you're more powerful. That will be, I think, the meaning of power in the twenty-first century. It's power that comes from the completion of self, from the incorporation into your behavioral repertoire of the other person's (or culture's) "secrets." And there's an interesting flip side to this: it is finding in yourself what you hate in your "enemy." For we only hate in others—whether in individuals or whole peoples—what we cannot accept in ourselves.

What was the source of this understanding in your own experience?

While teaching in a Black ghetto high school in Seattle in 1967, I came to feel that I was somehow incomplete as a person. There was something in these black teenagers, something they embodied, that I was attracted to

For all their historical and ideological differences, these two peoples—the Russians and the Americans—complement each other: they need each other; they can enrich each other; together, granted the requisite insight and restraint, they can do more than any other two powers to assure world peace. The rest of the world needs their forbearance with each other and their peaceful collaboration. Their allies need it. They themselves need it. They can have it if they want it.

—George F. Kennan

All mankind is divided into three classes: those that are immovable, those that are movable, and those that move.

—Arabian proverb

53

The wish is always father to the thought. Feeling always precedes thinking— as the body precedes the clothes. Change the feeling in an individual, and his whole method of thinking will be revolutionized.

—Swami Ram Tirtha

Is not the whole of human life turned upside down; and are we not doing, as would appear, in everything the opposite of what we ought to be doing?

—Plato

Peace is not an absence of war, it is a virtue, a state of mind, a disposition for benevolence, confidence, justice.

—Spinoza

and wanted to hang around. I noticed also that there was something attractive about me to them, something about me that they wanted to hang around. It was here that I first experienced the notion of the complementarity of cultures, and that's been a central idea for me ever since: that you can make yourself more whole and complete by assimilating the truths borne by other cultures. We need our enemies in order to complete ourselves. It's interesting to trace the first stages of this process. As the sense of threat diminishes, we redesignate our former "enemies" as adversaries. With the first hint of positive mutual value, "adversaries" become "rivals," a term which acknowledges each as a secret teacher of the other. Finally, "rivals," recognizing their mutual dependency, come to see themselves as "partners." Completeness is also a key concept in mathematics, so it's been with me since my formative intellectual years as a student of science. One learns that a set of things, a set of mathematical objects, can be complete or incomplete. If you want to say where something is located, you need three numbers; if you use only two, your knowledge remains incomplete. And if you want to locate an *event*, you need four numbers—three spatial coordinates plus time. The notion of completeness is central in science and I believe it is central to the present human predicament.

So this is how you relate to other cultures now?

Yes, in looking at Black, Islamic or Russian culture, I try to identify that aspect of the truth they bear most prominently. Our ini-

54

tial reaction to other people is often negative because we see that they fail to embody something we take as supremely important. Only after getting through this can we appreciate what it is that they have to offer. I don't expect ever to assimilate fully into my perspective the way a Chinese sees the world or landscape, or the way Muslims feel about their friends. But to begin to see what such qualities are, and to square another way of seeing or being with your own so the two are not in contradiction, is the work that the world has urgently to get on with. Otherwise we're going to react out of our initial distaste and annihilate the differences.

In a sense we commit a kind of psychic suicide, then, by severing ourselves from other cultures?

I think so—by making them wrong, by humiliating them, by invalidating them. They in turn become angry with us. We cut ourselves off from engaging with other cultures and try to crush and expunge our differences instead of celebrating them. We need only reinterpret the old French maxim, "Vive la Différence," to have the best anti-war cry imaginable.

In short, the activities that outmode and replace war must deal with incompleteness, whether it be of the body, mind or soul. No one activity embodies all these aspects. Nonetheless, to deal with want in any of its forms is to move towards bypassing war; and conversely, not to deal with want is to court war. We begin to see the outline of another grand human game on the horizon, coaxing us away

Ultimately, our troubles are due to dogma and deduction; we find no new truth because we take some venerable but questionable proposition as the indubitable starting point, and never think of putting this assumption itself to a test of observation or experiment.

—Will Durant

The greatest danger in any argument is that real issues are often clouded by superficial ones, that momentary passions may obscure permanent realities.

—Mary Ellen Chase

55

Going Beyond War

Why not go to the Soviet
Union and say to them,
"What if you could take
your sixth of the land
surface of the earth and
all your minerals and
your educated people and
infrastructure and just
build the best society you
know how? What would
you do?" And then ask
the same thing in the
U.S. What would we do
with our society if we
weren't spending ourself
into an enormous deficit
building all these exotic
weapons? It's an interesting challenge. I'd like to
see people actually talking
about it. Because by hav-
ing a vision, by seeing
how much would be pos-
sible, you begin to open
up the mind again and, if
the vision is attractive
enough and if some ways
begin to become obvious
for moving toward that
vision, then you have
another star to steer by.

—Craig Comstock on
audio cassette, "Beyond
the Boundaries"

from the thrills of the battlefield. It is the discovery and completion of one's own self as experienced in one's culture, and one's self as manifested in one's supposed enemy or shadow. This may well be an activity exciting enough and profound enough to supplant war. Completing ourselves is actually what we've always wanted; in fact, it is partly what we've sought for in vain through the cruel instrumentality of war. We now, finally, have the wisdom to get at these nurturing, self-completing truths directly. Hegel expressed this over a century ago:

"Each . . . part lives only by participating in and eventually giving itself up to the whole . . . the 'self' or identity which is given up, however, is only the claim on the part of a fragment to be the whole, a truth claiming to be truer than it is. . . ."

What kind of "warrior" will be needed for this new game you're proposing?

What the world needs now are *nonpartisans*—people who specialize in introducing different cultures to each other, people who develop the skill to create in antagonistic nations or cultures the capacity to hold in check that ancient familiar impulse to fight. And this involves a philosophical shift in thinking away from dualistic, possessive presuppositions to a more inclusive world-view. In traditional political or economic terms, the focus has been on who has what privilege, what right, what "stuff," what power. Those issues tend to be divisive because the prevailing view, at least in the past, has been "If I've

56

got something, you don't have it" or "If I control this, you don't"—categories of exclusion which make for dispute. But mathematics has taught us about non-zero-sum games. A zero-sum game is one in which my gain exactly equals your loss, whereas a non-zero-sum game is one in which it's possible that we both gain. It's going to become a central value in politics to move past this zero-sum game framework and hold out for that solution in which everybody experiences a win simultaneously.

Help thy brother's boat across, and lo! Thine own has reached the shore.

—Hindu proverb

Getting to Know
the Other Side

2

For the leader of a superpower, summitry means briefly meeting his counterpart, surrounded by a circus of foreign policy aides, security agents, and reporters, amidst widespread hope that somehow the discussions will make war less likely. Four out of ten Americans confess to expecting a major world war within the next decade. It's no wonder many people dream of a breakthrough during a fireside conversation, a walk in the woods, or a quiet dinner in an embassy. Sometimes leaders sign a meaningful agreement at the summit, yet the "spirit" of the occasion always seems to dissipate not long after the leaders fly home.

Photograph by Joel Schatz

In general, summitry simply means going to the top. We ordinarily think of the top as being occupied by officeholders rather than by citizens. Since war is conducted by nations, it's assumed that peace is likewise necessarily created "at the highest levels." All that citizens can do, according to this theory, is vote for the best available leaders and then acquiesce in what they do, unless their actions become flagrantly counterproductive.

A different perspective was offered, in striking terms, by Dwight D. Eisenhower, who had commanded a great army and who, when he spoke, was President of the U.S. "I like to believe," he said in 1959, "that people in the long run are going to do more to promote peace than are governments." He may have liked to believe this because he knew from direct experience how awful wars are—how awful they were even prior to the nuclear age—and also how awkward governments have generally been in preventing them.

"Indeed," he continued, "I think that people want peace so much that one of these days governments had better get out of their way and let them have it." Is this a bit of populist chatter from an old Kansan, or does Eisenhower have a deeper message than may at first appear? What would it mean for governments to "get out of [the people's] way"? And how could ordinary people possibly go about contributing to peace?

If Eisenhower was, as revisionist historians argue, a thoughtful and even crafty statesman who often concealed his best moves, his words would merit close attention. Perhaps the President really meant to imply that, with regard to peace, governments have a natural tendency to stand in the way. In his Farewell Address, Eisenhower returned to this theme when he warned against allowing excess power to the "military-industrial complex." In a draft of this address, he had also mentioned Congress as part of the complex.

Eisenhower clearly thought not only that the people "want" peace more than their governments, but also that, in some unspecified way, they would "do more to promote peace." Many observers have taken this to mean that, as voters, people would demand that their representatives and their President take actions, on the official level, to reduce the risk of war and create more constructive relations with other countries, including adversaries. However, Eisenhower appears to have gone beyond this in his own thinking. After all, he did not say the people would "demand" peace or "support" it; he said they would "promote" it.

I do not know exactly what Eisenhower had in mind, but it seems clear that he would have been fascinated by the recent greening of grassroots diplomacy or, as our title says, "citizen summitry." Obviously, not many citizens can go to meetings of top leaders and anyway they are forbidden, by law, from negotiating on behalf of their country. But thousands of citizens have begun a new kind of diplomacy—taking care not to speak for their government, but showing openness, persistence, and flair in representing much that's best and most creative about America. These citizen diplomats enlarge the opportunities for productive relations between peoples and, by extension, between their governments.

In the view of citizen diplomats, it would be absurd for two enormous countries to relate solely through their top leaders and the bureaucracies that supposedly serve them. Formal treaties must of course be negotiated by official representatives. However, nations actually touch one another in many other ways. For example, they trade. Citizens travel; they study or work abroad; they write and speak; they meet with colleagues in and from other countries; they take part in international associations and projects.

Sometimes when official relations are hostile or limited, other kinds of relations can nonetheless be rich and relatively constructive. While the Logan Act expresses a worry that a private citizen may be tempted to act as if he or she were the Secretary of State, one of the great advantages citizens have is that they are free *not* to do that; they aren't expected to speak for their government. This frees them to act on behalf of interests that cut across national lines.

Assume for a moment that, as some conservative and libertarian theorists argue, the most basic role of government is defense. In defending ourselves effectively, as we must take care to do, our government must watch for threats and take care not to be fooled; this easily leads in the direction of paranoia. A paranoid often has trouble making friends. Therefore, it follows that the agency with the necessary job of watching out for threats should not be solely relied upon to create constructive relations. If we fail at creating them, the penalties, in this nuclear age, are about as severe as they can get. If the government is taken up with the responding to threats, who can hold a positive vision that another approach is possible?

Ordinary citizens can, and America is as well suited as any major power to take advantage of this possibility. As Tocqueville noted, our culture favors voluntary associations and supports a rich, constantly changing network of them. We also have a tradition of individualism which, despite its faults, encourages people to act on their own initiative.

By contrast, the Soviet Union in general has favored official bodies such as its "peace committees" and has frowned upon unofficial initiatives by individuals; it has even openly suppressed them. Most Soviets who have substantial contact with foreigners act as members of some official body. In theory, there's a "line" on every question, and everyone is expected to follow it.

However, we know that, as in any society, an official line in the Soviet Union is often the outcome of a process of debate or differing initiatives within a complex establishment; and that once it takes shape, it's subject to various interpretations. Citizen diplomats often work in the space opened up by these legitimate differences, and may find that speaking unofficially gradually encourages others to reciprocate.

As compared with a government, a citizen may seem to have little power. He has no military forces to put on alert. Alternating genders, let's add that she cannot sign a treaty. His personal budget is miniscule as compared with that of the state, nor does she have a huge bureaucracy working for her. In short, a citizen enjoys none of the usual prerogatives of power. However, an individual has the enormous power to speak from the heart. It's overly harsh to say that an ambassador is "sent abroad to lie for his country," but in politics there's often an official reality that's understood to differ from what an ordinary individual would straightforwardly see, or say.

At their best, officials can prevent war; in a sense, however, they are seldom able to make peace of a profound sort. We want

61

them to, but we may also want them to act out our paranoia and hostility; they can't always do both. We are heartened when Reagan and Gorbachev enjoy the roar of a fire together, without aides. It's as if they could be friends. We resist the advice of our own first President who told us that states don't have friends, or at any rate not permanent ones; they only have interests. In contrast, ordinary people can make friends and can weave a fabric of shared projects.

It's true that citizen diplomacy has been dismissed as an illusion, a sideshow for tourists who are self-deceiving idealists or megalomaniacs who think that their efforts, as much as anyone's, are keeping the missiles in their silos or bringing about historic change in the Soviet Union. Critics also say that while the U.S. is capable of generating citizen diplomats, the Soviet Union puts forward only agents of a highly centralized society devoted to ruthless power seeking. Therefore, any exchanges are doomed to hurt us while helping them.

It may come as a surprise to some that President Reagan has a different view of citizen exchanges. In November of 1985 he asked us to "imagine how much good we could accomplish . . . if more individuals and families from our respective countries could come to know each other in a personal way." Calling for "bold new steps," the President explained that "we could look to increase scholarship programs; improve language studies; conduct courses in history, culture, and other subjects; develop sister-cities; and yes, increase athletic competition." Nothing wrong with competition, but "let it be on the playing field and not on the battlefield."

In this speech, which mentioned other specific ideas, the President beautifully caught the spirit of citizen summitry. "Such exchanges can build in our societies thousands of coalitions for cooperation and peace." Of course this program would require government facilitation, but "governments can only do so much; once they get the ball rolling, they should step out of the way . . . ." Here Reagan seemed to echo the Eisenhower who had said, "one of these days governments had better get out of their way and let them have [peace]."

What's so distinctive about Reagan's imagination, in this speech, is its humane particularity. Instead of simply referring to peace in the abstract, he envisions people from the two cultures getting together "to share, enjoy, help, listen, and learn from one another." And he goes further. He dreams that "our children and grandchildren can someday travel freely back and forth between America and the Soviet Union; visit each other's homes; work and study together; enjoy and discuss plays, music, and television; and root for teams when they compete."

If America were fully to act upon the vision set forth in the President's speech, this initiative could exceed in historic significance the founding of the Peace Corps by John F. Kennedy. There are serious problems in any exchange, but Americans and Soviet people need to know one another. Part of the answer is an exchange of artists, scientists, and other professionals. Part is trade.

Another part is accurate information about the other society. Reports don't need to be magnanimous; it would be a major advance if they were simply neutral instead of grudging, tendentious, or hostile. Beyond that, it would help if we showed even the most basic level of compassion for the other country's history and struggles, as President Kennedy did in 1963 at American University. Reminding us of the Soviet experience in World War II, he observed that if the U.S. had suffered a comparable disaster, it would have involved severe destruction from the East Coast as far west as Chicago. While finding Communism "profoundly repugnant as a negation of personal freedom and dignity," Kennedy praised Soviet achievement in various fields, "in science and space, in economic and industrial growth, in culture, and in acts of courage." Pointing to a "mutually deep interest in a just and lasting peace and in halting the arms race," the President announced a cessation of nuclear testing in the atmosphere, inviting Soviet reciprocation. Less than two months later, the limited test ban treaty was signed.

Above all, it would help if relations were to go beyond official speeches and events, into the ordinary lives of people. We need to travel more in each other's country and share a slice of our lives. Among other promising initiatives, President Reagan has proposed an exchange of students. Why not? Some say that the Soviets treat any exchange mainly as an opportunity to spy. Others note the major

63

restrictions upon travel within the U.S.S.R. and upon contacts there. But restrictions can be eased and espionage contained. The question is, to what positive effects could an exchange lead?

Reluctance to engage in people-to-people diplomacy may spring in part from realization that nuclear threats would come to seem incongruous to the growing network of people with friends in the other society, as well as to the larger public that would watch this phenomenon develop. At a certain point, while acknowledging the enduring conflicts between the two governments, people would nonetheless begin to ask, "Why is my government threatening to blow up my friend Mikhail in Leningrad?" and "Why is *mine* preparing to incinerate young Michelle in Boston?"

—*Craig Comstock*

Americans talk and write *about* the Soviet Union all the time, but how many of us have ever spoken with or written a letter *to* anyone in that country? To most people, even this question seems odd—to whom under the sun would you send such a letter and how would you go about it? Larry Levinger writes an open letter to a generic Russian, to "Dmitry, my invented friend" who, like the correspondent, is a father. It's as if he composes the sentences in his mind while putting his children to bed. As we do with friends, he imagines Dmitry's responses and takes account of them, exploring the myths that have held each of them captive and then pushing beyond.

Letter to a Russian

Larry Levinger

I cannot forecast to you the action of Russia. It is a riddle wrapped in a mystery inside an enigma, but perhaps there is a key. That key is Russian national interest.

—Winston Churchill

YOUR COUNTRY DOMINATES THE MAP, its vast borders muscling unpredictably into Europe and the East, curling boldly at the North Pacific and North Atlantic Seas. This is the geographical image we Americans have of you: this vast space squatting on the top of the world. Once we kissed your continent but drifted, say the geologists; now we know you at great distances: on maps, in our American film images of you—*Doctor Zhivago*, *Reds*— and in the dance of the cold war.

Given our data about you, we predict what it is you might do—though we are not sure you will do it. But if you should do it, then we have a plan for what we will do. And we will do certain things believing you will do nothing. If you do not do what we think you will do, we have bombs to keep you from doing what you might do. It matters not that

65

Today we are faced with the preeminent fact that if civilization is to survive, we must cultivate the science of human relationships—the ability of all peoples, of all kinds, to live together in the same world at peace.

—Franklin D. Roosevelt

He who rides a tiger finds it difficult to dismount.

—Chinese proverb

To constitute a dispute there must be two parties. To understand it well, both parties and all the circumstances must be fully heard; and to accommodate the differences, temper and mutual forbearance are requisite.

—George Washington

this is a dance into nothingness. What matters is that, at great cost, we can prevent our nightmare of you with a nightmare more horrifying than the one we imagine of you. We understand you from the perspective of a missile. From high in the air you look just like you do on the map—bold, vast, unpredictable.

At moments, we imagine you are not in the world, and that our country's great resources now put to war are returned to our people and to the hungry and needing of the world. We imagine this perhaps at night, when we go to cover our children in their beds and hate you for the world you are making for them to live in.

We fail to realize we have done little to prevent such a world. We do not wish to confront our complicity: without you we would still make bombs and bad deals, topple regimes, send arms and advisors, and cajole and trick with our arrogance the delicate balance of life on earth. Like you, we have learned to entreat, exploit, engage the commerce of power, the art of disguise. We are more like you than the distance would allow. We drift ever toward you, as if geological time had been reversed.

But we do not know you. Your faces escape us. You are the communist in the courtroom we tried for treason. You are your Krushchev, with his rumpled coat and triumphant belly, his pouting countenance and porkpie hat. You are vodka and stroganoff, Tolstoy and ballet, bad winters and bad karma—a bad affair from the Bolsheviks on. Marx is buried in the university, but Lenin is loose; like a paroled gangster he roams the Third World.

To Marx we ascribe the idea; to Lenin the method. When we think of you, it is of the method we think. Which is the issue. Which is the reason for the bombs.

Yet we thirst for you, your pulse and your yearnings, which for all our contradictions, we sense are like ours. Your poet, Yevgeny Yevtushenko, speaks for us too:

> I'm awkward, shy, and rude,
> nasty and good natured . . .
> Many opposites meet in me:
> from West to East,
> from envy to delight . . .
> Frontiers are in my way. I am embarrassed not
> > to know Buenos Aires and
> > New York;
> I'd like to walk at will through London
> > streets
> and talk with everyone I want, even in
> > broken English . . .
> I like to skate in winter . . . and carry a
> > woman across a street;
> I bite into books, and carry firewood;
> I can feel depressed, and know vaguely
> > what I seek.
> In hottest August I love to crunch
> an ice-cool slice of watermelon . . .

Is this you, my feared and hated Russian? Off the record, off the map, would we discover that we are the same in our failings and eagerness, our personal and public quests, our contrasts and yearnings, our desires and appreciations down to the moment of thirst quenched by fruit in the blaze of summer? Is it possible that all this time we have been comparing

We need men who can dream of things that never were, and ask why not.

—George Bernard Shaw

Intolerance betrays want of faith in one's cause.

—Mahatma Gandhi

Getting to Know the Other Side

ourselves only in the quality of our warheads?

Dear Dmitry. Dear Nikolai. Dear Leo. Dear Boris. These are our names for you from our movies. They are names that come to us quickly when we think Russian: Leo as in Tolstoy, Boris as in Pasternak. I am naming you Dmitry because it rings, sounding warm, familiar. I am inventing you. We are good at inventing Russians.

Our picture of you: walking briskly in Red Square, poker-faced, huge overcoat, square hat, snowflakes the size of flapjacks, and in the background, your gray, gothic facades, turrets growing up from them like enormous apples on tops of trees. No grass. No flowers. Magnitude. Power. Exaggeration. And you—resilient, stoic, your face fixed for war and weather. This is your exterior self, the self in harness and chore.

In your novels you are long-suffering, unruly, cagey; with your lovers and your vodka, your soil and your ideals, you are warm, generous, sentimental. In your novels you are like us, but this is not our enduring image of you. We remember you as a huge and boisterous crowd cheering as line after line of your missiles pass in review, your red flags beating the frigid air.

We cannot imagine you at work, other than as bureaucrats or thankless drones in headscarves and aprons, so many teeth in factory gears. We suspect you have toilet paper and forks, but we are not sure. Perhaps if you have them, you use them differently, or not at all. We learn your food and clothing are expensive, your housing cheap and meager.

68

You suffer unpredictable disappearances of toothpaste, towels, axes, locks, vacuum cleaners, plates, irons, rugs, shoes, meat. Your free medical care is inept, your refrigerators and washers break down and you have no parts for them. Your wages are low and your goods unstylish, and you stand in long lines to get little for your rubles. Most of you do not know what it is to drive a car.

This pleases us, this contrast between your shortage and our abundance. We like the fact that you have attained only a small percentage of superpower life. In our abundance we need a donkey. We have this image of you as a hulking figure in a heavy coat obeying the only option he has—a military one. We never see you at your kitchen table, where, like our Midwesterners, you socialize, creating the center of your home. Perhaps a small, intimate, overcrowded table, where, over cabbage and brown bread, broth and potatoes, salted or smoked fish, and strong, amply sugared black tea, you are open, candid, loving. Here, your well-supervised public life dissolves, yet here also the state may, if it wishes, invade your table—and often does, with informers who may be your friends. Here, at your table, sits the ghost of repression and purge. Seeing you here, can we not admire the endurance of your families in the face of raw disclosure, torture, death? Are yours not the same heart-strengths and thought-filled passions that have made us a country, too? Would we not, if we could, raise our vodka to you in admiration and respect? If we are to blow each other to particles, will the act

Man has learned to live with the thought of his own mortality. And he now has accommodated to the thought that all may die, that his children and grandchildren will not exist. It's a capacity for accommodation at which we can only marvel. I suspect that our minds accept the thought but do not embrace the reality.... A commitment to this reality is now the supreme test of our politics. None should accept the easy evasion that the decision is not ours...For after the first exchange of missiles...the ashes of Communism and the ashes of Capitalism will be indistinguishable. Not even the most passionate idealogue will be able to speak of the difference, for he too will be dead. In an age when so much is uncertain, there is one certainty: this truth we must confront.

—John Kenneth Galbraith

be no more than annihilation of our truest and most similar selves?

I imagine you writing back. You call me capitalist-moralist. The nature of capitalism, you inform me, is ruthless individualism masked by goodwill. In the name of love and God, you explain, the capitalist takes for himself the riches of the earth. You ask me if I would be willing to divide and share those riches with the rest of the world? You ask me if in my thirst to know you, to break from this primitive isolation and embrace my world, I would be willing to diminish, to allow the importance of others to increase?

It is a good question. I am possessive of what I have and of the right to obtain more, though what I have is inevitably at the expense of someone who has not. I am an American. To be an American is to be blessed in riches and cursed with the immutable fact that for each of our riches, many suffer. The act of living well on the backs of others is a nearly unconscious one in my country. Yet I confess to you a willingness, a blind, earnest, idealistic impulse toward our diminishment and the world's increase. If we are to make of history something other than it has been, then we must perceive it as a moral universe—not something to be filled with power, ideas, abstractions, but something active, moving, hopeful, from which human destiny is derived.

I want to share with you who and what we Americans are. For two centuries we have been isolated: by two oceans, by the grace of not one bomb falling on our shores, by our amazing and rapid success, which, like yours,

We must learn to live together as brothers or perish together as fools.

—Martin Luther King, Jr.

70

prevails upon us responsibilities we fail to comprehend. If you are a country that would hope to undermine the legend of God, then we are a country imagining ourselves brought forth by His hand. A godless society does not concern itself with overthrowing God; a God-wrought country does not jeopardize His creation. Like you then, we are a country deceived by our central notion of ourselves. Our power is the noise that keeps the world awake at night. It is in our weakness that our truth is told: like you, we are an enormously resourceful people, cowering before the obligation to make peace in the world.

Thus we invent ourselves, as we invent you. Like Mark Twain's *Huckleberry Finn*, we are living, we believe, a great adventure, rafting through our feuds and cons, inequities and clever deals with a homegrown explanation for each. We perceive our nation sprouting in genius like a magical, hybrid crop; our people, like Huck Finn, are heroic. They navigate excess and delusion and power with all the innocence and élan of Huck navigating through flood and fog. What makes Huck Finn like us is his playfulness in the midst of dire consequence. If you would understand us you must know of this playfulness. We are a huge nation of Huck Finns playing with our bombs, with your life and with our own.

It is a remarkable bubble we live in, one of rainbows and guilt, naïveté and achievement. It floats just off the surface of the twentieth century, weighted by collapsing images of ourselves. Now the bubble collapses; we emerge sharing the century with you. It is our

What is the spirit of moderation? It is the temper which does not press a partisan advantage to its bitter end, which can understand and will respect the other side.

—Judge Learned Hand

If what we call human nature can be changed, then absolutely anything is possible.

—Shirley MacLaine

Getting to Know the Other Side

Whatever you do, you need courage. Whatever course you decide upon, there is always someone to tell you you are wrong. There are always difficulties arising which tempt you to believe that your critics are right. To map out a course of action and follow it to an end, requires some of the same courage which a soldier needs. Peace has its victories, but it takes brave men to win them.

—Ralph Waldo Emerson

The first problem for all of us...is not to learn, but to unlearn.

—Gloria Steinem

century, yours and mine, beyond our power to make sane and orderly despite our bombs; beyond us in our isolation; beyond us in our complexity; simply beyond us, though we are toying with the future. To realize how willing we've become not merely to kill, but to end all human hopes requires outlandish courage of every individual. "Individual life," said your Stalin in 1934, "is a piece of reactionary petty bourgeois absurdity. . . . " I am saying to you that this is a time for the individual to come forward, that in individual life—not capitalist life or communist life—but individual life, you may touch the heart and deliver it to others.

We do not wish to take the risk of that touch, of learning from one another, speaking to one another. We prefer an arsenal to speak for us. We hold up our bombs with one hand while we go about our business and pleasures with the other. This leaves us only one hand for life: the bomb denies us half our resources and we are put to sleep by its silence. We relinquish to technology the creative impulse, the responsible course. With one hand I write to you, Dmitry, my invented friend; with the other I hold the bomb.

All over America, Dmitry, we are making plans. Myself, I plan to remodel the bathroom. A woman in Des Moines plans to return to school. In Montana, someone plans a woodstove for the basement, in Mississippi, an end to erosion, and in Kansas, a new well. Three people in Philadelphia plan a move to the country. There are people with a plan to end cancer and war, hunger and acid rain. Someone plans to descend a volcano, grow zucchini in rows. Everything moves for the better and the just. In each hovering moment we are ahead of ourselves by two.

We are simply people with plans, scratching our way along. At night our heads hit the pillow with big schemes: another rack of hardware for the store, disposable shoes; next time, less cruelty to a friend. In the morning our cars whistle and turn over and the white smoke from the tailpipe follows us down our streets to a job or a bar, an unemployment line or the cleaners. Inside ourselves is a little future capped by death, one in which our soul is perfected in work and wage, our skin meets the skin of another in pleasure, our children and those we are fond of are happy and at ease with plans of their own. Each small department and factory line holds within itself the good of the man or woman with a plan.

All over America we are struggling to know. Is a Honda better than a Volkswagen? Can computers sell cows? Does Saturn have air? Do prunes cause diabetes? Will magnetism heal bones? We want to know how to bake righteous muffins and grow back hair, how to discipline our dogs, dreams, urges, how to jog without body odor, and who is doing what to whom when, and why there are stones. We are just a curious people poking around the house, reading the cornflakes label and answering the phone. We are so well informed our attention span has lapsed and we lull it into flame with whatever we can. I make no apologies for us: we are, most of us, well-intended people seeking out minor destinies in

A partial truth is sometimes more dangerous than falsehood; a truth that has had its day blinds one to the reality of the present.

—Jawaharlal Nehru

*Coming together is
a beginning; keeping
together is progress; working together is success.*

—Henry Ford

*If I were asked to name
the most important date
in the history of the
human race, I would
answer without hesitation,
6 August, 1945. From
the dawn of consciousness
until 6 August 1945,
man had to live with the
prospect of his death as
an individual; since the
day when the first atomic
bomb outshone the sun
over Hiroshima, he has
had to live with the prospect of his extinction as
a species.*

—Arthur Koestler

which we champion our own. It is our lot to make both smog and compost, instant breakfast and polio vaccine. We are just grinding out a little hope and happiness, convenience and concern. We are no different from the Massai or the Tasaday; we want things better in the cave. If not better, sufficient. If not sufficient, passable. If not passable, painless.

All over America we are making plans and struggling to know.

But we do not want to know what the Pentagon knows: how to make and deploy such efficient fire that not a drop of blood will boil but merely vaporize. And we do not want to know what the Pentagon plans: to trade our minor lives of small schemes for a larger and more manageable scheme. We are going to give up human history—past and future. We are going to give up breathing and eating and copulating and discovering and even being silly, for an idea. And the idea is simply, my friend Dmitry, that you shall not have your way with us.

I want to see the men of the Pentagon as I see myself—a lover of big plans, odd knowledge, gadgetry, and small revenge. I want to say: these are Americans—basically good-intended people with a thirst to know and a right to plan. I want to believe we are a country of rights and that therefore these new-age moles, chewing away at the roots of civilization, represent the right of any American to scheme and make plans and tinker with the known. Deep in the heart of America, however, there is an underground fortress, a technological dream-zone with indoor plumbing, racquetball and red phones. Each room in the fortress has a window carved into rock. On the windows are painted surfaces of real life above ground: forests and waterfalls and fishing boats amid the tides. This is where the Pentagon will go when the trade is made—our lives for their scheme. This is where the new world will begin.

Recently, when a Nazi war criminal was on trial, a Jew was brought to testify and upon seeing his old tormentor from forty years past, he was thrown to the floor of the courtroom in convulsive recognition. What threw him to the floor, he explained, was that the man on trial was not the beast he had remembered forty years, but a man, like any man. Not insane. Sane, but without compassion. If I am to take your life, or you mine, if we are to take the lives of each other's children, it will be an act of measurable sanity in which we failed not in mind, but in will. It requires will to love others' children as our own. Not morality. Not even principle. Will. In the long run, compassion is a matter of will. As is our future.

Now it is time to close. My children, like yours, speak to me in their sleep of their complete trust in us: that there will be a world for them to inherit. In their beds they breathe their deep sighs of long and playful days. They breathe our names. It is as if, in the small midnight whisperings of sleeping children the distance closes: *Dmitry. Daddy. What will we do tomorrow?*

The lights begin to
  twinkle from the rocks:
The long day wanes: the
  slow moon climbs: the
  deep
Moans round with many
  voices. Come, my
  friends,
'Tis not too late to seek a
  newer world.

—Alfred Lord Tennyson

It is never too late to give up your prejudices.

—Henry David Thoreau

75

Not long ago, the Soviet Union appeared on U.S. television mainly in the form of geriatric leaders freezing above Lenin's mummified body as they watched rocket launchers roll over snowy cobbles swept with birch brooms by babushkas. Now we are accustomed to seeing interviews by space satellite from Moscow, but still we seldom get images of ordinary life over there. In many eyes Moscow remains a city of dour government spokesmen attacking the West and withholding information to make their own system look good. What about the enormous majority of ordinary people who are not employed to create impressions? What about workers trying to meet quotas in the factories of this "workers' state," scientists studying the universe that flows past political boundaries, mothers taking the kids to school, bureaucrats trying to solve a problem, doctors working in a clinic, students preparing for university exams or going to a dance? What about young people getting married? We are spending a fortune to be ready to destroy these people's country if their leaders ever push us too far, but we don't even know who the people are. As a self-appointed citizen diplomat, Joel Schatz applied for a visa and boarded a plane to get to know some of them. Here are his first impressions.

Through the Eyes of a Citizen Diplomat

Joel Schatz

The clear sky.
The green fruitful earth
*   is good;*
But peace among men
*   is better.*

—Wawan (Native American) Song

STEPPING ONTO SOVIET SOIL FOR THE first time, I was shocked by the diversity of everything. I somehow expected a monolithic visual impression. Color, especially, was fascinating. Not that I would have expected there to be fewer frequencies of the spectrum in the Soviet Union than anywhere else, but most of the pictures I had seen of that country were black and white photographs, especially from World War II. So I was surprised by something

76

as obvious as blue sky, red and purple flowers, and colorful clothing, as well as by the beautiful pastel buildings.

I had heard from many people that Moscow was a dreary, oppressive place, where people walked slowly and wore large, dark garments as they moved ponderously through the totalitarian state. In fact, I found people who looked no different to me than in any city I'd ever visited—folks holding hands, businessmen with briefcases eating ice cream cones, kids in strollers looking wide-eyed at their environment, a man and a dog walking through a park, little girls dancing in the street, people sitting on park benches in animated conversation—*people*.

Photographing these people was a particular joy for me because I had been warned by the U.S. State Department, in literature sent to me when I first applied for my visa, that there were serious restrictions on the use of cameras. It was in my nature to test those restrictions, to find out how far I could go. I was fully prepared to relinquish my film at any point, so I did take pictures of bridges, and of military personnel; I took pictures of everything I felt like taking pictures of. I was very conspicuous taking pictures. Carrying several cameras with telephoto lenses, tape recorders, lots of western gear, we were clearly not Russian citizens on vacation. No one ever asked me not to take pictures of anything and consequently, I took about 2500 photographs on several trips there.

On my return to the States, I shared these slides with hundreds and hundreds of

When you meet God be ready for two questions: "What did you do for my other children? And did you have fun?"

—Frank Rubenfeld

We are wide-eyed in contemplating the possibility that life may exist elsewhere in the universe, but we wear blinders when contemplating the possibilities of life on earth.

—Norman Cousins

All men are liable to err;
but he shows wisdom and
earns blessings who heals
the ills his errors caused,
being not too stubborn;
too stiff a will is folly.

—Sophocles

people in lectures and found that nothing I said about the Soviet Union was as meaningful as the impressions people received from looking with their own eyes at these photographs. People would remark, "Gee, I didn't realize that there were women in stylish clothing there. I had no idea that there was makeup. I didn't realize that the cars were modern. I didn't realize there were beautiful fountains."

I came to realize that over the years Americans have deprived themselves of direct access to reality in the Soviet Union to the point where we have developed and reinforced impressions of that culture which are very limited. Somehow they've been portrayed as a culture oppressed to the point of not smiling, of not falling in love, not raising families, not enjoying themselves on picnics, not bicycling in the countryside, not pursuing careers that excite them. It's a different culture, totally different from ours, but the spirit of the ordinary people, their warmth and love, is as great as anywhere on the planet.

Most of the stories written for western audiences by western journalists rarely dwell on the normal human side, the successful side of life in the Soviet Union. Journalists, almost by training or tradition, are interested in looking under stones for problems. So we see a very lopsided view of life in the Soviet Union. Their stories are reinforced by pronouncements from high levels of our own government, and by other media people, which leave us no doubt, for the most part, until we physically go there ourselves and say, "Hey, this is not exactly what it has been claimed to be by our press and by our politicians."

Take for example something as simple as Red Square. Many of the photographs of people that appear with this article were taken in Red Square. Almost all of the images of Red Square seen by Americans show military parades and rockets and tanks rolling through. These events occur several times a year. All of the other days, Red Square is a meeting place, a tourist environment where people of every type congregate. Many of them are Russians on vacation to Moscow, out with families looking at the museums and old churches, shopping at the department store. There's plenty of color around and there's no sign of military might.

Photographic documentation is, I think, critical for being able to assemble a more complete understanding of what life is like there. If you could have access to time-lapse photographs from the beginning of World War II through the calamity that occurred there, through the reconstruction years, and into 1985, you would see steady progress. You would see larger and more plentiful automobiles, apartments becoming larger, increased variety of consumer goods, much more western clothing fashion, more appreciation for western music, particularly popular rock music, more variety of musical tours from the west, a greater influx of business people looking for new ways to exchange goods and raw materials. It's a changing culture which is, above all, as human as our own.

Most of the Russians I'm working with are people I've met through friends and through

If I died in a nuclear war I wouldn't have to think about it. But if my friends or my family died, then I'd feel scared and all alone. The arms race means mass killing, mass murder, and it's wrong to kill. People say we have to kill the Russians. But if the Russians are bad people because they have nuclear bombs, then we're bad people too because we have nuclear bombs. And everybody is not bad. Everybody is just the same. People are good. We have weapons because we all think the other people are bad. If we all thought the other people were good, then probably we could be friends. We could live in peace. So we have to change the way we think.

—Daniel Fox, an American child, at age 10

What is the use of a house if you haven't got a tolerable planet to put it on?

—Henry David Thoreau

business encounters and in social environments where someone looked interesting and I would seek him out or someone said, "Hey, if you get to Leningrad, there's a friend of mine there you'd enjoy looking up." It isn't any different than with the people I know here in San Francisco. The photographs of these people are natural extensions of those newly formed relationships.

In a way almost impossible to describe, I have found Russians to be more like Americans in basic ways than people from any other country in which I've ever traveled. In both the U.S. and the Soviet Union the national psyche seems to have mostly to do with the scale and robustness of the human spirit. The vision there is as grand in scale as our own. We are the superpowers. The people seem to me so much like Americans in their psychology, their humor, their emotional climate, their dreams, their flair for experimentation, the depth of their theoretical abilities. Their playfulness with reality models seems to occur at a level higher than in any other culture I've ever experienced before. Yet we have managed to push our cultures to the point where we either have to exchange the things that are of greatest value that we've developed or we annihilate each other.

There's great strength in the Russian people, great patience and a sense that life, however strange by many American values and American standards, is steadily improving. Life is getting better compared to where they've been, and it's reflected in their faces. I've also seen a tremendous change since Gor-

Office workers enjoying the sun in Gorky Square, Moscow.

Cityscape from a visitor's hotel window, looking toward the skyscraper of Moscow University.

Veterans of World War II participating in the opening day ceremony at a Soviet school.

Newlyweds following the custom of laying flowers at a memorial for the 20 million Soviet citizens who died in World War II..

bachẹv has ascended to power. There's more lightness in people, more playfulness, more sense of motion, and a relief that some of the boldest dreams may yet be realized.

Prominent among these dreams is opening up to the West. In my view the most revolutionary tool for opening up East-West communication is the computer. Until very recently the Soviets have resisted computers; now they are making every effort to catch up. The computer represents a potential for decentralizing information and control. That's exactly what it's done in the West. Gorbachev has ordered 50,000 computers within the next year for high schools. There's talk in Moscow of building a teleport for facilitating all forms of telecommunication between the Soviet Union and the rest of the planet.

This is all good news for everyone, for the Russians, for the Americans, and for the

Son of a Russian mother and Greek father, taking the air in Moscow.

rest of the world population. It means inevitable applications of high technology communication for increased diversity and volume of information exchange. The Soviet Union appears to be opening up. This isn't to say that miracles will occur and they will abandon the Marxist-Leninist philosophy. It only means that there is coming to be tacit approval for experimenting with and utilizing every new channel of communication to link people in both political camps. I think this is the beginning of a revolutionary period of development on the planet.

The way to normalize relations between the two cultures is not to send old men to Geneva or any other part of the world to sign

Boy from Tashkent visiting Moscow on holiday.

Moscow girls having a giggle.

85

A boy in Moscow.

pieces of paper claiming that they will trust each other into the future. The only way to normalize relations is for Americans and Russians to develop normal relations with each other.

For the most part, Russians are better informed about Americans than Americans are about Russians. They study this country more systematically than we do theirs. There's much more news on Soviet television about life in the U.S. than there is news in the U.S. about life in the Soviet Union. A lot of it comes through the propaganda filters of the Soviet bureaucracy, but that's offset by the direct experience that Russians have when

Mother and daughter sharing a picnic on the first day of spring, 1985, in the woods outside Moscow.

A Moscow father repairing his daughter's toy.

Getting to Know the Other Side

A day in the park.

Indian summer along a Leningrad street.

Young Pioneers.

Moscow teenagers.

they meet Americans. They may be told in political cartoons that the American system is out to get them, but they make a distinction between the American government and the American people.

They are totally fascinated by Americans. When they meet an American they do not assume he or she is a CIA operative. They take people as they are. They welcome Americans into their homes. I have never been treated with such instant warmth and hospitality anywhere in the world as I have been treated in the Soviet Union. The level of emotional commitment to strangers is just incredible. One can say, "Well, what does this have to do with the government? The government is separate from the people." I don't buy that. All systems interact one way or another, and many of the people I work with at the official level in the Soviet Union have influence with their government. In the strangest ways, through the strangest connections, people influence each other.

89

Getting to Know the Other Side

Uzbek man, among the 50 percent of the Soviet people who are not Russian.

I really believe it's a numbers game at this point. The more people from both cultures who meet each other, the greater the inevitable influence there will be on respective governments that are now operating almost detached from the human compassion that exists in both cultures. I really do believe

that the only possibility for averting a catastrophe in a nuclear weapons race is for Americans and Russians by the tens of thousands to form normal working relationships with each other, in every sphere of human activity. It's possible to do that. The Soviet government is not prohibiting these kinds of people-to-people relationships. I'm talking about mega-patterns of trade, of high technology, of new forms of exchange and collaboration—in fields such as cancer research and earthquake prediction—exchanges of top musicians, direct communication of school children in both cultures via computer, and shortly by television satellite. All of these possibilities are now unfolding, with the promise of introducing large numbers of people to each other.

Uzbek grandmother.

Art restorer descended from a line of well-known Russian painters.

91

Getting to Know the Other Side

Americans have an opportunity to go over and talk to everybody they can about what they consider to be a better way to live. There's nothing stopping us from doing that. The Russians do not prohibit us from doing that. If we are willing to die to defend the right to have freedom of speech, we should at least consider visiting less fortunate parts of the planet to show people what we think life would be like if they were a little more free to speak. That's why I'm doing what I'm doing; that's why so many Americans are traveling there now.

Both cultures have problems. We have not solved all of the riddles of life any more than the Russians have. We all have a long way to go. Americans are always interested in reminding the rest of the planet that we're

Soviet citizens discussing global telecommunications project in coffee shop of Moscow's International Trade Center, which is named after Armand Hammer.

Yevgeny Yevtushenko reading one of his poems by telephone to a Los Angeles radio audience from a Moscow apartment.

Workers repairing a step outside Lenin's tomb in Red Square.

93

Since August 1983, Scientific American *has been translated into Russian.*

American citizen-diplomats joining Soviet friends for dinner in the home of a Moscow art collector.

Starting on July 17, 1975, the American Apollo spacecraft and the Soviet Soyuz docked in space long enough to make 29 revolutions of the earth.

somehow more skilled at everything. We would do well to pay attention to a few things here and there that might be working better in some other cultures. I'm not saying we should ignore the things that are wrong in those cultures, but to focus solely on human rights violations or military policy to the exclusion of so many things that are right and that are working is to pay grave disrespect to tens of millions of people in that culture and in other parts of the world who are slowly attempting to improve the conditions of life on the planet. It's happening everywhere in spite of all of the political problems.

95

In the Soviet Union I found a real sense of community and warmth amongst strangers, even in the streets, that I do not see often enough in our own culture. You cannot dictate that kind of feeling and empathy. I think it's a direct function of the severity of the calamity in the Russian experience. The only way they have survived is by taking care of each other. They are a very proud and determined people who are working through some horrible experiences in their past and trying to somehow deal with the ultimate question of how to survive in a world which has now come to the brink of a catastrophe.

They're very concerned about the possibility for accidental war, even more so than

Soviet and American fishermen visiting one another's trawlers at sea.

deliberate war. This is not what they have struggled for all these centuries, to come to the end of the script. They've buried too many millions dead in war and improved their life millimeter by millimeter from the devastation caused by Hitler. In talking with an American, they are haunted by the questions, "Do you think we're going to kill each other? Do you think there's any hope? Is it ever possible to persuade the military-industrial complex to make profits selling things that aren't so destructive?"

There's almost a transcendent quality to spending time with Russians on their own soil, as there is when we've entertained Russians here in the U.S. You look at each other and you almost don't have to say anything. You know how absurd the situation is and you know that on a one-to-one basis everything is OK. At a distance Russians and Americans distrust and fear each other, but up close they tend to love each other. It's no different from the human process everywhere, where strangers operate at a distance either with no knowledge or with misinformation.

The future of this planet is interactive communication, not sitting back in isolation assuming that you know the way things are somewhere else. To me isolation is a very limited, non-exuberant, and uncreative way to move into the future. It doesn't make any sense whatsoever. On a recent trip I went into the countryside with Russians on a picnic. I could have been in Colorado or in Brazil or any place else on the planet—with good friends, drinking fine wine and eating great

The war-drum throbb'd no longer,
and the battle-flags were furl'd
In the parliament of man, the federation of the world.

—Tennyson

I am only one
But still I am one.
I cannot do everything,
But still I can do something;
And because I cannot do everything
I will not refuse to do the Something that I can do.

—Edward Everett Hale

Whatever you can do, or dream you can, begin.
Boldness has genius, power and magic in it.
Begin it, now.

—Goethe

food, watching birds, exchanging pleasantries and feeling at home on the planet.

Then you look aside and say, "but there are missiles everywhere." What do you do about that? The missiles are a direct function of lack of contact, of distrust, of isolation. The only solution to this problem is rapid increases in communication among the people of the planet. We've been stymied because the channels of communication linking these two populations are practically jammed with politicians, journalists and bureaucrats. And a few tourists. The point is, if we widen those channels to include more volume and more diversity, then a whole new pattern of understanding and rearrangement will necessarily occur.

The first problem for all of us ... is not to learn, but to unlearn.

—Gloria Steinem

All photographs in this chapter were taken by the author, except for the Apollo-Soyuz hookup, which is courtesy of NASA, and the Soviet and American fishermen, which is by Tobey Sanford.

98

About 50,000 Americans are now visiting the Soviet Union each year. Probably only a few think of themselves as citizen diplomats. Most visit with another purpose or else with the lack of purpose that marks the casual tourist. But there's an increasing number of Americans who are determined to go beyond Intourist programs, who seek broad contacts with unofficial Soviets and informal contacts with officials. After years of relative neglect, the U.S. media have begun to give this phenomenon the attention it deserves. What follow are two news reports from papers in the San Francisco Bay Area. Among citizen diplomats, the experiences recounted here are quite ordinary. The stories could be multiplied by the hundreds.

Meeting the Soviets Face-to-face: News Reports

You don't promote the cause of peace by talking only to people with whom you agree. That is merely yes-man performance. You have got to meet face to face the people with whom you disagree at times, to determine whether or not there is a way of working out the differences and reaching a better understanding.

—Dwight Eisenhower

Sarah Seybold and Neil Forney each is something of an enigma to Intourist, the Soviet travel agency that arranges hotel rooms, meals and sightseeing for visiting foreigners.

They don't want to go on cruises on the Volga. They aren't interested in seeing the onion-shaped domes of St. Basil's Cathedral in Moscow anymore.

When they go to the Soviet Union, they want to go their own way, meet people and talk about similarities and differences between the United States and the Union of Soviet Socialist Republics. They are searching for some common ground.

These Bay Area residents, who have visited the Soviet Union three or four times in the past year, are a part of the stream of 60,000 Americans a year who visit the Soviet Union.

99

Getting to Know the Other Side

You cannot shake hands with a clenched fist.

—Indira Gandhi

The human race is a family. Men are brothers. All wars are civil wars. All killing is fratricidal. As the poet Owen put it, "I am the enemy you killed, my friend."

—Adlai Stevenson

We must face what we fear; that is the core of the restoration of health.

—Max Lerner

They see themselves as "citizen diplomats" who have decided that the American and Soviet governments being at odds over arms control, Afghanistan and Central America doesn't mean ordinary citizens can't get together and trade views.

The State Department has taken no official position on this citizen diplomacy, but officials say they are skeptical about the likelihood of Americans actually influencing Soviet policy.

They do say, however, that the contacts can't hurt anything.

Seybold, who lives in the Oakland hills, is a nurse, mother, college instructor and a former Peace Corps volunteer in Turkey and Brazil.

She has gone to the Soviet Union three times in the past year, raising part of the money from friends and acquaintances who believe in what she is doing. She plans to spend a month in Leningrad next spring studying Russian.

"I think there's no country on earth we have need to know more about than the Soviet Union," Seybold said in an interview at her home. "I feel there's an urgency to the arms race. . . . I feel I can make a very small contribution to educating people to dispel the ignorance that breeds fear."

On most citizen diplomacy trips, Americans try to spend no more than half their time in organized sightseeing arranged by Intourist.

The rest of the time, there may be discussions with local Soviet "peace committees" and time to go out on their own and meet with ordinary citizens, often in their homes.

Most Americans hold plenty of stereotypes about the U.S.S.R.—that it is uniformly grim, that the people are alike, hard-edged and mean, and that control of the individual is paramount.

Seybold said what she found on her first visit, though, was "a pluralistic society with many layers."

"The minute you say one thing about it, you can find an exception," she said. "I think it's like the onion domes. You peel away layer after layer after layer."

She has been back twice since; in August, she led a group of twenty Catholics from Oakland, San Francisco and Sacramento, and she visited again last month with eleven other people who are doing a similar kind of work to prepare for more trips.

These private citizens, who usually speak on their experiences when they return to the United States, are occasionally criticized as dupes who are being manipulated by Soviet propagandists without their knowing it.

Seybold, however, rejects the suggestion that she has been brainwashed or is too uncritical.

"I don't think they're wonderful in the Soviet Union," she said. "I've been with refuseniks (Jews who have been denied exit visas to leave the country) in their homes, I've been with dissidents, I've talked with artists in the Baltic republics who wish they could visit the West.

"I don't have any illusions. I know they have a very different idea about human rights,"

There are deeper myths, born of the permanent and universal aspirations of men, such as the dreams of a future human fraternity. Such myths as these...are never mere mythology, because they are founded on a literal and present truth.

—William Ernest Hocking

Always forgive your enemies; nothing annoys them so much.

—Oscar Wilde

101

Peace is our passion.

—Thomas Jefferson

There are admirable potentialities in every human being. Believe in your strength. . . . Learn to repeat endlessly to yourself: "It all depends on me."

—André Gide

she said. "I still think the bottom line is we have to co-exist."

Forney, a 47-year-old interior designer who lives in San Francisco, has visited four times so far and says Americans can get too rosy a picture the first time they go.

"The first time I was lied to. . . . I was given a whitewash," Forney said. "A one-time traveler to the Soviet Union is going to get a certain amount of a snowjob. A traveler should know that's true all over the world."

Forney first decided to go to the Soviet Union on New Year's Eve 1982, after he and some friends were discussing the arms race and the nuclear freeze and the inevitable question came up: What about the Russians?

In preparation, the group studied the Russian alphabet and language and awaited their departure, set for mid-September 1983. Then, a few days before their departure, a Korean Air Lines flight was shot down by a Soviet jet fighter, with 269 lives lost.

"Two people backed out, one because of family pressure," Forney said. "The other twenty-seven of us went anyway."

Forney said some peace and nuclear freeze supporters go to the Soviet Union with the idea that they will instantly find a common ground and discover the Soviet people are just like Americans in what they want. That is ridiculous, he said.

"We bleeding-heart Americans can be taken in so easily," Forney said. "An American who goes over to find that the Soviets are exactly like us will find that, but it's not true.

"They're nothing like me. Their thought patterns are different. We have to acknowledge each others' differences and learn to respect them. We're not going to change them and they're not going to change us."

Forney said the biggest difference between the two societies is human rights. In the United States, individual rights are paramount, but in the Soviet Union, people are trained from a young age to think of the group first.

"I couldn't live there, I wouldn't survive," Forney said. "I'm too much of an individualist."

Another big difference is that Russians are baffled and repulsed by Americans who come to the Soviet Union and criticize the United States, he said.

"They do not respect us when we knock our own government. . . . We're considered a bunch of kooks (when we do that)," Forney said.

Normally, the trips are problem-free, but on one, Forney said, a member of the group invited a Russian student to eat dinner with them in the hotel, which was normally off-limit to Soviets.

Afterward, the student was escorted away in a taxi by plain-clothes police.

"They need to please us tourists so we'll come back, but they really don't want their citizens to see how we're treated," Forney said.

Where would these citizen diplomats like their efforts to lead?

Forney cites a quotation from Gandhi, the Indian leader who believed in non-violent

Surely civilization is old enough, surely mankind is mature enough so that we ought in our own lifetime to find a way to permanent peace. . . .

Peace can be contributed to by respect for our ability in defense. Peace can be promoted by the limitation of arms and by the creation of the instrumentalities for peaceful settlement of controversies. But it will become a reality only through self-restraint and active effort in friendliness and helpfulness.

—Herbert Hoover

If we do not change our direction, we are likely to end up where we are headed.

—Chinese proverb

action: "When the people lead, eventually the leaders will follow."

In the short run, though, he said he hopes for a free flow of tourists between the two nations. He thinks relations will improve during President Reagan's second term.

"I don't think Reagan is a bad person," he said. "I think the man would like to leave a mark in history. He believes in dealing from strength, but I think he believes in dealing.

"I think citizen diplomacy can help; it can't be ignored any more," he added. "It's really happening."

The next step, though, is for Americans to learn the language. "I think language is prime, totally essential to get any further than we have," Forney said.

Seybold, who plans to take a delegation of 100 to 150 high school and college students to the Soviet Union next summer, also sees momentum building.

"In a year, it's just caught fire. People are asking, 'Maybe I need to go and see about it myself. . . . ' We have to realize our interdependence in a global way."

In Washington, D.C., State Department officials say they question whether the citizen contacts can lead to anything substantive.

"We haven't taken any position (on the visits), this being a free country and all," said Charles Sylvester, a public affairs advisor in the department's Bureau of European Affairs. "We're dubious, of course, about the effects. An American who goes over is really limited as to who you can see and how much you can influence their system.

"I don't think it hurts any," Sylvester said.

Forney said he was told that, too, by an official in the consular section of the U.S. Embassy in Moscow. He quoted the official as saying, "Frankly, at the moment, it's the only thing happening. You can't do any harm."

Some U.S. officials, however, suggest the contacts are, as much as anything, a form of personal therapy for Americans worried about nuclear war.

If people feel that the issue of nuclear annihilation is out of their control and someone else will decide whether they live or die, then a trip to the Soviet Union may at least give them the satisfaction of knowing they've tried to do something.

—Craig Staats

TIME WAS WHEN SHARON TENNISON believed what she now calls a myth, a nightmare myth about nearly 300 million people in the largest country on earth. The myth goes like this: "The Soviet people are our enemies, and their way of life, the incarnation of evil. They are a brainwashed people who hate Americans. They live in mute fear of being sent to Siberia. And they want war."

The San Francisco nurse says she knows it's a myth, because she went to see for herself.

Now, Tennison—intensive care nurse, businesswoman and mother of four—is devoting her life to myth-busting among her friends and friends' friends. She firmly believes it's the only hope for world peace.

The creation of a thousand forests is in one acorn.

—Ralph Waldo Emerson

Even in a quarrel, leave room for reconciliation.

—Russian proverb

105

Getting to Know the Other Side

When Tennison isn't presenting programs about "The Other Side of the Enemy," she's leading three-week trips to the Soviet Union. She's taken four so far and has five scheduled this year.

Tennison calls her groups—made up of teachers, doctors, lawyers, business people, firemen, psychotherapists, ministers, housewives—"grass-roots diplomats." On the trips, they meet with Soviet community leaders and make the obligatory visits to monuments and museums. But the heart of their method is the forays they make on their own—in the subways, on the buses, on the streets—meeting everyday people and observing Soviet life as it is being lived.

Tennison's U.S./U.S.S.R Initiatives is one of a number of citizens' groups that have sprung up in the last year or two to promote peace by visiting the Soviet Union and getting to know the Soviet people.

The State Department cautiously endorses such efforts. "It would be a wonderful thing if we could find out we had more in common than divides us," said Raz Bazala, a Soviet affairs specialist for the State Department in Washington. Bazala expressed concern, however, that the Soviets "may use groups like this for propaganda purposes." He said the State Department does not monitor their trips.

Tennison doesn't believe her groups are being used. "But, if it's in the interest of peace on earth, I'm willing to be used," she said.

The nurse took her first trip to the Soviet Union just a year and a half ago. At the

106

disarmament programs she'd been presenting since 1980 for Physicians for Social Responsibility, people kept saying, "But what about the Russians?"

"They asked with such fear and condemnation," she said. "And I had to tell them, 'I don't know anything about the Russians.'"

So she decided to go and see for herself.

Tennison returned from her first three-week trip—starting just days after the Soviets shot down a Korean Airliner, killing several Americans—disturbed and confused.

"It's true, they don't see life the way we see life, politically or economically," she said. "Their rights are to housing, education, medical care, food and safe streets, not to freedom of speech, freedom of assembly, freedom of religion, like ours. Personal freedom is not as important there, and it may never be, because their value system is different. Everyone there is working to make sure that everyone has enough. There are a lot of differences. But they're not evil, just different."

What shook Tennison the most was her contact with individual Soviets. "They were friendly, curious, eager to know more about America and Americans," she said. "And they were terribly concerned about peace, terribly afraid of nuclear war."

The nurse found that peace is a ubiquitous theme in the Soviet Union. Everywhere she looked there were giant posters and murals promoting "Mir" (peace) or "Mira" (world peace). School children wrote essays on peace, drew pictures of what peace would look like. Even the Soviet soldiers she talked to spoke

There is perhaps no phenomenon which contains so much destructive feeling as moral indignation which permits envy or hate to be acted out under the guise of virtue.

—Erich Fromm

When I'm getting ready to reason with a man, I spend one-third of my time thinking about myself and what I am going to say—and two-thirds thinking about him and what he is going to say.

—Abraham Lincoln

It takes two to speak the truth—one to speak and another to hear.

—Henry David Thoreau

107

The man who never alters his opinion is like standing water, and breeds reptiles of the mind.

—William Blake

The world is my country, all mankind are my brethren, and to do good is my religion.

—Thomas Paine

yearningly of peace.

"How do they reconcile their concern for peace with their involvement in Afghanistan and Poland?" a woman at one of Tennison's recent presentations asked.

"They see it differently," the nurse replied. "They see it something like we saw Vietnam, as an unfortunate necessity."

Even zealous American "hawks," such as a retired Air Force colonel who went on one of their trips, came home saying that their preconceptions about the Soviet people were off base, Tennison said.

"We need to give the Soviets the same leeway we give ourselves," she went on to say. "There are parts of our society that work well and parts that don't work at all. That's true there, too."

What works in the Soviet Union?

Child care and education, Tennison said without hesitation. "They have excellent protective laws for mothers and children. All children get a classical education, no matter where they live. And they learn languages from the earliest grades."

She also applauded the Soviet public transportation system, which she said is safe, clean and efficient, and the wealth of cultural activities—concerts, plays, ballet—accessible to everyone at low cost.

And what doesn't work?

"I have to change spectacles to answer that," Tennison remarked. "Through American spectacles, they have to live in very small, standardized apartments. Few people have private cars. There are shortages of consumer goods. Everyone has something, but no one has a lot. We would not be satisfied with that. As an American, I also wish they would open their borders and change their treatment of political dissidents. They will do anything to shut political dissidents up."

"Through Soviet spectacles, the bureaucracy is the worst thing. The length of time it takes to get anything done drives them crazy."

Tennison said her groups have had no difficulty moving freely in the Soviet Union. They followed a child to school, dropped in unannounced and were invited to stay and observe English classes. They attended a Baptist Church prayer meeting. Raised a Southern Baptist, Tennison says she shivered to hear the congregation singing "What a Friend We Have in Jesus" in Russian. . . .

Tennison's group followed some rules and broke others. They sold no blue jeans or dollars, but they did leave the city unescorted. "They say you can't leave the cities," she said. "So we did."

The nurse and her companions took a commuter bus packed with peasants, hopped off out in the country and hiked up into the hills, where they met a gnarled old shepherd. He led them to his cottage to meet his family. With few words in common, the Americans and Soviets discovered a new and universal language: Polaroid.

Tennison calls Polaroid pictures the second most powerful weapon in the citizen peacemaker's arsenal, second only to the "peace button." The button, on which the word "friendship" appears in English and in Rus-

The central question is whether the wonderfully diverse and gifted assemblage of human beings on this earth really knows how to run a civilization.

—Adlai Stevenson

Peace is a daily, a weekly, a monthly process, gradually changing opinions, slowly eroding old barriers, quietly building new structures. And however undramatic the pursuit of peace, that pursuit must go on....

But peace does not rest in the charters and covenant alone. It lies in the hearts and minds of all people. And if it is cast out there, then no act, no pact, no treaty, no organization can hope to preserve it without the support and wholehearted commitment of all people. So let us not rest all our hopes on parchments and on paper—let us strive to build peace, a desire for peace, a willingness to work for peace in the hearts and minds of all of our people.

—John F. Kennedy

sian, was worn by each American on the trip. It produced smiles on the subway, invitations to dinner, and in at least one case, a reprieve from a ticklish situation.

Robert Sturdivant, a San Jose city planner, was taking pictures of Soviet citizens standing in line to buy melons, when KGB (secret police) agents scooped him up and took him to a small back room of his hotel to interrogate him. "When I showed them our 'friendship' button they brightened and said OK," Sturdivant recalled. "They felt we were people of good will."

When Tennison and the others tell their Soviet travel tales back home, they sometimes run into angry disbelief.

When Palo Alto businesswoman Jenny McLaughlin got back from the Soviet Union, she tried to discuss her experience with friends.

"People felt I had been duped," McLaughlin said. "It's almost as though, if their system isn't all bad, that means there's something wrong with ours."

Tennison admits she can't prove that she and her traveling companions aren't simply the beneficiaries of the ancient Russian art of *pokazuhka*, a practice with a single goal: to give a favorable—and false—impression of the country.

Tennison's hope is that, when enough Americans and Soviets get to know each other, they will put pressure on their leaders to enact life-supporting rather than life-negating policies, such as disarmament instead of an arms race. It's sometimes called the trickle-up theory.

110

It could happen in the United States, where the political system allows for the possibility of trickle-up policy-making. But do Soviet citizens have that kind of influence on their government?

"They feel like they do," Tennison said. But do they really?

"I don't know," she said quietly.

What if they don't? What good does all the traveling and lecturing and writing do?

"I don't know," she said again. "But I am completely clear that I have to do it. I couldn't live with myself if I didn't. I have to try."

—Jennifer Donovan

No man is an island, entire of itself; every man is a piece of the continent, a part of the main.

—John Donne

Granting that citizen diplomacy is enjoyable and probably harmless, some observers ask, "What, if any, deeper significance does it have? Does it have any disadvantages? How might it develop further?" Michael Shuman is a graduate of Stanford Law School and president of the Center for Innovative Diplomacy in Palo Alto, California; Gale Warner is a free-lance writer in Boston. Together they have written *The New Diplomats* (Crossroad/Continuum, January 1987), which tells the stories of a variety of Americans who have engaged in people-to-people explorations in the Soviet Union.

Effectiveness of the New Diplomats

Michael H. Shuman
Gale Warner

I like to believe that people in the long run are going to do more to promote peace than are governments. Indeed, I think that people want peace so much that one of these days governments had better get out of their way and let them have it.
—President Dwight D. Eisenhower
September 1959

WHAT IMAGES COME TO MIND WHEN thinking about the Soviet Union? For many Americans, these images include processions of tanks and rockets rolling through Red Square on a bitter cold October day, long lines of faceless peasants in dark rags being watched by KGB agents, and snowy gulags where exhausted dissidents lift heavy bricks at gunpoint. Most of us suspect these images are incomplete and misleading, but they are still the landmarks of our psyches, the framework in which we process all geopolitical facts. British historian E.P. Thompson has written, "We think others to death as we define them as the Other: the enemy: Asians: Marxists: non-people. The deformed human mind is the ultimate doomsday weapon—it is out of the human mind that the missiles and the neutron warhead come."

Over the past forty years, despite intermittent efforts by American and Soviet leaders to improve relations through summit meetings, trade agreements, and arms control treaties, the two most powerful nations on earth have remained locked in a "Cold War." During the best of times, the so-called "superpowers" could do no better than "détente," a term meaning a relaxation of tensions; "entente" or cooperation has always been out of the question. The principal architect of "détente," former President Richard Nixon, recently wrote in *The Real War*, "It may seem melodramatic to treat the twin poles of human experience represented by the United States and the Soviet Union as the equivalent of Good and Evil, Light and Darkness, God and Devil; yet if we allow ourselves to think of them that way, even hypothetically, it can help clarify our perspective on the world struggle."

At the worst of times, mutual animosities have struck such shrill notes that the superpowers seemed to be edging perilously close to war. In the early 1980s, Americans were outraged by the Soviet Union's invasion of Afghanistan, its suppression of Solidarity in Poland, and its shooting down of a Korean

People who develop the habit of thinking of themselves as world citizens are fulfilling the first requirement of sanity in our time.

—Norman Cousins

The U.S. already has enough nuclear submarines to sink everything on the ocean.... We must expect that when war breaks out again, we will use the weapons available. I think we'll probably destroy ourselves. I'm not proud of the part I played.

—Adm. Hyman G. Rickover

113

Hope is the capacity to live with danger without being overwhelmed by it; hope is the will to struggle against obstacles even when they appear insuperable.

—Pastoral letter of the United States Bishops on War and Peace, 1983

Never ascribe to an opponent motives meaner than your own.

—Sir James Barrie

Every gun that is made, every warship launched, every rocket fired, signifies in a final sense a theft from those who hunger and are not fed— those who are cold and not clothed.

—Dwight D. Eisenhower

747 airliner with 269 people aboard (including a U.S. Congressman). At a March 1983 gathering of evangelical ministers, President Ronald Reagan castigated the Soviet Union as an "evil empire." Soviet reaction to the United States' invasion of Grenada, military involvement in Central America, and deployment of intermediate-range cruise and Pershing II missiles in Western Europe was hardly more charitable. By 1984, three of America's most renowned experts on the Soviet Union— Averell Harriman, Clark M. Clifford, and Marshall D. Shulman—were moved to write: "[O]ur situation has become deeply troubling: there has been a total breakdown in negotiations with the Soviet Union while we have rushed into the largest peacetime military buildup in our history. Some regard these developments with complacency, even satisfaction, but, ignoring the lessons of history, they are blind to the dangerous trends now set in motion."

As relations have waxed and waned, the Cold War has inexorably continued, providing the ideological basis for an arms race unprecedented in human history. In the forty years since two nuclear bombs vaporized the cities of Hiroshima and Nagasaki, the arsenals of the United States and the Soviet Union have swelled to more than 50,000 nuclear weapons—arsenals large enough to fuel a Hiroshima-sized blast every second for nearly twelve days. Recent reports by a renowned international team of scientists, confirmed by the U.S. National Academy of Sciences, suggest that the detonation of even one percent

114

of these stockpiles could plunge the world into a dark, deadly "nuclear winter" and imperil the survival of *homo sapiens*.

The prospect of nuclear winter has convinced a growing number of Americans and Soviets that they must learn to live together or they will die together. The emerging realization is that both nations' fate, indeed the world's fate, now teeters on the ability of the superpowers to resolve their differences through discussion, negotiation, and compromise instead of through saber-rattling, missile-building, and nuclear war-fighting. The Cold War, in other words, must give way to a new era of cooperation.

Some hope that cooperation will arise from more enlightened national leaders. Jerry Hough, a noted Soviet specialist from Duke University, has pointed out that the two leading practitioners of foreign policy for the superpowers in the early 1980s, Ronald Reagan and Andrei Gromyko, "were in their mid-thirties when the atomic bomb was dropped and in their fifties when intercontinental ballistic missiles were deployed, [and] it has been difficult for them to grasp the impact of nuclear weapons on war and international relations." Only when these leaders and their successors begin awakening to the realities of the nuclear age, Hough and others argue, will the superpowers be capable of putting their Cold War to rest. They breathed an enormous sigh of relief when President Reagan and Party Chair Gorbachev finally sat down in Geneva during November of 1985 and reached several preliminary agreements for new cooperation on arms

It is more difficult to organize peace than to win a war, but the fruits of victory will be lost if the peace is not well organized.

—Aristotle

Next to knowing when to seize an opportunity, the most important thing in life is to know when to forego an advantage.

—Benjamin Disraeli

115

Seize upon truth, wherever it is found, among your friends, among your foes, on Christian or on heathen ground; the flower's divine where'er it grows.

—Isaac Watts

Governments, like clocks, go from the motion men give them, and as governments are made and moved by man, so by them they are ruined also. Therefore governments depend upon men rather than man upon government.

—William Penn

control, air safety, environmental protection, and citizen exchange.

Anyone following the topsy-turvy course of American-Soviet relations, however, cannot be too optimistic that leadership alone can melt the Cold War. Superpower relations seem destined to remain volatile until cooperation receives the full support of the American and Soviet publics. Without public support, enlightened policies can easily be swept away by new demagogues playing upon old Cold War fears.

When the superpower leaders call one another an "evil empire," they are reflecting not just their own feelings but those of their people. A 1983 Gallup Poll found that only 9 percent of the American public had favorable views toward the Soviet Union—the lowest level since 1956. In another poll, taken by Daniel Yankelovich, most Americans expressed their belief that Soviets would attack us or our allies if we were weak (65 percent), that the Soviets treat U.S. friendly gestures as weaknesses (73 percent), that "the only language the Soviets understand is force" (62 percent), and that we should weaken the Soviets at every opportunity "because anything that weakens our enemies makes us more secure" (46 percent). While similar public opinion polls are not available for the Soviet Union, numerous Westerners visiting there report that many Soviets are similarly fearful that, if given the chance, the United States would try to dominate and conquer the world. Only when *people* in the superpowers begin to reject these confrontational views will their national leaders have the political incentive to move toward long-term cooperation.

Since the Soviet Union was founded, a few courageous Americans have quietly begun building small bridges to the Soviet Union to replace mutual ignorance, fear, and hostility with mutual awareness, respect, and trust. Americans have reached out to every stratum of Soviet society, from the highest level Politburo members to the lowest level peasants. Some have settled for developing just friendships with Soviets, while others have sought to enter business deals, joint scientific projects, and new forums for political dialogue.

Twenty thousand years ago the family was the social unit. Now the social unit has become the world in which it may truthfully be said that each person's welfare affects that of every other.

—Arthur H. Compton

While their numbers were at first very small, in recent years thousands of Americans have joined them. Their ages range from 13 to 87. Their walks of life include law, medicine, business, education, farming, journalism, psychology, nursing, and junior high school. Their politics range from liberal to conservative, with some considering themselves apolitical. What they share is a belief that Americans must take personal responsibility for healing our ideological rifts with the Soviet Union and preventing a nuclear war. These are the men, women, and children whom we call the "new diplomats."

If they want peace, nations should avoid the pin-pricks that precede cannon-shots.

—Napoleon

How Does Citizen Diplomacy Work?

The new diplomats are more than tourists, for unlike most of the 50,000 Americans traveling to the Soviet Union each year, they have a strong sense of *mission* that guides their trip—before, during, and after. Since they do

117

Getting to Know the Other Side

not represent the United States government, they are not quite diplomats either. In many ways, however, their activities are very similar to those of traditional diplomats.

Hans Morgenthau, a well-known international relations scholar, once defined "diplomacy" as the principal instrument national governments use for "establishing the preconditions for permanent peace." Traditional diplomats serve as the nations' legal representatives, who can negotiate and enter authorized agreements; they serve as symbolic representatives, who show respect for other nations' diplomats through lavish ceremonies and parties; and they serve as "the nerve center of foreign policy, . . . [the] outlying fibers maintaining the two-way traffic between the [home country] and the outside world."

The new diplomats also serve these functions in their own pursuit of "permanent peace." While the new diplomats never claim to represent the United States government, they often do represent smaller chunks of America—churches, businesses, civic groups, local governments, or other Americans of like mind. The new diplomats enter binding contracts or other agreements on behalf of the Americans they represent. They demonstrate their respect and goodwill for Soviets through informal opportunities to sing, dance, play, and drink with them. And they maintain their own two-way traffic of information and impressions by reporting back home on their view of events in the Soviet Union and convey to Soviets the foreign policy views of those they represent. In short, while traditional diplomats serve as conduits between American and Soviet leaders, the new diplomats serve as conduits between the American and Soviet people.

In a seminal article on citizen diplomacy in the Winter 1981-1982 issue of the quarterly *Foreign Policy*, William D. Davidson, a psychiatrist specializing in foreign affairs, and Joseph V. Montville, a Foreign Service officer in the State Department, defined the official channel of governmental relations as "track one diplomacy" and the unofficial channel of people-to-people relations as "track two diplomacy." Their definition reflected their belief that the two tracks run parallel. Track two diplomacy, they wrote, is "a supplement to the understandable shortcomings of official relations." In track one diplomacy, national leaders "must assure their followers they will defend them against enemies—other tribes or nations—who want to conquer or destroy them." Unfortunately, this "necessary and predictable leadership function often gets tribes—and countries—into conflict." To defend their nation's interests, track one diplomats must make worst-case assumptions about an adversary's intentions, but these very assumptions may set in motion a chain reaction of mutual distrust, threats, and hostilities that can culminate in war. Track two diplomats, Davidson and Montville argued, create an alternative set of relationships that can prevent this kind of chain reaction: "Track two diplomacy is unofficial, nonstructured interaction. It is always open-minded, often altruistic, and . . . strategically optimistic, based on the

A great many people think they are thinking when they are merely rearranging their prejudices.

—William James

You can't escape the responsibility of tomorrow by evading it today.

—Abraham Lincoln

119

For countless ages the sun rose and set, the moon waxed and waned, the stars shone in the Milky Way, but it was only with the coming of man that these things were understood. Man has unveiled secrets which might have been thought undiscoverable. Much has been achieved in the realm of art, science, literature and religion. Is all this to end because so few are able to think of man rather than of this or that group of men?

—U Thant

best case analysis. Its underlying assumption is that actual or potential conflict can be resolved or eased by appealing to common human capabilities to respond to goodwill and reasonableness."

When track one diplomacy is stuck because one side perceives the other side's gain as its own loss, track two diplomacy can help identify common ground that might increase both sides' gains. Often the new diplomats can engage in informal, freewheeling discussions that can help identify new possibilities for official agreement, possibilities that might have remained hidden in traditional formalities. The new diplomats, therefore, try to open new areas for accommodation that can be developed, negotiated, and finalized by the traditional diplomats. "Both tracks," Davidson and Montville concluded, "are necessary for psychological reasons and both need one another."

At the most basic level, the new diplomats operate by spreading information about the viewpoints, politics, culture, and personalities of the citizens of one country to the citizens of the other. They aim to close the enormous information gap that now exists between the United States and the Soviet Union.

Soviet images of the United States, for example, are simultaneously too glorious and too critical. Soviets adore American art, film, literature, fashions, and music, and yet they also believe that America is a virtual war zone. Their news continually tells them about race riots, massive poverty, handgun crimes, political corruption, and U.S. misconduct abroad. They are incredulous that we could tolerate such anarchy and insecurity.

Yet most Soviets are also highly skeptical of their sources of information and eager—indeed, often ecstatic—to learn more by meeting and speaking with Americans. In this sense, an afternoon with an American is like tasting a delicious forbidden fruit. Comments Michael Murphy, co-founder of the Esalen Institute and an active citizen diplomat: "Every day the Soviet media is pounding in how absolutely awful life is in the West—massive unemployment, unjust poverty, dreadful insecurity. It's like a Catholic girls' school where the nuns pound in day after day after day how awful, evil and sinful sex is—it gets the girls so steamy they can't wait to get out and try it." Every American visiting the Soviet Union is a walking banned book, containing facts and opinions at odds with prevailing "party lines." What's more, Americans often carry with them actual books, magazines, or news clippings containing information that Soviets might otherwise not see.

As bad as the average Soviet's information is about the United States, the average American's information about the Soviet Union may well be worse. While Soviet people tend to be familiar with the latest in U.S. fashion, music, and literature, Americans are ignorant about nearly every aspect of Soviet life. Columnist Ellen Goodman writes that "in the United States, it is private citizens who self-censor Russian language literature, politics. . . . Maybe the notion that our shelves

The shortest and surest way to live with honor in the world is to be in reality what we appear to be; and if we observe, we shall find that all human virtues increase and strengthen themselves by the practice and experience of them.

—Socrates

The ultimate good desired is better reached by free trade in ideas.

—Oliver Wendell Holmes

121

are full of facts dulls our appetite." Senator Dan Quayle, a conservative Republican from Indiana, has remarked that even the U.S. Congress is pervaded by an "incredible lack of knowledge about the Soviet people and Soviet history." A recent survey showed that 44% of all Americans did not know that the Soviet Union fought against Nazi Germany in World War II, and more than half of incoming freshmen at a major university pointed to Central America when asked to place the Soviet Union on a map. Another survey revealed that, in contrast to the more than four million Soviets studying English, only 25,000 Americans are studying Russian. An oft-cited statistic is that there are more Soviets teaching English than Americans learning Russian.

The information gap between the superpowers is so wide that even if Americans traveling to the Soviet Union did nothing more than take some notes, snap some photographs, speak with several Soviets on the streets, and tell what they learned to their friends—what might be called "active tourism"—they would be serving an extremely valuable function. At a minimum, they would be teaching themselves and other Americans about the Soviet Union, as well as teaching the Soviets they have encountered about the United States.

Many American new diplomats, however, go many steps farther. When Sharon Tennison, for example, returned from her first trip to the Soviet Union, she began speaking and showing slides about her experiences to audiences throughout America. Today, hundreds of the new diplomats are conveying their

Let us overcome the angry man with gentleness, the evil man with goodness, the miser with generosity, the liar with truth.

—Mahabharata

122

experiences on radio talk shows, television news programs, and local newspaper articles, not just in American mass media but also in the Soviet mass media as well. Although the Soviet media are government controlled, many American new diplomats have addressed large public crowds in the Soviet Union, had their points of view reported in Soviet newspapers, and appeared on Soviet radio and television. Dr. Bernard Lown, for example, helped organize a special round-table discussion on the medical consequences of nuclear war that was broadcast on Soviet prime time—twice. Similarly, Soviets who visit the United States often describe their impression to audiences and write articles about their experiences in the Soviet press, as well as speak before American audiences and appear in American media.

The new diplomats are closing the information gap with a host of new, cheap global communications technologies. Through the wizardry of modern satellites, Columbia University now presents its students with live Soviet television; at any time of the day, students and faculty can sit and watch the latest Soviet news, movies, drama, or music. At Stanford University, where a similar facility is being built, several local cable companies are planning to carry these programs as entertainment for Bay Area residents. Nearly a dozen "space bridges," pioneered by Americans like Jim Hickman and Kim Spencer, have brought thousands of Americans and Soviets face-to-face via large video screens. With proliferating short-wave radio, many Soviets are now listening to the BBC and Radio Tokyo. As hun-

One day we must come to see that peace is not merely a distant good that we seek but a means by which we arrive at that goal. We must pursue peaceful ends through peaceful means.

—Martin Luther King, Jr.

123

Getting to Know the Other Side

As human beings, our greatness lies not so much in being able to remake the world—that is the myth of the "atomic age"—as in being able to remake ourselves.

—Mahatma Gandhi

With the proper flow of commerce across the borders of all countries it is unnecessary for soldiers to march across those borders.

—Thomas J. Watson

Don't put a loaded rifle on the stage unless someone intends to fire it.

—Anton Chekhov

dreds of thousands of personal computers enter the Soviet Union and begin linking with international electronic mail networks, a whole generation of young Soviet "hackers" may soon be communicating with one another and with outsiders in ways their parents never dreamed possible.

Technologies for global communication and transportation are literally shrinking the world and irreversibly diminishing the ability of anyone—whether bureaucrat or journalist, whether American or Soviet—to control information. These technologies, once affordable only by a very few Americans, are now within the reach of millions. Overseas flights now cost a sixth of what they did in 1940; overseas telephone calls cost a hundredth of what they did in 1935; and overseas cables cost a thousandth of what they did in 1866 (and a tenth of what they cost in 1970). As more and more Americans visit and communicate with Soviets—and carry modern technologies with them—people in both superpowers will increasingly be able to influence their nations' relations.

The new diplomats are also providing superpower leaders with better information that can enable them to respond to international emergencies. While the long-term goal of American and Soviet leaders is to normalize their relations, the short-term goal is to prevent, manage, and transcend crises—events like the shooting of the Korean Air Liner Flight 007 which, if handled poorly, could trigger a war. As recently as the early 1980s, the so-called hotline directly linking American and Soviet leaders was nothing more than a clumsy teletype. Thanks to the creative lobbying of Americans like Roger Fisher, William Urey, and Richard Smoke, Americans and Soviets are now connected by more advanced telecommunications and may soon be further assisted by a jointly run "crisis management center."

Knowing more about one another can reduce the risks of war but, alone, cannot eliminate these risks. We must use our knowledge, the new diplomats believe, to build a strong, complex, and durable web of relationships between the United States and the Soviet Union—indeed among all nations. Few Americans fear the nuclear weapons possessed by Great Britain or France, even though their weapons could wipe us off the map. Even China, a nuclear-armed country widely regarded as a "yellow menace" in the late 1960s, has since become a friend because of what Arthur W. Hummel, Jr., the U.S. Ambassador to China in the early 1980s, has called "an amazing web" of relationships. "As others have said, we no longer need to plan for the possibility of a war with China. . . . The multiplicity of relationships which we have—perhaps the majority of them having nothing to do with the U.S. government—is a genuine stabilizing force and a force which through the decades will produce much better understanding." The new diplomats aim to build relationships with the Soviet Union so that a Soviet-American war becomes as unthinkable as a Franco-American war or a Sino-American war.

If rational men cooperated and used their scientific knowledge to the full, they could now secure the economic welfare of all.

—Bertrand Russell

It is now thoroughly understood that the development of a nation's resources in peace is the only road to prosperity; that even successful war makes a people poor, crushing them with taxes and crippling their progress in industry and useful arts.

—Rev. W.E. Channing

125

Getting to Know the Other Side

A childlike mind, in its simplicity, practices that science of good to which the wise may be blind.

—Schiller

Nations have no existence apart from their people. If every person in the world loved peace, every nation would love peace. If all men refused to fight one another, nations could not fight one another.

—J. Sherman Wallace

In developing relationships with Soviets, the new diplomats have learned that successful relationships must pass through two very different stages—one ecstatic and the other tumultuous. The first stage is the affirmation that those on the other side "are real people, too," people who are, in many ways, "just like us."

Putting a human face on the enemy may seem a rather trivial accomplishment until one realizes, as the new diplomats have, how deeply both Americans and Soviets have dehumanized one another. As anthropologist Margaret Mead has noted, "our unfortunate capacity" is that we "define half the human race as not human." For Americans, a quick glance through the movie pages or a television guide quickly reveals our images of a subhuman and diabolical enemy. The 1984 film *Red Dawn* portrays Colorado high school students resisting a brutal invasion by Soviet paratroopers. The 1985 film *Rambo* depicts Soviets as sadistic torturers in Vietnam who are ultimately blown away by a heroic anti-Communist veteran. In 1987, the American Broadcasting Company intends to broadcast an epic television series about life in the United States after a bloodless Soviet conquest entitled *Amerika*. With images like these, it is easy to see how Americans can come to view the Soviet Union as an "evil empire" by dismissing its people as robots, Commies, nonhumans, and expendable. The thought of blowing up millions of Soviet children in the name of national security is not unthinkable if we never know who those children really are.

Similarly skewed and dehumanized images of the United States are presented by Soviet media and films. A 1984 ten-part Soviet television series called "Tass is Authorized to State" pitted clever and daring Soviet intelligence agents against a group of ruthless CIA spies. A 1983 film, "Incident in Quadrant 36-80," depicted Americans as violent psychopaths in a drama in which a U.S. submarine accidentally fires missiles at Soviet warships.

Despite these negative images, most Americans and Soviets regard the true source of "evil" as one another's leaders. In a 1983 *Time*/Yankelovich poll, nearly 90 percent of the American public agreed that "the Russian people are not nearly as hostile to the U.S. as their leaders are and, in fact, the Russians could be our friends if their leaders had a different attitude." Similarly, travelers to the Soviet Union are struck by the high regard most Soviets have for the American people.

Citizens in both superpowers are eager to establish relationships with their counterparts abroad. This revelation—that the once dark, mysterious "enemy" really looks, talks, thinks, dresses, worries, and behaves in all too familiar ways—can be profoundly shocking, visceral, and even euphoric. Perhaps more than anything, both Americans and Soviets are relieved to learn how much the enemy really fears nuclear weapons and, as the rock star Sting sings, how much they "love their children, too."

Yet in recognizing their mutual humanity with Soviets, the new diplomats achieve

I pray that the imagination we unlock for defense and arms and outer space may be unlocked as well for space and beauty in our daily lives.

—Adlai Stevenson

127

The conference table, though scarred by many past frustrations, cannot be abandoned for the certain agony of the battlefield. Disarmament with mutual honor and confidence is a continuing imperative. Together we must learn how to compare differences, not with arms, but with intellect and decent purpose.

—Dwight D. Eisenhower

Social progress makes the well-being of all more and more the business of each.

—Henry George

less a relationship and more an infatuation, a sudden rush that can easily and quickly evaporate. If these relationships are to succeed, many of the new diplomats have discovered that they also must learn about and come to terms with their significant cultural and political differences from the Soviets. This step can be as painful and confusing as the first step was euphoric and clarifying. The turning point often comes when, after the handshakes, toasts, speeches, and agreements, Americans criticize their own government and expect the Soviets to reciprocate. In nearly all formal settings (and even many informal ones), the Soviets will simply agree with the Americans' criticisms and say nothing critical about their own government. If the Americans have not yet come to appreciate Soviet political thinking, they may feel betrayed and frustrated and conclude that "they are really government propaganda mouthpieces, after all." If the Americans keep pushing, the Soviets then may feel betrayed as well, concluding that "they're really just trying to subvert our government, after all."

As in marriage, both an appreciation of similarities and a respect for differences are necessary for a long-term relationship. If a relationship is to last beyond the honeymoon, each partner must accept the other's imperfections, unpleasant mannerisms, and differing beliefs. To preserve the relationship, both partners must learn to cope with each other's faults and idiosyncrasies—while still not giving up entirely, perhaps, a secret hope of eventually changing the other. Explosive quarrels

128

filled with recrimination and regret will get nowhere. A thoughtful, sober relationship must be the nature of American ties with the Soviets. Given the current arsenals of nuclear weapons, the two societies are in a very real way married; divorce court is not an option.

Most of the new diplomats believe in the importance of *long-term* relationships. If Americans and Soviets simply have short diplomatic encounters, they may be able to exchange information and improve their mutual understanding, but they will never truly appreciate— let alone be capable of permanently tolerating and cooperating with—one another's differences. This is why the new diplomats are increasingly committed to spending many years, even decades, nurturing their ties with Soviets. While it is still too early to be sure how these ties can strengthen superpower relations, there are early indications they are succeeding in three important ways.

First, as more and more Americans and Soviets form relationships they care about, separation becomes more costly and unlikely. Each citizen relationship, by itself, has very little impact. But as more and more little strands tie the two nations together, a sturdy fabric is woven that no one international incident can easily rip apart. For example, the many Midwestern farm interests that benefitted from grain sales to the Soviet Union in the 1970s became among the most vocal advocates of restoring relations after President Carter imposed a grain embargo in 1979. By 1983, according to William Bundy, editor of *Foreign Affairs*, President Reagan "responded

Progress toward universal and enduring peace, as I see it, lies along three roads—organized international cooperation, mutual international understanding and progressive international disarmament. All must be traveled simultaneously.

—Dwight D. Eisenhower

Every heart that has beat strong and cheerfully has left a hopeful impulse behind it in the world, and bettered the tradition of mankind.

—Robert Louis Stevenson

We didn't all come over on the same ship, but we're all in the same boat.

—Bernard Baruch

to heavy domestic political pressures from the U.S. farm belt" when he scrapped the embargo and signed a new five-year contract "with a guarantee against interruption for political reasons." Citizen diplomats sometimes use the image of the Lilliputians tying down the giant Gulliver with thousands of tiny strands. As more and more Americans and Soviets do business together and enjoy the benefits of economic cooperation, as they make the commitment to learning something about the others' language, culture, and viewpoints, and as they become closer friends, the possibility of cutting these relationships off— let alone incinerating these people in a nuclear war—becomes increasingly unpopular.

Second, the high quality of even a few citizen diplomacy initiatives has helped the superpowers reach new accommodations. Thanks to people like Norman Cousins, high level Soviets and Americans have been able to gather once a year at the Dartmouth Conferences to discuss security issues in an informal setting. These track two discussions have culminated in track one agreements banning above-ground nuclear tests, installing the original "hot line," allowing direct flights between the United States and the Soviet Union, and expanding trade. When the superpowers reached an impasse over the release of six dissident Pentecostalists who hid in the U.S. embassy in Moscow, they called upon Olin Robinson, the President of Middlebury College, to mediate and resolve the dispute.

Finally, citizen diplomacy is improving superpower relations by delegitimating nuclear war and, indeed, all war. By creating relationships in which more and more Americans and Soviets *care* for one another in a serious way, deep enough to transcend crises, citizen diplomacy is gradually transforming the act of launching nuclear weapons into an act of murdering friends. It was this insight that once prompted Roger Fisher to recommend implanting the launch code near the heart of the military attaché who normally carries it in a briefcase. This way, the President would have to gore at least one human being before ordering the slaughter of millions. If the new diplomats can make people and leaders in both superpowers appreciate that the objects of their abstract policies are real people, then perhaps that can make a decisive difference in humanizing their policies.

There is a long, painful, slow, but very persistant historical movement from stable war into unstable war into unstable peace into stable peace. The main object of peace policy is to speed up the transition by deliberate decision.

—Kenneth Boulding

How Have Governments Reacted To Citizen Diplomacy?

Citizen diplomacy has essentially been an American innovation because American citizens, unlike their Soviet counterparts, enjoy relatively broad freedoms of speech, assembly, and travel. Yet in matters of foreign policy, the traditional policy-makers in both superpowers have been reluctant to relinquish their former autonomy to the new diplomats, though this now may be changing.

In the early days of the Cold War, the U.S. government frequently denied passports to Americans trying to travel to the Soviet Union. Those who were able to travel—people like William Mandel—often returned to inquisitions by the FBI and by Congressman

It is a puzzling fact that international conduct is so often judged by far lower standards than are the acts of individuals...Men who would not think of assaulting another to gain an end—who would indeed suffer great loss, and be proud to suffer it, rather than obtain their rights by such a method—feel that a nation should be ever ready to assert its claims by blows.

—George Malcolm Stratton

131

Joseph McCarthy's Committee on Un-American Affairs and then found themselves immediately unemployed. McCarthyism receded by the mid-1950s, but it was not until détente in the 1970s that the U.S. government actively supported people-to-people contacts between Americans and Soviets.

When détente collapsed, official hostility toward citizen diplomats flared once again. When the Reagan Administration first came to office, it banned most trade with the Soviet Union, suspended Aeroflot flights, refused to renegotiate several key cultural and scientific exchange agreements, cut the budgets of continuing exchange programs, restricted the movement of Soviet visitors to the United States, denied entry visas to some Soviets, and intensified its anti-Soviet rhetoric about "fighting limited nuclear wars" against an "evil empire." Unlike the 1950s, however, this period goaded thousands of citizen diplomats into action.

By the mid-1980s, the attitudes of the Reagan Administration began to soften. Many officials were not sure what good it really could do and feared that some Americans might be fooled by Soviet propaganda, but they were no longer opposed to Americans going over and doing their thing. To be sure, there were exceptions. In mid-1985, for example, Reagan appointees to the Corporation for Public Broadcasting (CPB), a private non-profit organization created to channel public funds into the nation's public broadcasting system, refused to provide funds for a delegation of Public Broadcasting Service executives to visit

Tsze-King asked, "Is there one word which may serve as a rule for practice for all one's life?" The Master said, "Is not reciprocity such a word? What you do not want done to yourself, do not do to others."

—Confucius

Moscow and discuss arrangements for exchanging television shows. CPB Chair Sonia Landau argued, "I just don't want the CPB name associated with it. Russian TV is not exactly the BBC. We are talking about the same guys who shot down the Korean jetliner." Despite these exceptions, however, the U.S. government became increasingly supportive of citizen diplomacy.

The biggest convert was President Reagan himself, who came to recognize that the new diplomats embody what's best about America—pluralist thinking, independent initiative, and global responsibility. In June 1984, President Reagan said: "We should broaden opportunities for American and Soviet citizens to get to know each other better. . . . The way governments can best promote contacts among people is by not standing in the way. Our administration will do all we can to stay out of the way and to persuade the Soviet government to do likewise."

A few days before President Reagan met with Mikhail Gorbachev at a November 1985 summit, he shocked political commentators with what has since been dubbed his "People to People" speech:

Imagine how much good we could accomplish, how the cause of peace would be served, if more individuals and families from our respective countries could come to know each other in a personal way. . . .

I feel the time is ripe for us to take bold new steps to open the way for our peoples to participate in an unprecedented way in the building of peace. . . .

A period of high civilization is one in which thoughts fly freely from mind to mind, from one country to another—yes, from the past into the present.

—Gilbert Highet

In times like the present, men should utter nothing for which they would not willingly be responsible through time and in eternity.

—Abraham Lincoln

133

Instead of resisting increased economic interdependence, we should be embracing it wholeheartedly. In my view, it is our great hope for peace.

If we get sufficiently interlaced economically, we will most probably not bomb each other off the face of the planet. For example, I suggest that we are so economically intertwined with Japan that if we have any problems with Japan today, we are going to work them out. I think the same will be true globally. We should welcome increased trade with the Soviet Union, all the developed nations, and the Third World, as world trade moves us closer to world peace.

—John Naisbitt

We could look to increase scholarship programs; improve language studies; conduct courses in history, culture, and other subjects; develop new sister-cities; establish libraries and cultural centers; and yes, increase athletic competition. People of both our nations love sports. If we must compete, let it be on the playing fields and not the battlefield.

In science and technology, we could launch new joint space ventures, and establish joint medical-research projects. In communications, we'd like to see more appearances in the other's mass media by representatives of both our countries. . . . [P]eople-to-people contacts can build genuine constituencies for peace in both countries. . . .

Such exchanges can build in our societies thousands of coalitions for cooperation and peace. Governments can only do so much; once they get the ball rolling, they should step out of the way and let people get together to share, enjoy, help, listen, and learn from each other. . . .

It is not an impossible dream that our children and grandchildren can someday travel freely back and forth between America and the Soviet Union; visit each other's homes; work and study together; enjoy and discuss plays, music, and television; and root for teams when they compete.

President Reagan's speech echoed the same points citizens had been making for years. And it was more than just rhetoric. The speech presaged several important agreements that came out of the summit—agreements

134

renewing a number of U.S.-Soviet exchanges, resuming direct commercial flights between the countries, and opening new consulates in Kiev and New York. How much support the U.S. government will offer track two diplomacy in the years ahead is uncertain. At a minimum, however, the government seems unlikely to begin radically curtailing citizens' rights to communicate and travel abroad— the rights that will enable them to launch track two initiatives on their own.

The Soviets' reaction to citizen diplomacy has also been complex. Like their American counterparts, Soviet leaders presiding over the early stages of the Cold War were adamant about keeping foreign influences away from the Soviet people; their authoritarian power enabled them to repress citizen diplomacy far more effectively than in the West. Foreign radio signals were jammed, foreign literature and letters were confiscated, foreign telephone calls and telex messages were delayed or cancelled, and foreign visa applications were often denied. The old guard was also extremely reluctant to allow Soviets to leave the country; even during the heyday of détente, no more than 14,000 Soviets received visas to visit the United States.

As American citizen diplomats began descending upon the country in the early 1980s, the views of Soviet leaders began shifting. "Initially hesitant in 1980," states a 1985 report from the Kennan Institute for Advanced Russian Studies, "the Soviets have responded energetically to the increased interest of private American organizations to engage in

Vast and fearsome as the human scene has become, personal contacts of the right people, in the right places, at the right time, may yet have a potent and valuable part to play in the cause of peace which is in our hearts.

—Winston Churchill

135

Getting to Know the Other Side

We should be careful to get out of an experience all the wisdom that is in it...not like the cat that sits down on a hot stove lid. She will never sit down on a hot stove lid again...and this is well...but also, she will never sit down on a cold one anymore.

—Mark Twain

cultural exchanges of all types."

But resistance by the old guard remains high. In 1984, for example, the government passed several new repressive laws against foreign contacts—one that punished any Soviet giving shelter, transportation, or other "services" to a foreigner without official permission, and another making illegal acceptance of "money or other material value from foreign organizations or persons acting in the interest of those organizations." While there have been no verified cases of these laws actually being enforced, they are still on the books and could be activated at any moment.

With the emergence of Mikhail Gorbachev, however, the Soviet government may be beginning to open itself to a degree unprecedented in its history. The verdict will not be in for some time, but Gorbachev and his contemporaries seem to see—unlike their predecessors—three important reasons for cooperating with the new diplomats.

First, the new Soviet leaders have learned that citizen diplomats can help facilitate dialogue with the U.S. government. During the early years of the Reagan administration, when government-to-government communication had practically disintegrated, citizen diplomats provided one of the few "back channels" they had for relating to the United States. Even though official relations have since improved, many Soviets remain eager to keep these back channels open, both to improve their communications with Americans and to use in the future should the official channels close again.

Second, as Samuel Pisar, a noted international lawyer, has written, "The new Soviet leaders know that the choice before them is fateful: either to face up to the challenges of an advanced economy, with the free movement of ideas, people and goods that this presupposes, or to isolate themselves in an armed fortress condemned to obsolescence." The old guard may still try to restrict foreign "ideas, people and goods" from the general Soviet populace, but the fact remains that hundreds of thousands of foreigners entering the country for economic intercourse will necessarily foster other ties with millions of Soviets. "If writers cannot publish, if scientists cannot travel, if intellectuals cannot communicate," Pisar continues, "then inventors cannot innovate and managers cannot manage."

The declining relevance of the old guard's resistance to opening up the country was revealed at the 27th Soviet Communist Party Congress in March 1986. Victor Cherbrikov, head of the KGB, announced a new crackdown on video recorders because they were spreading "ideas alien to us, a cult of cruelty and violence and amorality." He was apparently incognizant that the previous day Yegor Ligachev, the chief ideologist at the Politburo, announced that "measures have been formulated to start large-scale production of video technology."

Finally, many Soviets are honestly concerned with preventing war and see citizen diplomacy as a promising avenue for "peaceful coexistence" with the United States. No

American-Soviet trade as a strand in the expanded web of involvement of the Soviet economy in the global system can nurture domestic change in the Soviet Union. But the changes to be anticipated will be only steps in the gradual opening up of the Soviet Union to global society and of less confrontationist policies toward the West. Trade relations cannot be expected by themselves to form the basis for an enduring peace between the superpowers; political and cultural efforts are needed as well. Trade relations cannot ensure peace, but they can contribute to the process of building peace.

—Cyril E. Black and Robbin F. Laird, "The Impact of Trade on Soviet Society," in *Securing Our Planet*

Getting to Know the Other Side

The realization that our small planet is only one of many worlds gives mankind the perspective it needs to realize sooner that our own world belongs to all of its creatures, that the moon landing marks the end of our childhood as a race and the beginning of a newer and better civilization.... It is not easy to see how the more extreme forms of nationalism can long survive when men have seen the Earth in its true perspective as a single small globe against the stars.

—Arthur C. Clarke

American can leave the Soviet Union without being overwhelmed by the nation's sense of its past. Many commentators have observed that World War II—and the loss of twenty million Soviet people—seems like only yesterday. Memorials, paintings, songs, pins, and icons all commemorate the "Great Patriotic War." True, much of this rhetoric is aimed at obfuscating public scrutiny of the Soviet government's own militaristic behavior. But the memories of the horrors of war are also very real and motivate many Soviets, both inside and outside government, to do what they can to prevent another cataclysmic war. There is a growing recognition within the Politburo that security in the nuclear age depends more on constructive economic relations with the West than on having the latest military gadget. "A Western Europe [, for example,] that can offer technology," Jerry Hough argues, "is more useful to the Soviet Union than a conquered Western Europe that must be communized and provides not technology but political headaches."

Revulsion to warfare and a longing for economic prosperity, therefore, are leading the Soviets to overcome their long tradition of xenophobia and open themselves up to more foreign influence. To be sure, there are other, more subtle barriers to a massive expansion of citizen diplomacy. To give just two examples, both governments are reluctant to provide any funding for citizen diplomacy and Soviet hotels may soon reach full capacity. Yet these are precisely the areas where citizen diplomats might be able to do constructive lobbying in the future. Certainly the U.S. Congress might be persuaded that financing a hundred thousand U.S. visitors to the Soviet Union might buy more national security than an equivalently priced aircraft carrier. Likewise, the Soviet government might be convinced a billion rubles earmarked for heavy missiles might be better spent on new hotels. If the past is any guide, future obstacles to citizen diplomacy will arise, but creative Americans and Soviets will find ways around them.

What About Those Nagging Criticisms?

No matter how many modest successes the new diplomats can claim, many Americans have castigated their efforts. Typical of these criticisms were those leveled against the Nobel Prize Committee, which, in 1985, awarded its peace prize to the International Physicians for the Prevention of Nuclear War, a group founded by Drs. Bernard Lown, a cardiologist at the Harvard School of Public Health, and Yevgeni Chazov, a high-ranking Soviet cardiologist, to educate their publics on the medical consequences of nuclear war. *The Wall Street Journal* chastised the Nobel Committee because "the Soviets use the group to foist one-sided calls for disarmament on their Western dupes." *The New Republic* scolded: "There is an elaborate pretense that Soviet bloc doctors are, like Western doctors, an independent group for influencing public opinion and pressuring government at home. The Western doctors do not seem to notice, or perhaps to care, that their East bloc col-

In the long run you hit only what you aim at. Therefore though you should fail immediately, you had better aim at something high.

—Henry David Thoreau

My interest is in the future because I am going to spend the rest of my life there.

—Charles F. Kettering

139

> There is no security
> on this earth. Only
> opportunity.
>
> —Gen. Douglas
> MacArthur

> There are misreadings of
> the adversary's intentions—
> sometimes even the refusal
> to consider them at all.
> There is the tendency of
> national communities to
> idealize themselves and to
> dehumanize the opponent.
> There is the blinkered,
> narrow vision of the pro-
> fessional military planner
> and his tendency to make
> war inevitable by assum-
> ing its inevitability.
> Tossed together, these
> components form a pow-
> erful brew. They guide
> the fears and the ambi-
> tions of men. They seize
> the policies of govern-
> ments and whip them
> around like trees before
> the tempest.
>
> —George F. Kennan

leagues never take a position contrary to the current Soviet line." Soviet physicians who *do* take positions critical of the Soviet government, protested Sergei Batovrin, founding member of the Moscow Group to Establish Trust, a much harassed independent Soviet citizens group, are "subject to harsh persecution." Implicit in these criticisms are three themes—that citizen diplomacy is useless, immoral, and dangerous.

Since the Soviet people have virtually no influence over their government, critics first allege, how can the new diplomats expect to change anything by establishing closer ties with the Soviet people? "Our problem with the Soviet Union is not the absence of communication," writes *Christian Science Monitor* columnist John Hughes, "it is the antithetical character of their society to democracy." Conservative professor Irving Kristol goes further: "'Liberalization' remains a fantasy. True, the more insane 'excesses' of Stalinist terror have themselves been 'liquidated,' but these were never integral to Leninist rule. The party still rules supreme, its Leninist orthodoxy intact; the Soviet peoples remain sullen, intimidated and coerced into passivity."

While the Soviet people certainly have less power than their American counterparts, assertions that the Soviet government is an Orwellian monolith are serious exaggerations. On issues that escape our attention—especially local issues like the quality of consumer goods, medical care, or schools—public debates rage every day in Soviet media; *Pravda*, for example, contains a lively "letters to the editor" section. Public outrage over the pollution of Lake Baykal, the largest fresh water lake in the world, led to the closure of many industrial facilities operating there. Vociferous complaints from city dwellers over air quality led the government to move many smokestack industries to the periphery of these cities.

Even over such high level matters as nuclear weapons policy, public debates have been brewing. As Dusko Doder of *The Washington Post* observes:

"Lost in the unfolding East-West propaganda exchanges over the past two years is the extraordinary fact that the question of nuclear weapons has gradually entered Soviet public debate. For a country devoid of real political discourse and given to obsessive secrecy, particularly about military matters, this is a significant turn of events. . . . "

Thus, while the new diplomats recognize the limits of Soviet public opinion, they hope to exert whatever influence is possible. This also explains, however, why the new diplomats often choose to work with those in power —why, for example, Dr. Lown decided to work with Dr. Chazov. Those within the Soviet government, while ostensibly unified behind a "party line," are still people with many diverse values, interests, and opinions that change in subtle ways as they meet and work with Americans. By working with Dr. Chazov, for example, Dr. Lown was able to open up public debate on the unwinnability of nuclear war.

Many new diplomats have also chosen to work through the many government-spon-

The risks inherent in disarmament pale in comparison to the risks inherent in an unlimited arms race.

—John F. Kennedy

141

*Do not condemn the
judgment of another
because it differs from
your own. You may both
be wrong.*

—Dandemis

*Never one thing and
seldom one person can
make for a success. It
takes a number of them
merging into one perfect
whole.*

—Marie Dressler

sored organizations that make up the fabric of
daily Soviet life—organizations like the Soviet
Peace Committee, the US-USSR Friendship
Society, the USA-Canada Institute, and the
Soviet Committee of Women. While these
organizations espouse official viewpoints, the
new diplomats have chosen to work through
them because often they are staffed by thoughtful Soviets eager to take innovative, sometimes even risky initiatives that do help improve relations. The Soviet Peace Committee
assisted Chris Senie as his group of Americans,
Soviets, and Scandinavians bicycled for peace;
Gostelradio helped Jim Hickman put together
the early space bridges; and the Soviet Sports
Committee supported Cynthia Lazaroff's efforts to lead a mountaineering expedition for
both American and Soviet youths.

The new diplomats recognize that no
matter whom they work with—whether Soviets on the streets, middle level bureaucrats,
or upper level officials—change in the Soviet
Union will only come gradually. As frustrating
as they sometimes find it to work with officials
who refuse to criticize their government (at
least overtly), they realize that only through
patient, persistent, and respectful dialogue will
the system ever really change.

The second theme of critics is that it is
morally abhorrent for Americans to work with
members of the Soviet Communist Party who
so flagrantly violate the human rights of "independent" peace activists and other dissidents. They often point to the case of Sergei
Batrovin.

On June 4, 1982, Batrovin, a Moscow

artist, and several other Soviet citizens announced the formation of what he called "The Group to Establish Trust Between the USSR and the US," whose express purpose was to develop "a four-sided dialogue" among the governments and people of the United States and Soviet Union. Nearly 1000 people signed the group's founding appeal; sister groups sprang up in Leningrad, Odessa, Novosibirsk, and elsewhere. The Soviet government, however, decided that this group was a threat and began harassing group members by confiscating an exhibit of 88 anti-war paintings and placing the group's leaders under house arrest. Batrovin was placed in a Moscow psychiatric hospital, where, he says, "they told me that in the Soviet Union only the government can work for peace." When what remained of the group put a list of U.S. peace organizations in one thousand Moscow mailboxes, hoping to get correspondence started between concerned citizens of the two countries, the government accused them of being linked to the CIA and Batrovin was hand-delivered an exit visa with instructions to leave the country in a week.

With the Batrovin incident—as with countless other instances—the Soviet Union has made clear that it will not tolerate an *independent* citizen diplomacy movement. The Soviet view is not dissimilar to that of large American corporations. In the same way that management of General Motors would purge disgruntled employees who tried initiating their own public relations program, the leaders of the Soviet Union try to squelch citizens who

Times of general calamity and confusion have ever been productive of the greatest minds. The purest ore is produced from the hottest furnace, and the brightest thunderbolt is elicited from the darkest storm.

—Colton

Friendship is a plant of slow growth and must undergo and withstand the shocks of adversity before it is entitled to the appellation.

—George Washington

143

begin operating outside established government organizations. To us, running a country like a large corporation is reprehensible, but this is the reality of Soviet life.

Critics quickly retort that the Soviet reality is so inherently evil that Americans' only moral recourse is to confront, challenge, and harass these Soviet managers. Many of the new diplomats share critics' concerns about Soviet society, especially its human rights violations, but disagree completely on tactics. They believe that the confrontational approach is a guaranteed loser. They point out, for example, that Jewish emigration from the Soviet Union reached its peak during the late 1970s as a result of détente; when relations between the superpowers soured in the early 1980s, Jewish emigration slowed to practically zero. American courtships with Soviet dissidents and refuseniks, they also point out, can often increase harassment of them.

Unlike their critics, the new diplomats adopt the assumption that the Soviet Communist Party will be in power for the foreseeable future. In working with Soviets, they are not endorsing the nation and its policies—any more so than President Reagan was endorsing the Soviet Union by meeting with Mikhail Gorbachev at the Geneva summit—but, instead, they are recognizing that top Soviet government officials are the people with most of the power to decide whether to build, scrap, or launch nuclear weapons. To ignore or needlessly antagonize official Soviet leadership is political suicide. While many new diplomats hope to reform the Soviet

Blessed are the peacemakers, for they shall be called the children of God.

—Matthew, V. 9

If anyone is not willing to accept your point of view, try to see his point of view.

—Lebanese proverb

Union—as well as the United States—they believe that these reforms, whatever form they might take, must grow out of a cautiously constructed web of cooperative relationships with people at *all* levels of Soviet society—dissidents and Politburo members, artists and factory workers, party bureaucrats and children.

By cooperating with those working *within* the Soviet system, the new diplomats are neither supporting nor denigrating the activities of dissidents working outside the system. The new diplomats simply acknowledge that for every courageous dissident there are many courageous Soviets who are working more quietly but no less profoundly for change, some of whom are Party members and some of whom are not. Cutting off communication with Soviets because of official human rights abuses is a lose-lose strategy. It's a strategy that would accomplish about as much as various Soviet committees would were they to cease working with Americans until the U.S. government committed itself to improving conditions for urban blacks and native Americans.

The new diplomats believe that we do not have to choose between working to improve human rights within the Soviet Union and working to reduce the risk of nuclear war. The evidence of the last fifteen years strongly suggests that improved relations between the superpowers accomplishes both goals. A lessening of tensions not only helps the cause of Jews and Soviet dissidents, it helps guarantee the ultimate human right for the people of the planet—the right to life itself.

A final criticism against the new diplo-

The art of life lies in a constant readjustment to our surroundings.

—Kakuzo Okahura

Qui tacit, consentit. (He who is silent consents.)

—Unknown

145

Peace itself is not a static state. Change and development, conflict and synthesis are all part of it. What is important is how we deal with conflicts. If they are repressed or suppressed they will emerge later in one form or another and sour notes will sound at unexpected times and places. If we begin to listen to ourselves, and listen to others, then the possibility of a dynamic peace or harmony arises. Then as different notes emerge, they interact in such a way as to create a new whole, which transcends the sum of the parts.

When we are at peace with ourselves, we are not in our own way; when we are at peace with others we get out of their way and appreciate them.

—Frank Rubenfeld, psychotherapist

mats is that they have become "dupes" who naively accept the official version of Soviet life and policy. As these Americans and their constituents get captured by Soviet views, America's "resolve" will be weakened, leaving our nation open to Soviet hegemony and, ultimately, domination.

It is certainly true that, in the past, the Soviets have fooled Americans. In the 1930s and 1940s, as Paul Hollander's book *Political Pilgrims* meticulously documents, many noted Americans were shown model facilities for health care, education, farming, and even criminal rehabilitation, and returned home to proclaim the wondrous accomplishments of the Soviet state—completely incognizant of the exceptional nature of what they saw. In 1944, for example, Henry Wallace, then vice-president of the United States, and Owen Lattimore, professor of Johns Hopkins University, were given a tour of Magadan, one of the most sinister forced labor camps, and later described it as "a combination of TVA and Hudson's Bay Company."

Today's new diplomats are acutely aware of how their predecessors were deceived. Unlike dupes, however, whose agendas and contacts were all carefully orchestrated by the Soviet government, most new diplomats have a great deal of latitude in setting their own agendas and arranging their own contacts. Most seek a variety of perspectives, some inside the party and some outside, to help inoculate themselves from receiving—let alone swallowing—any "big lie." Paradoxically, the one guaranteed way of foiling any potential deceptions is to have even more citizen diplomacy. The more Americans who travel, meet, speak, and work with Soviets, the more likely mass deception will be exposed and deterred in the future.

Rather than promote the interests of either the United States or the Soviet Union, as dupes might do, the new diplomats are consciously encouraging both nations to recognize and enter agreements on their common interests—in exchanging culture, expanding trade, and preventing war, to name a few. Many U.S. critics simply deduce that these agreements are in the interest of the Soviet Union and conclude, *ipso facto*, that they are against the interest of the United States. "The thrust of American foreign policy," Irving Kristol admonishes, "should be to inflict a series of defeats, however minor, on the Soviets." This is precisely the destructive Cold War logic that track two diplomacy is trying to eliminate.

The dupe charge seems even more tenuous in the face of all the ways many new diplomats are trying to change Soviet society. Many of the new diplomats are deeply concerned with improving human rights for Soviets, reversing the Soviet arms buildup, and reducing the power and ambitions of the Soviet military. These suggestions go over no better in Moscow than their analogues do in Washington, D.C. Yet because the new diplomats offer criticism *in the context of cooperation,* superpower leaders are increasingly open to their proposals.

The only way Americans will certainly be duped is if they cut themselves off from the

Everyone has a stake in this, and the obligation to become informed....It is strange...that we are vocal and determined on issues like taxes, inflation and unemployment. Yet on the basic issue of survival, many of us feel ignorant and powerless and, therefore, remain silent.

—John Filer
Chairman, Aetna Corp.

I think that we may safely trust a good deal more than we do. We may waive just so much care of ourselves as we honestly bestow elsewhere.

—Henry David Thoreau

Today the real test of power is not capacity to make war but capacity to prevent it.

—Anne O'Hare McCormick

147

The worth of a state, in the long run, is the worth of the individuals composing it.

—John Stuart Mill

A man is a little thing while he works by and for himself; but when he gives voice to the rules of love and justice, he is godlike.

—Ralph Waldo Emerson

Soviet Union altogether and return to the Cold War. If our information sources are reduced to U.S. media that rarely venture beyond their inner press circles in Moscow, to Soviet media that only boast about what's best in Soviet society, and to Soviet emigrants who highlight their own worst experiences, we will be left with the same distorted impressions of the Soviet Union we have had for nearly seventy years. If we refuse to enter relationships with the Soviets in areas like trade or scientific research, other less paranoid democracies like Japan, Canada, Great Britain, West Germany, France, and Italy will simply take our place. If we deny ourselves the opportunity to build new ties with the Soviets and prevent a nuclear war, we—and the rest of the world—will be the big losers.

The reign of top-down diplomacy is undergoing a profound transformation. The question is not whether citizen diplomacy will come of age; the era of citizen diplomacy has already arrived. The new diplomats are here, multiplying in number and growing in power. The only real questions are who will join next and when.

What is most significant about citizen diplomacy is that it gives each of us a concrete, realistic task for tomorrow. We no longer need to despair that nuclear war is inevitable and we as individuals can do nothing about it. We can now join hands with our neighbors and transform our enemies, one by one, into our friends and partners. The power to rebuild the wreckage of U.S.-Soviet relations into an exemplar for a new era of global peace is now within our grasp. As Albert Einstein wrote at the advent of the nuclear age: "We cannot leave it to generals, senators, and diplomats to work out a solution over a period of generations. . . . Today lack of interest would be a great danger, for there is much the average man can do."

There are people still alive who were children when Marconi managed to send a single letter, in Morse code, across the ocean. Now we can talk to Moscow as if we're in the same room. Probably the most dramatic form of citizen diplomacy is the space-bridge, a name for exchanges conducted over television between participants in two countries who are linked by space satellite and who view one another, generally, on large screens with simultaneous translation. Space-bridges began in 1982, and are among the amazing untold stories—untold mainly because, in contrast to the Soviet Union, the U.S. has broadcast very few of the space-bridges that have occurred. On this side most of them were seen only by people at a rock festival or a scientific conference or an award ceremony. One of the major exceptions, the Live Aid concerts, had only brief Soviet participation. It was Phil Donahue who created one of the first Soviet-American space-bridges that was widely broadcast in the U.S. Behind his success lies a remarkable story of initiatives that have created a new form of superpower communications. The authors of this chapter are close to the leading pioneers on the American side.

Space-Bridge Pioneers

Jim Garrison
David Landau
Roger Macdonald

with the staff of the Esalen Soviet-American Exchange Program and of the Institute for Soviet-American Relations

The time has passed when foreign affairs and domestic affairs could be regarded as separate and distinct. The borderline between the two has practically ceased to exist.

—Walter Bedell Smith

TELECOMMUNICATIONS IS IN SOME ways as mighty a force in today's world as are the nuclear arsenals of the two superpowers. Everyone knows that the superpowers now possess a destructive capability equal to tens of thousands of times the firepower that was expended in all of World War II. Not many people know that in only a few seconds a single advanced communications satellite is able to transmit back and forth between the Soviet Union and the United States all the information contained in the entire *Encyclopedia Britannica*.

A recent study for the United States Arms Control and Disarmament Agency, produced by the Harvard Nuclear Negotiation Project, asserts that the use of audio-visual telecommunications to link U.S. and Soviet decision-makers in times of crisis could be instrumental in stopping a nuclear outbreak. But that is only the most obvious way in which satellite communications could be a force for peace. If U.S. and Soviet leaders could talk regularly, face to face, in everyday settings, without the public pressure that attends in personal summit meetings; if scientists and health professionals, without having to leave their respective countries, could share information with each other on humanitarian projects; if university faculties and students could exchange lectures, seminars and ideas; if the two peoples could gain an understanding of each other's history, tradition, culture, and home life—how, then, would the superpowers' confrontational posture change?

The spread of information by electronic means has remade our own society more than once, and the process continues to develop rapidly. Microelectronics, computer graphics, speech synthesis, data-base management, satellite television, and artificial intelligence, have

Our problems are man-made. Therefore, they can be solved by man. And man can be as big as he wants. No problem of human destiny is beyond human beings. Man's reason and spirit have often solved the seemingly unsolvable—and we believe they can do it again. I am not referring to the absolute, infinite concepts of universal peace and goodwill of which some . . . fanatics dream. I do not deny the value of hopes and dreams, but we merely invite discouragement and incredulity by making that our only and immediate goal. Let us focus instead on a more practical, more attainable peace—based not on a sudden revolution in human nature but on a gradual evolution in human institutions—on a series of concrete actions and effective agreements which are in the interests of all concerned.

—John F. Kennedy, from a 1963 speech reprinted in *Securing Our Planet*

151

only begun to make their presence felt. America has come to be known as an "information society." More than half our Gross National Product is expended in the production, processing and dissemination of information; more people are employed in this vast enterprise than in manufacturing, agriculture, and mining combined. By the year 2000, as much as two-thirds of our national work force will be employed in, or allied with, the information and knowledge industry.

The technological reach of telecommunications is indisputable; however, the uses to which it will be put are far from evident. Harvard sociologist Daniel Bell has remarked that after the discovery of human speech, the invention of writing, and the advent of printing, electronics is creating the fourth great revolution in man's ability to communicate. Historically, telecommunications has arrived on the scene at a time when the paramount issue is nuclear war versus human survival. Political institutions are not yet making full use of the technical advances of satellite communication. Even so, as the recent history of Soviet-American satellite linkups shows, the governments of both superpowers are more open to the possibilities of increased telecommunications than the record of their political relationship suggests.

What, then, would be the best use of the present opportunity? In a word, education, in the broadest sense of the term. We and the Soviets are separated by physical distance, cultural non-awareness and historic mistrust. Our political leaders cannot seem to discern

We must build spiritual and scientific bridges linking the nations of the world.

—Albert Einstein

152

each other's intentions. Our science and technology exchanges, which were flourishing in the late 60s and 70s, are now greatly reduced. A minimum of trade passes between our countries. Little exists to oppose the escalation of political conflict and the drift toward war.

An ongoing program of Soviet-American telecommunications could provide a forum for discussion between political and business leaders; it could bring together researchers and thinkers to explore various approaches to problems in a host of fields; it could create educational exchanges between students and faculty members in universities, high schools and grade schools of the two countries; it could make possible a wide range of joint performances between entertainers and athletes. Overall, it could allow Soviet and American citizens to get to know each other and learn about each other's societies without the interference of propaganda and political disputes. A program of concrete cooperation could bring the people of the superpowers together.

Telecommunications is one of those discoveries that, by its nature, suggests a transcending of artificial boundaries and political arrangements. It reshapes the way we see ourselves, each other, and the way we relate to our surroundings. Even in the worst of times, it can promote an exchange of knowledge—in science, education, medicine, health, environment, business and politics—so as to lay a groundwork for productive cooperation between people.

In dealing with Soviet people, it is important to understand that while at one level

The greatest danger of war seems to me not to lie in the deliberate actions of wicked men, but in the inability of harassed men to manage events that have run away with them.

—Henry Kissinger

The whole world is learning that treaties, constitutions, ordinances and bonds are good only to the extent that they are made coincident with basic human relationships which have the approval of that sensitive, quick acting and dominant power, the public opinion of the world.

—Owen D. Young

153

Americans and Soviets share a common humanity, at another level, fundamental differences divide us. Unless we can appreciate both our commonality *and* our differences, we can not hope to develop successful long-term relations with the Soviets, whether at the level of building space-bridges or at the level of Geneva arms control talks.

A major difference in our societies is described by anthropologist Edward Hall, who divides cultures into "high context" and "low context" types. Americans are a very low context society. *What* is being said is more important than the larger context in which the message is being sent and received. We emphasize specificity of content, and because we are relatively unconcerned about context, we value the qualities of honesty, flexibility and initiative. When confronted by a complex problem, we tend to want to break it down into its component parts.

The Soviet Union, on the other hand, is a very high-context culture. For Soviets, the setting in which a message is sent and received is as important as the message. If we seek to break complex problems down, they tend to emphasize the general setting out of which complex problems emerge. It is nearly impossible to talk about a contemporary political issue with a Soviet official without the official at some point mentioning the heavy Soviet losses during World War II. Soviets emphasize the general over the particular, the sweep of history over the immediate political concerns. The Soviets know how to wait, something foreign to Americans whose whole political

Let the competition between America and Russia descend from outer space and extend to the more crucial area of the peaceful resolution of all international differences here on earth.

—Israel R. Margolies

We need above all to learn again to believe in the possibility of nobility of spirit in ourselves.

—Eugene O'Neill

economy is predicated on taking the waiting out of wanting.

Psychologist Steven Kull offers the images of a motorboat and a sailboat to explore the differences between how Americans and Soviets view themselves. Americans are like motorboats. We are inwardly motivated and emphasize our uniqueness and individuality. We assume that we are acting in an autonomous, inner-directed way, independent of external forces. We therefore tend to emphasize personal initiative and creativity over conformity and cooperation. For us, truth is an absolute perspective that we arrive at individually. We value one-to-one loyalties above group loyalties. For us, the bigger the entity, the weaker our allegiance to it.

Soviets, on the other hand, are more like sailboats. Rather than being inner-directed, they are much more aware of the effects of the environment, metaphorically the wind and the movements of the sea. They stress the situation they are in as the causal factor in their behavior. For them, truth is derived more from social consensus than from an inward process. For them, group loyalty is preeminent, especially when dealing with foreigners.

The above statements are, of course, rough generalizations. No culture is exclusively high- or low-context. Yet for Americans working with Soviets, the observations by Edward Hall and Steven Kull can be useful. The comparisons are offered not for the sake of judgment but in the interest of enabling us to understand the enormous differences in how Americans and Soviets perceive them-

Nothing splendid has ever been achieved except by those who dared believe that something inside them was superior to circumstance.

—Bruce Barton

155

selves. Respecting these differences between our cultures and value systems makes it possible to build cooperative projects that can benefit both sides.

This is not the place to explore these complexities further. We need to underscore, however, the importance of getting to know the Soviets as we work with them. Their culture, politics, history, geography and economy are completely different from ours. As a result, when Soviets and Americans meet each other there will be an extraordinary amount of creative tension. There will be guilt, there will be dreams, there will be suspicion, there will be hope. Our mutual hurt must be dealt with while we experience the excitement at discovering new emotions in and with each other.

In this spirit, during the past few years, a small number of American citizens have pioneered a new frontier of intercultural communication. While professional diplomats have been working primarily through official channels, citizen diplomats have been creating alternative channels of communication, with funding they have generated by themselves. Because the citizen diplomats have no official responsibilities, they have often had more room to maneuver, especially in times when official channels have been blocked by bad relations. On the other hand, because few have been professionally trained in the art of diplomacy, they have had to learn their lessons from the school of hard knocks: trying, failing, trying again with a new idea, perhaps failing again, but in the end succeeding because of their dedication and willingness to

Citizen diplomats have two essential functions. One is to spread information and the second is to establish relationships. The spreading of information goes both ways—Americans bring information over to the Soviet Union and Americans bring information about the Soviet Union back to the United States. In a way you can think of Americans going to the Soviet Union as [if they were] human banned books out of Fahrenheit 451. *Every individual American who goes there is a storehouse of information containing many ideas that are subversive to the Soviet state. At the*

156

work as equals with their Soviet counterparts in an innovative way. The following narrative attempts to capture some of the spirit of these first steps toward building space-bridges between the Soviet and American peoples.

The First "US" Festival (9/5/82)

The pioneers of satellite communications links between the United States and the Soviet Union were Richard Lukens, an independent producer working at the time with the UNUSON Corporation (founded by Steve Wozniak, inventor of the Apple Computer), and Jim Hickman, the Executive Director of the Esalen Institute Soviet-American Exchange Program. On Labor Day weekend in 1982, they arranged a live satellite linkup between a music and technology festival in southern California and Soviet musical performers playing in the Moscow studios of the Soviet "State Committee for Television and Radio," known as Gosteleradio.

In early 1982, UNUSON Corporation executives had hit upon the idea of bringing high-tech and rock and roll together over Labor Day in a huge Woodstock-like "US Festival" just outside Los Angeles, to symbolize the transition from the "me" generation of the 1970s to the "us" generation which the UNUSON Corporation hoped would characterize the 1980s. After preparations for the "US" Festival were well under way, another idea had come: what better way to promote peace *and* demonstrate high-tech than to exchange music via satellite between the United States and the Soviet Union?

same time Americans bring back lots of information about the Soviet Union that helps eliminate all of the stereotypes and misperceptions that we talked about earlier, that Americans have about the Soviets. Some people think of citizen diplomacy as a lot like Gulliver, where the Lilliputians each wrap their little threads around the huge giant. No one thread would hold the giant down but all of these threads would hold the giant down. I think that giant is the cold war and those little threads are cultural relations, economic relations, scientific relations.

—Michael H. Shuman on audio cassette, "Beyond the Boundaries'

Lukens took on the task of obtaining Soviet cooperation. Peter Ellis obtained approval from the UNUSON Corporation to pay all broadcast expenses, some $100,000 as it turned out, in exchange for Soviet participation. The question then became one of finding someone both familiar with the Soviets and willing to act as middle man in the negotiations with them.

Our country is the world, our countrymen are all mankind.

—William Lloyd Garrison

This is where Jim Hickman came in. Along with Michael and Dulce Murphy, cofounders of the Esalen Institute Soviet-American Exchange Program, he had been developing contacts with the Soviets for several years in the course of developing programs between Esalen researchers and Soviet academics on issues that included bioenergetics, physical fitness, mass communication, health care, ecology, and international relations. In the process, Hickman and the Murphys had developed a network of influential supporters and funders who adhered to the common aim of improving Soviet-American relations on a personal and cultural, rather than merely political, basis. Reached by Lukens just as he was about to embark on another of his frequent working trips to the Soviet Union, Hickman agreed to discuss the proposal in Moscow with officials he knew at Gosteleradio.

No nation can rise above the level of the ideals of its citizens.

—Brooks Fletcher

Meanwhile, Lukens split his time between San Francisco, Los Angeles and New York trying to set up a satellite linkup between the two countries. It took him several weeks of extended phone calls and travel to discover how it was done and then actually to begin the process of arranging the satellite time and

158

organizing all the technical help necessary at the festival site in San Bernardino, California. He persisted in the face of consistent advice from all quarters that despite the idealism behind it, setting up a live satellite exchange with the Soviets could not be done, given the short time frame and the state of Soviet-American relations.

In Moscow Hickman obtained approval from the Soviets. It might seem surprising that the Soviets would entertain a proposal for an unscripted, spontaneous international satellite broadcast, but Hickman had developed a high degree of rapport and trust over the years and they were willing to move with him into uncharted territory. To be sure, they also had solid political reasons for wanting to cooperate. The Soviets' satellite equipment had already been set up for the 1984 Olympics, and they were eager to make use of it. Through UNUSON they were interested in broadening their contact with the world of American computer technology. In addition, the Soviet Embassy in Washington had investigated UNUSON and determined that they were an independent American group who, like Hickman and the Murphys, desired improved Soviet-American understanding in a period of very poor official relations.

Hickman returned to the United States in early August, just weeks before the "US" Festival was to begin. Negotiations continued over the phone with Gosteleradio as Lukens lined up the American technical team. With only days left, Lukens and Hickman flew to Moscow after a stop in Washington where

So great has been the endurance, so incredible the achievement, that, as long as the sun keeps a set course in heaven, it would be foolish to despair of the human race.

—Ernest L. Woodward

We must never forget that international friendship is achieved through rumors ignored, propaganda challenged and exposed, through patient loyalty to those who have proved themselves worthy of it, through help freely given where help is needed and merited.... Peace is more a product of our day-to-day living than of a spectacular program, intermittently executed.

—Dwight D. Eisenhower

159

Getting to Know the Other Side

I would like to see exchanges [in which] auto workers and teachers and physicians, people in all walks of life, from every class in societies, swap roles with each other for a year or two and learn about the other culture, so that we develop an alternative to thinking of them in war-like terms, so we think of them as "those people I lived with that year," with all the problems and all the pleasures of having done that. And that thought itself develops enough weight so it displaces our tendency to think of them in simplistic terms of enemies and friends. It becomes more interesting, actually a better game than the other way of [regarding] them. Return visits would happen, the world would finally come to know itself, and this situation that's lasted throughout all of human history, where we only really know a small part of our own [global] culture, would change for the first time.

—Robert Fuller on audio cassette, "Beyond the Boundaries"

they had made a sizeable down-payment for several segments of satellite time. Upon arrival, they met with Soviet officials from the foreign relations section of Gosteleradio in a Red Square hotel room to negotiate the Soviet part of the telecast and coordinate it with the American festival. Speed was imperative. The satellite window to the California festival would be opening just two and a half days hence.

Six people, two Americans and four Soviets, worked in the hotel room until midnight, outlining a sequence of broadcasts: the first a one-way from Moscow to California, and the others two-way, with full audio-visual contact on both sides. The first broadcast would be Hickman's and Lukens' "Hello from the Soviet Union," an introduction to the country; the others would be a group of Soviets and a group of Americans playing music and dancing together—an unscripted, unchoreographed celebration via satellite, to honor the UNUSON festival's theme of cooperation through technology.

The following morning, Thursday, Hickman, Lukens and their Soviet counterparts met with the Deputy Ministers of Gosteleradio to present their plans and obtain the necessary permissions for the telecast. Approval had to be granted by both the technical and foreign relations sections; then the Minister himself; and finally, a representative of the Communist Party leadership. The Deputy Ministers gave their approval that morning. What followed were hours of continuous frenetic activity, involving not only Hickman, Lukens and Gos-

160

teleradio in the Soviet Union, but UNUSON executives back in the U.S., particularly Peter Gerwe, the music and entertainment producer for UNUSON. It took literally hundreds of people to accomplish the task.

At 9:00 Saturday morning Moscow time, 10:00 Friday evening Los Angeles time, the Soviet commentator, Joe Adamov, went live with Hickman and Lukens in the first of the satellite broadcasts. The signal traveled from the Gosteleradio studio in Moscow over the Russian land mass to the Soviet earth station at Dubna; from there, it leapt some 22,300 miles to the INTELSAT satellite orbiting the equator over the Atlantic, then plunged to the COMSAT gateway in West Virginia. From there, it sped over land lines to an RCA earth station in New Jersey, where, again, it shot 22,300 miles into space for its "bounce" across the American continent by RCA satellite to Burbank, California. From Burbank, it was borne by specially installed land lines to the "US" Festival site in the desert outside San Bernardino, where it materialized as a clear television-like image on a huge, 90-foot-wide screen. The signal had journeyed well over a hundred thousand miles in less than a second.

In the "US" Festival amphitheater some 300,000 people were awaiting the main event: a performance from a band that bore the unlikely name of The Police. First, however, there came a live greeting from the Soviet television studio. The broadcast then showed a tape of Lukens and Hickman touring Moscow, along with an overflight of the Soviet

Progress might have been all right once, but it went on too long.

—Ogden Nash

There never was a time when, in my opinion, some way could not be found to prevent the drawing of the sword.

—Ulysses S. Grant

161

Until you have become really, in actual fact, a brother to every one, brotherhood will not come to pass.

—Fyodor Dostoyevski

Government alone cannot meet and master the great social problems of our day. It will take public-interest partnerships of a scope we cannot yet perceive.

—Joseph Califano, Jr.

Union. But at this point, things went askew. Because there had been only two and a half days to put the entire show together, Lukens and Hickman in Moscow had been working primarily with Gerwe in San Bernardino. Outside of a very small group of people, few knew that a satellite broadcast was to take place or what it would be like. Unfortunately, one of the festival producers had not been informed of the Moscow link. He happened to be on stage when the live greetings came in from Moscow, and thinking the incoming signal was spurious, the producer quite simply and literally pulled the plug on stage. The transmission, while continuing to be received by the mixing truck backstage, ceased to appear on the huge video display screen that the rock fans were watching. When Gerwe discovered what had happened, he rectified the situation and the tape was later played several times from the big stage.

The second two telecasts the following night were scheduled to be live interactive pieces between Soviet and American musicians. Again, problems arose: Gerwe could not get any of the groups performing at the "US" Festival to play live with a Soviet band via satellite. Just the thought seemed preposterous to most, and without knowing with whom they would be playing and having never rehearsed with them, the bands were unwilling to volunteer in front of several hundred thousand screaming fans. So while what came in from the studios of Gosteleradio was live, the music Gerwe was forced to send back was performances taped earlier in the day, one being

Eddy Money. There were live pans of both audiences, however, which gave a feeling of immediacy and intimacy to both sides.

The last half hour, by all accounts, was the best. The Soviets poured enormous feeling into a variety of performances, from Russian folk dancing and jugglers to Dixieland jazz. The Moscow audience could see the "US" Festival crowd watching them, which heightened their feelings of connectedness. In spite of mix-ups, the euphoria at just *connecting* Moscow with San Bernardino live via satellite was enormous. Soviet and American citizens had worked together with incredible energy and a shared sense of the exceptional opportunity that was briefly available to establish positive communication between societies otherwise so much at odds.

A measure of the program's success was that the Soviet evening television news, "Vremya," broadcast a three-minute summary of the linkup throughout the Soviet Union. An estimated 200,000,000 people watched the report. In the United States, the significance of the event was unrecognized and there was almost no media coverage.

"Linking US Together" (5/28/83)

UNUSON Corporation executives were so pleased with the results of the first live broadcast that they decided to invest in an even more dramatic satellite exchange for the next "US" Festival. In February 1983, Hickman returned to Moscow at UNUSON's behest to open talks with Soviet officials on a second satellite exchange. His approach, which

Our representatives depend ultimately on decisions made in the village square. We must carry the facts. From these must come America's voice.

—Albert Einstein

163

The Soviets tend to think that the United States is both too wonderful and too awful. They, on the one hand, love everything that's American in terms of culture—they love American art, American music. When I was in Moscow I met kids who were in their teens who were singing Bruce Springsteen's "Born in the USA." They love American clothes; that's why they wear American jeans. They like American television stars. There are now bootleg copies of American videos— including "Rambo," by the way—that are circulating through the Soviet Union. On the other hand, the Soviets think that the Americans are living in a virtual war zone. They think that the multinational corporations run everything in American life, top to bottom. They think that the political

he expected would win a favorable reception from the Soviets, was: "Together we did this successful thing. Let's try it again. What do you think would be the best thing to do?" The Soviet answer was a disappointment: "We're not interested in talking to you about that. Tell us what you want, and we'll tell you whether or not we'll do it. Maybe we could do it again, but you really don't have an idea of what you want to do. Come back to us when you've got some plan."

The Soviets, in other words, were not ready to collaborate until the Americans made a specific proposal. The reasons were manifold. As Hickman and Lukens were soon to find out, the front line of the Soviet television bureaucracy was not free to work with foreigners on unapproved proposals. Once the higher authorities had endorsed a particular effort, all other personnel would work with incredible energy to move the project forward. Until that magical moment, however, the would-be initiator faced a brick wall. The fact that the earlier broadcast had registered a success, more pronounced in the Soviet Union than in America, seemed to be of little interest to the Gosteleradio officials. For whatever reasons, the Americans found themselves in the disheartening position of having to start all over again.

The proposal the Americans finally made was full of risks, the goals of the new telecast would be more complex than before, the new satellite exchanges would go beyond merely demonstrating the technology of Soviet-American teleconferencing. The satellite link would devote itself to practical ends, as well as to adventurous means of expression, such as groups of American and Soviet musicians, 10,000 miles apart, jamming with each other. It was also proposed that studio audiences and select panels in both countries engage in direct, unscripted conversations with each other in the same broadcast. To allay Soviet concerns about unplanned discussions on live television, the Americans proposed that controversial policy topics be ruled out in advance. No one would be allowed to engage in polemics about Central America, Afghanistan, the Cold War, or human rights. The tone of the dialogues would be friendly; the purpose would not be to win a debate, but to develop better ways of communicating and building relationships.

In addition to studio audiences talking with each other, the Americans proposed three-person panels in Moscow and in California. Each panel would include: an educator; someone of influence in the worlds of both science and politics; and "a kind of colorful figure who commands great respect from the viewing public," in Hickman's words. In making their proposal as specific as possible, Hickman and Lukens nominated not just the American panelists, but also—guided by unofficial suggestions from Soviet friends—the prospective Soviet panelists. For the educators, they chose Maurice Mitchell, a long-time pioneer of radio networking who directed the Annenberg School of Communications at the University of Pennsylvania, and Zoya Malkova, a member of the U.S.S.R. Academy of Sci-

action committees are basically manipulating all of our politicians. They think that we are always having race riots. They think that our streets are just flooded with nothing but pornography and drugs. They see all the down sides of freedom without responsibility and they say, "How can you tolerate such abuse?"

—Michael H. Shuman on audio cassette, "Beyond the Boundaries"

ences, whose specialty, pedagogy, had made her a leader in formulating Soviet textbooks and curricula. In the area of science and politics, they picked Evgeny Velikhov, Vice President of the U.S.S.R. Academy of Sciences and an expert in computer technology, and Congressman George Brown, Democratic Congressman from California, who had a special interest in science and space exploration. For the "colorful figures," they decided on an astronaut and a cosmonaut. These were Rusty Schweikert and Vitali Sevastianov, with whom Hickman had recently been working on a proposed astronaut/cosmonaut exchange project.

When given this proposal, the Soviet authorities approved it. Nevertheless, the Americans were never sure—as they had not been sure in the first "US" Festival broadcasts—that the hook-up had been given *final* approval. They proceeded with their plans, working with Gosteleradio staff for 20 hours a day, knowing that things could be stopped at any time. Hickman and Lukens experienced phenomenal support in some areas and bizarre obstacles in others. The liberty they enjoyed was a remarkable display of Soviet forbearance, in exchange for something the Soviets badly wanted: favorable exposure in America.

In this telecast, as in the previous one, the intricacies of music were at least as critical as the subtleties of politics. The centerpiece of the musical exchange was to be a jam session between two groups, one Western and one Soviet, who had never rehearsed with or even met each other. Since the audio-video

We know a few things that the politicians do not know.

—Albert Einstein

166

signals would have to follow an earth-and-satellite pathway more than 100,000 miles long, the delay might throw off the musicians' timing in a distracting, embarrassing way.

On Saturday evening Los Angeles time, May 28, 1983, the first live-by-satellite rock and roll jam session bridging the superpowers took place between a tent at the "US" Festival in California and a studio in Moscow. According to those who saw and attended, it came off beautifully. The Soviet band, Arsenal, played to wild applause from the several hundred thousand people gathered at the "US" Festival; and a Festival band, Men At Work—from Australia—received a wild reception from Moscow.

The more "intellectual" parts of the broadcast were perhaps tame by comparison. With one exception the conversations between studio audiences and panelists were important more for the fact that they happened than for anything that was said. As someone has written on another subject, when one applauds dancing elephants, one applauds not because the elephants have danced well but because they've danced at all. Whether it was an American asking the Soviets at what age they learn English, or Soviet youngsters talking about rock music and Atari, the occasion transcended the points of discussion and gave rise to a spirit that brought stony-faced people to tears.

The high point of the dialogue, by all accounts, was Velikhov's statement on behalf of disarmament: "I would like to say that today we're not only talking about the fact that

We are 90 percent alike, all we peoples, and 10 percent different; the trouble is that we forget the 90 percent and remember the 10 percent when we criticize others.

—Sir Charles Higham

Getting to Know the Other Side

The recipe for perpetual ignorance is: Be satisfied with your opinions and content with your knowledge.

—Elbert Hubbard

A decent boldness ever meets with friends.

—Homer

it's possible to talk to one another; we're actually doing it. It's no accident that this conversation takes us back about forty years ago—at that time I was nine years old. I came from Stalingrad to Moscow. This was in the spring of 1944 and I saw something which I have remembered for my whole life—very much the same kind of pictures that we're looking at today: Soviet and American hands joined together; Soviet and American flags joined together." (The American audience begins to applaud.) "At that time we conquered a very terrible enemy, but at the same time another enemy arose who is unfortunately still here with us. This is nuclear weaponry. Sometimes it seems to us that these are muscles. But of course they aren't muscles; this is really a cancer, and we have to perform an operation as quickly as possible to liberate ourselves from this cancer." (Tumultuous applause, people standing.) "In order to have the courage to go through with this operation, we have to build bridges, we have to talk with each other; each one of us has to be able to feel his own responsibility for what is happening in the world. This, I think, is what we have managed to achieve here today."

Writing in the November 1983 issue of *Soviet Life*, the English-language Soviet pictorial magazine, Vladimir Pozner commented on the second Moscow-"US" Festival broadcasts: "In my years as a journalist, I have had my share of television exposure. This has often been an exciting experience, sometimes even a dramatic one. But nothing came near matching the sheer emotional impact of this hook-up. There was something incredibly moving in the meeting that spanned eleven time zones and over 10,000 miles. The air was charged with excitement, and both audiences were physically jolted to their feet when they first saw each other on those two large screens. The immediacy of it, the proximity, and yet the huge distance, created a blend of special magic. Some people might call it a technological miracle, and I think that would not be an exaggeration. But the more I think about it, the less I tend to dwell on the technology. For the truly striking element was the undisguised joy on both sides of being able to communicate directly, to look into each other's eyes."

It was probably this feeling that led Pozner—by now a prime mover in two-way telecasting between Moscow and the US—to initiate the next space-bridge between the U.S. and the U.S.S.R.

"Children and Film" (7/20/83)

The program arose in discussions between Pozner and Michael Cole, a professor in the Department of Communications at the University of California at San Diego and fluent in Russian, who, along with his wife Sheila, a writer and journalist, had traveled to Moscow to attend a Soviet-American-sponsored conference on human development. The Coles had met Pozner some twenty years before while studying on an exchange program in the Soviet Union. In informal, late-night-over-vodka meetings, which took place in mid-June 1983, Pozner gave stirring accounts

We always have time enough, if we will but use it aright.

—Goethe

No small part of the cruelty, oppression, miscalculation, and general mismanagement of human relations is due to the fact that in our dealings with others we do not see them as persons at all, but only as specimens or representatives of some type or other....We react to the sample instead of to the real person.

—Robert J. MacIver

of the second "US" Festival telecasts.

The proposal Pozner and the Coles worked out called for an exchange centered around the Moscow Film Festival, which would start in a month's time. Children in each country would meet live on video satellite, would watch American and Soviet film clips together, and would then discuss the clips with the directors and with each other. It was at once an exciting and terrifying proposal: exciting for the obvious reasons, and terrifying for all the obstacles—logistical, financial, political—to be surmounted in so short a time. By the end of their stay, the Coles, impressed by the Soviets' enthusiasm over the second "US" Festival broadcast, had committed themselves to the project.

Once back in America, they appealed to foundation executives in New York for financial support. They received sympathy but no cash.

Man is a gregarious animal, and much more so in his mind than in his body. He may like to go alone for a walk, but he hates to stand alone in his opinions.

—George Santayana

It was with some urgency then that Michael Cole turned to his colleagues at UCSD. Were the broadcast facilities of the university equal to the technical demands of a Soviet-American satellite exchange? More critical still: would the university back the project with financial, logistical and personnel support? The answer to both questions was a resounding yes. Everyone Cole contacted—notably the university's chancellor, Richard Atkinson, and the Communication Department chairperson, Helene Keyssar—leapt onto the bandwagon. Once the university had made the project its own, foundations began to take notice. Within days, the Carnegie

Foundation and the Foundation for Child Development had each committed $5,000 to the broadcast, making up most of the $15,000 budget for transmission costs and some equipment rentals. The Soviets were to pay for their satellite time and production costs.

As is typical in such bold undertakings, time was woefully short. It was already the beginning of July, and the broadcast was to take place on the 20th. No official Soviet confirmation of the hook-up had yet reached San Diego; hence, no one had booked satellite time for the event. No written script had materialized, in spite of Soviet promises to provide one; and even the American technicians who were to set up this side of the satellite link were stymied in their efforts to get questions answered. "With no script, no official positive telegram, admissions of difficulty but assurances that everything would work out, we were forced to make a difficult decision about booking the satellite time," the UCSD Final Report relates, in admirable deadpan tone. With moral and financial backing from the UCSD Chancellor's office, the staff sent a $5,000 check to the satellite company to reserve the time.

Not until Saturday the 16th—four days before the broadcast—did the UCSD team, in a phone conversation with Vladimir Pozner in Moscow, learn that official permission had been given. Even then, confusion persisted on a number of fronts. The repeatedly promised Soviet script still had not appeared; San Diego had to negotiate every last detail over the uncertain phone line. To make things more

Man's capacities have never been measured. Nor are we to judge of what he can do by any precedents, so little has been tried.

—Henry David Thoreau

171

Outer space will never again be the geopolitical vacuum it once was. To make sure civilian space programs do not surreptitiously spawn weapons capability, a positive space security agenda should be pursued. Controlling space weapons can clear the stage for the use of space technology to improve both arms control verification and superpower relations. The most important items on a space security agenda are an improved Law of Space regime, an international satellite monitoring agency, and joint U.S.-Soviet space ventures. This last item, now perceived as irrelevant or at best symbolic of other changes, holds the greatest promise for defusing superpower conflict. Indeed, cooperation can link these over-armed societies in the pursuit of goals that transcend national differences, thus making the thorny verification question and breakout and peace conversion problems more tractable.

—Daniel Deudney, "Unlocking Space," in *Securing Our Planet*

complicated, American and Soviet satellite technicians could not agree on the telecast origination point in Moscow. The Americans thought it should be Gosteleradio; the Soviets said it would be Moscow Studio. Days went by before both sides realized they were talking about the same place! Just twenty-four hours before the telecast, San Diego learned that because of this confusion over the place-name, the satellite booking had not been confirmed. Since the agreed-on hour was now unavailable on the main INTELSAT route, an elaborate compromise was necessary. The broadcast would now begin a half hour later than planned. The San Diego-to-Moscow signal would have to travel a circuitous route that involved an added downlink and uplink in Germany, meaning another satellite "bounce" and a cost increase of around $5,000.

The telecast began with an exchange of taped footage, the Soviets sending clips of the Moscow Film Festival and of Moscow, the Americans sending pictures of life and work at UCSD and of Southern California. Thanks to the skillful camera work in the Moscow studio, where as many as a dozen cameras recorded the reactions of some 300 Soviet children, the Americans could watch the Soviets watching the transmission.

Like the Americans, the Soviets presented three films: the first, a kind of morality play about a young man with a Midas touch, the second, a Soviet adaptation of "Winnie the Pooh," and the third, an uproarious farce entitled "The Kindergarten Teacher With a Moustache." This fantasy created a group of

172

small schoolchildren who manage to program a computer so that a skeleton comes alive, prances around and terrifies their anatomy teacher. The sight of a skeleton cavorting in a Soviet schoolroom drew the loudest reactions, with children in Moscow and San Diego laughing and clapping in time to the music.

Everyone was so pleased with this telecast that the same sets of producers moved immediately to discussions of a new hook-up centered around the upcoming Moscow Book Fair in September. These discussions came to an abortive end, however, as a result of the Korean airliner tragedy, which happened in early September and ushered in an especially dark period in relations between the superpowers.

War is only a cowardly escape from the problems of peace.

—Thomas Mann

The Nuclear Winter Conference (11/1/83)

The idea behind this telecast was to provide a Soviet link to the Conference on the Long Term World-Wide Biological Consequences of Nuclear War. The conference, organized by Dr. Paul Ehrlich, Dr. Carl Sagan, and others, was scheduled for the end of October in Washington, D.C. Several Soviet scientists had taken part in the research effort behind the conference, and not all of them would be free to travel to Washington to attend in person. If these Soviet scientists could take part in the conference from Moscow, their presence would add to the symposium's effectiveness.

The proposal for the linkup came not from the conferees but from INTERNEWS,

It is when we all play safe that we create a world of utmost insecurity.

—Dag Hammarskjold

173

an independent production team which had extensive experience with satellite technology and which had been interested in the Soviet field for some time. INTERNEWS directors Kim Spencer and Evelyn Messinger developed a proposal for the Henry T. Kendall Foundation of Boston, which was a principal conference sponsor. Messinger would produce the American side, Spencer the Soviet side. Dr. Bernard Lown, the renowned Harvard cardiologist, agreed to make the telecast proposal to the Soviet scientific establishment. He forwarded the idea to his Soviet colleague, Dr. Evgeny Chasov, the leading Soviet cardiologist and personal physician to Brezhnev and Andropov. Chasov and Lown had co-founded International Physicians for the Prevention of Nuclear War, with some 70,000 members worldwide.

When it is dark enough you can see the stars.

—Ralph Waldo Emerson

In the aftermath of the KAL incident, negotiations were understandably difficult. The Soviets remained ambivalent. Both sides were aware of the importance of maintaining dialogue. As it turned out, the American team arrived in Moscow to negotiate last-minute details, and actually to stage the broadcast, only days after the American invasion of Grenada in December. The atmosphere, Spencer said later, was almost surreal. "In every newscast, they were doing the newsbreaks showing American soldiers holding submachine guns to the heads of little black boys. They thought that Reagan was moving on to conquer the world."

Because of the sensitive nature of the broadcast, the ground rules called for the discussions to be entirely scientific. There were to be no policy discussions and no audience applause. While everyone was working feverishly to assure order with less than an hour before broadcast time, one of the Soviet producers brought Spencer some troubling news. "We have got a message from our contacts in the United States," he told the Americans. "C-Span is planning to put this program next to an anti-Soviet film."

In the midst of all the last-minute details that had to be completed, this was at most a minor irritant. Yet it had to be dealt with, and quickly. The American cable television channel, C-Span, had contracted to replay a tape of the telecast twice in the coming week. The Soviets feared that the telecast was going to be used for anti-Soviet propaganda purposes.

Spencer reached his colleagues in Washington, using a reserved phone line called a "four-wire." The people in Washington immediately called C-Span and asked for clarification. The C-Span producers absolutely assured them that although other programs were scheduled, no propaganda misuse would be made of the conference tape. This information was in turn communicated back to Spencer and the Soviet producers via the four-wire.

That was not good enough for the Soviets. They wanted *written* assurances—a telex, to be precise. Luckily, the production truck in Washington had a portable communications terminal. Moments before the telecast, as the heads of Gosteleradio entered the con-

There is a time for departure even when there's no certain place to go.

—Tennessee Williams

We seek peace, knowing that peace is the climate of freedom. And now, as in no other age, we seek it because we have been warned, by the power of modern weapons, that peace may be the only climate possible for human life itself.

—Dwight D. Eisenhower

The war against war is going to be no holiday excursion or camping party. The military feelings are too deeply grounded to abdicate their place among our ideals until better substitutes are offered than the glory and shame that come to nations as well as to individuals from the ups and downs of politics and the vicissitudes of trade. There is something highly paradoxical in the modern man's relation to war.

—William James, "The Moral Equivalent of War," in *Securing Our Planet*

trol room, Spencer received the needed telex and could assure them in writing that no anti-Soviet propaganda was intended.

This small story is important for several reasons. First, the fact that Soviet intelligence knew about C-Span weekly television programming indicates the degree of concern the Soviets bring to Soviet-American space-bridges. Second, the use of the telex in laying the matter to rest shows not only the power of the printed word, something the Soviets in particular respect, but the importance of having at our disposal communication technologies that can respond at the speed of human events.

The broadcast began with the cameras focusing in close on the image of the earth the Soviets had set up in the Moscow studio, and then panning the panelists and audiences in both Moscow and Washington, D.C. This transmission came at the end of the two-day conference in Washington where an international group of 700 scientists, including Soviets, met to discuss the long-range effects of nuclear weapons. Enormous political and media attention had been generated. Working all night, Evelyn Messinger had condensed the proceedings down to a two-hour tape, which was telecast to forty scientists gathered in the large studio of Gosteleradio. The Soviet scientists in Moscow then discussed these findings via the satellite linkup with a panel of scientists in Washington, marking the first time Soviet scientists made a statement on the facts concerning nuclear winter.

Scientists in both countries had prepared

calculations of the effects of a war in which nuclear weapons with a total yield of 5,000 megatons were exploded, 80% over military targets and 20% over cities, half bursting in the air and half on the ground. A few of these weapons were assumed to yield 20 megatons, the rest in the 50 to 500 kiloton range. (A megaton equals the explosive power of a million tons of TNT; a kiloton equals a thousand tons.) The American and Soviet nuclear arsenals together contain about 50,000 megatons. The findings of the scientists indicated that nuclear winter would result if only 10% of existing nuclear stockpiles were detonated. The consequences would be equally disastrous if only one side detonated weapons.

The American study was prepared by Richard P. Turco (the atmospheric chemist from California who coined the term "nuclear winter"), Carl Sagan, and others, and presented to the Soviets by Sagan. The study found that the dust, smoke and debris hurled into the atmosphere by such a detonation of nuclear weapons would cause 80 degree (Fahrenheit) temperature drops in the Northern Hemisphere, with 90% of the sun's light cut off for a month or more. Normal conditions would not return for a year or more. All agriculture would cease and mass starvation would be inevitable.

The Soviet model showed that 40 days after the end of the war, temperatures would have dropped by 65 degrees in Alaska, 61 degrees in the eastern and midwestern United States, 92 degrees in Central Europe, and 100 degrees around Murmansk, in the far north

We must never relax our efforts to arouse in the people of the world, and especially in their governments, an awareness of the unprecedented disaster which they are absolutely certain to bring on themselves unless there is a fundamental change in their attitudes toward one another as well as in their concept of the future.

—Albert Einstein

I think it's factually correct that war has been a very attractive adventure for men, going back I suppose to primeval times. Today in the late 20th century I think we have to find a different kind of adventure and I think this quest, if you will, for true world peace, is maybe the greatest adventure that any of us could conceive of. It can be an adventure that is fun, enjoyable, thrilling, as well as extremely challenging.

—Don Carlson on audio cassette, "A Better Game Than War"

of the Soviet Union. The Soviets found that after an initial period of subzero cold, atmospheric radiation would bring temperatures up to hothouse levels.

The Moscow-Washington linkup ended on a much more somber note than had the earlier satellite exchanges. At the same time, it was by far the most significant event aired by live television transmission between the superpowers. It received wide coverage in the Soviet Union: highlighted mention on television and radio news, televised broadcast of a 60-minute version later in the year, and stories in all major periodicals. The exchange received attention from several major American newspapers and was replayed on Ted Turner's cable television channels on no less than four separate occasions. The conference highlights were also rebroadcast in Austria, Finland, Ice-land, Japan, Sweden, and the United Kingdom.

In a final statement from Moscow, as he had done at the 1983 "US" Festival, Academician Velikhov likened nuclear weapons to a cancer that must be excised from the body politic of the human race. Upon hearing this, the scientific audience in Washington spontaneously applauded in an emotional release that soon generated applause from the audience in Moscow. The long conference had been an exacting one. And yet, the combined power of the space-bridge linking scientists from the two countries that most threaten each other with nuclear weapons, and the discipline of the scientists themselves in keeping their remarks to the purely scientific, cre-

This world in arms is not spending money alone—it is spending the sweat of its laborers, the genius of its scientists, the hopes of its children.

—Dwight D. Eisenhower

ated a tremendous impact. The implications regarding policy and public pronouncements are only beginning to be felt in both countries.

The NOVA Space-Bridge (September 1984)

This telecast took place due largely to the longstanding friendship and professional contact between Gerard Piel, President of the American Association for the Advancement of Science and Chairman of the Board of *Scientific American*, and Sergei Kapitsa, editor of the Russian language edition of *Scientific American*, a noted Soviet physicist, and moderator of a well-known Soviet television program on science. The program was low-key and involved a panel of four American scientists in Boston and four Soviet scientists in a studio of Gosteleradio in Moscow who discussed a variety of areas where Soviet and American scientists have cooperated: fusion, seismographic research, astronomy, and biology.

Co-produced by WGBH, a public television station, this telecast was broadcast over the PBS national network as one of the NOVA series in October. While the Soviets had provided extensive media coverage, none of the other satellite linkups had been aired on national television in America.

The Beyond War Telecast (12/13/84)

Beyond War is an organization dedicated to the proposition that "working together we can move beyond war." Each year it gives an award—a Stueben crystal—to a person or

After the final no there comes a yes, and on that yes the future of the world depends.

—Wallace Stevens

179

*Our problems are directly
created by the way we
think. Problems are
directly created by the
dominant belief system in
the industrial societies, to
an extent that goes prob-
ably much farther than
most of us feel comfort-
able with right at first.
So to solve the problems
the beliefs have to change.
That's one realization
that we need to have. But
then the other one is the
power of holding the im-
age, the power of creating
a vision, the power of
seeing that we can have
a world without war and
without preparation for
war and without wide-
spread hunger and
without chronic poverty
and without tearing up
the environment all over
the earth. We can have
such a world and the first
step is to create the
vision, but that step is so
important that when we
have created the vision
we have already set the
forces in motion to bring
about the actualization of
that vision.*

—Willis Harman
on audio cassette, "A
Better Game Than War"

group who works in a particularly notewor-
thy way toward this goal. In 1983, the crystal
was given to the American Catholic bishops
for their pastoral letter denouncing nuclear
weapons. In 1984, Beyond War decided that
the crystal should go to the International
Physicians for the Prevention of Nuclear War
(IPPNW) for their work in educating the
public on the medical and biological effects
of nuclear war. As IPPNW was co-founded by
Dr. Bernard Lown, a cardiologist from Harvard, and Dr. Evgeny Chasov, Director of the
Cardiology Institute of the Academy of Sciences in Moscow, it seemed natural to have
a live telecast linking the award ceremony in
San Francisco, which is near the headquarters
of Beyond War, and Moscow.

Beyond War made the decision to award
the crystal to IPPNW in late September,
1984. The ceremony was planned for December 13th, not leaving much time. The organization turned to INTERNEWS, which had
helped to arrange the nuclear winter telecast.
Evelyn Messinger took on the task of producing the American portion and Kim Spencer
went to Moscow with a group from Beyond
War to produce the Soviet part. As with the
other telecasts, things were nip and tuck right
to the end. The task was expedited by two
factors, however. The first was Chasov's high
standing in the Soviet Union. To honor the
personal physician to Brezhnev, Andropov,
and Chernenko with an international award
was to honor someone very high in the Soviet
hierarchy. The second factor was the experience of Messinger and Spencer.

Beyond War booked two hours of satellite time for the evening of December 13th in San Francisco, which was the morning of December 14th in Moscow. Hosted by Beyond War organizers in both places, the bilingual award ceremonies began with a live exchange of greetings, followed by a pretaped history of IPPNW. The crystals were then given to Lown and Chasov who both made speeches, Lown from the San Francisco Masonic Auditorium, where six large screen projection systems had been set up, and Chasov from the Gosteleradio Concertina Hall in Moscow, which seats 600. The program drew to a close with Soviet folksinger Jenna Bichevskaya singing "Where Have All the Flowers Gone?" The finale came when the San Francisco Boys' Chorus, accompanied on saxophone by Paul Winter, sang the first verse of "Blue Green Hills of Earth," which had been inspired by the astronauts' first view of earth from space. The Gosteleradio Children's Choir responded by singing the second verse; then Gospel singer Etta James and the audiences in both cities joined in for the third verse.

An estimated 100,000 people in the San Francisco Bay area viewed the event, and viewer groups of up to 250 were arranged at "downlink" sites in Los Angeles, Visalia, Portland, Madison, Seattle, Denver, and Boston. The Beyond War broadcast marked the first time a space-bridge was transmitted live on American television. The Soviets provided excellent media coverage and an edited program was telecast in the spring of 1985.

The choice is between nonviolence and nonexistence.

—Rev. Martin Luther King, Jr.

We can't really envision a positive future until we have divested ourselves of these negative, uncomfortable, difficult feelings. And I have found this because the workshop begins with people imaging the future. I don't say a positive future or a negative future, I just say "in the future." And people draw pictures of very difficult, negative struggle, fire and brimstone and deserts— very, very pessimistic futures. In the process of the workshop, we begin to explore the feelings that we actually have. At the end we do the exercise again and then come the colorful, positive images of hope and comraderie, [images] to make the change happen.

—Chellis Glendinning on audio cassette, "A Better Game Than War"

181

"Remembering War" (5/7/85)

This space-bridge was produced by a partnership of the Roosevelt Center for American Policy Studies, the Department of Communication at the University of California, San Diego, KPBS-TV in San Diego, and Gosteleradio in Moscow. Negotiations for this linkup began in August 1984, when Helene Keyssar, Chair of the Department of Communications, UCSD, and Christopher Makins, Director of International Security Programs at the Roosevelt Center, traveled to Moscow to discuss with Gosteleradio officials the idea of a series of space-bridges on Soviet and American history, culture, and contemporary society.

In February 1985, Keyssar and Makins returned to Moscow to discuss an initial space-bridge on the occasion of the 40th anniversary of VE Day. They were accompanied by Kim Spencer of INTERNEWS, who had been hired as a design consultant on the technical details and structure of the space-bridge. During this visit, agreement was reached on the outline and date of the space-bridge. The linkup was to use documentary and narrative film, photography, music, and drama from the Second World War and the post-war era to stimulate discussion among the Soviet and American audiences. Participants were to include veterans, civilian officials, historians, war correspondents, workers on the home-front, and history teachers and their students. The space-bridge was to take place on May 7, 1985. In April, Keyssar and Makins returned to Moscow yet again for further de-

The superior man makes the difficulty to be overcome his first interest; success comes only later.

—Confucius

I am not struck so much by the diversity of testimony as by the many-sidedness of truth.

—Stanley Baldwin

tailed planning of the simulcast, and especially of the documentary and narrative films to be presented by the two sides during the planned program.

On schedule, the linkup took place between the studios of KPBS-TV in San Diego and the Gosteleradio studios in Moscow. Moderating were Frederick Starr, President of Oberlin College, and Vladimir Pozner, commentator for Radio Moscow. After brief introductions, audiences in both studios saw the same footage and discussed it with one another. The initial footage presented diverse faces of war. Successive sections of the spacebridge were introduced by footage of the start of the Moscow counter-offensive on December 6, 1941, and the attack on Pearl Harbor on December 7, 1941. This was followed by views of the war from the standpoint of common soldiers, both men and women; the homefronts; images that Soviets and Americans presented of their allies during the war; the meeting between Soviet and American troops on the Elbe River in April 1945; the course of the war after VE Day; post-war homecomings; and film clips to show how the Second World War has been represented in the post-war period. The simulcast ended with a poetry reading from San Diego and singing from Moscow.

The program was seen live at downlink sites in Washington, D.C., eight universities, and several of the University of California campuses. On May 11, KPBS-TV aired a two-hour edited tape of the space-bridge, and on June 22 Gosteleradio aired a 90-minute edit

The fateful question for the human species seems to me to be whether and to what extent their cultural development will succeed in mastering the disturbance of their communal life by the human instinct of aggression and self-destruction.

—Sigmund Freud

183

on Soviet national television. Discussions are under way between the Roosevelt Center, the UCSD Department of Communications, and Gosteleradio about doing another one. This will most likely be on aspects of Soviet and American contemporary societies, with special reference to young people.

"Live Aid" Concerts (7/13/85)

The most spectacular live satellite link-up to date was the "Live Aid" concert, designed to bring rock musicians from around the world to raise consciousness and elicit aid for people starving in Africa. Over one and a half billion people in 45 countries were able to view up to 16 hours of the live concert, not only from Wimbley Stadium in London and JFK Stadium in Philadelphia, but also from uplinks in the Soviet Union, Yugoslavia, Norway, West Germany, Holland, Australia, and Japan. Fourteen communication satellites were used to connect the musicians and to beam the concert around the world. The "Live Aid" concerts turned out to be one of the largest television events in history.

It was Bob Geldorf of Ireland, chairman of the board of Band-Aid, an organization dedicated to raising money for Africa, who developed the idea in the spring of 1985. Rock promoter Bill Graham was soon brought in to help, as was a newly formed company called World Wide Sports and Entertainment, set up by Michael Mitchell-Mitchell, who had served as Vice-President for Finance during the 1984 Olympics. Given the urgency of mass starvation in Ethiopia and the Sudan, and the

Today the most useful person in the world is the man or woman who knows how to get along with other people. Human relations is the most important science in the broad curriculum of living.

—Stanley C. Allyn

If the human race wishes to have a prolonged and indefinite period of material prosperity, they have only got to behave in a peaceful and helpful way toward one another, and science will do for them all they wish and more than they can dream.

—Winston Churchill

184

fact that media attention was high around the issue of world hunger, the promoters decided on a very short lead time to organize the concerts—only ten weeks. The concerts were to take place on the 13th of July 1985.

The format was deceptively simple. Each rock group was expected to pay its own way and perform for free. Corporate sponsors were invited to donate what they could and pay standard fees for their television commercials. For example, video tape was provided by Kodak, satellite transponder time was given by both system operators and leasors, while AT&T donated 800 (toll-free) phone lines for the telethon. ABC Television paid $2 million for rights and provided technical services. The only costs to "Live-Aid" were the actual production costs, which came to around $4 million, an amount more than offset by the more than $7 million in ticket sales at the stadiums and by the size of the television rights. Each country receiving the satellite feed was charged $30,000 for the entire 16 hours of concert time, although the Global Broadcasting Corporation subsidized the downlink costs of those African nations which could not afford it.

Richard Lukens, who had had the original idea for a space-bridge at the first "US" festival, was hired by World Wide Sports and Entertainment to coordinate the international component of the concerts. This initially meant seeking Chinese, Indian, and Soviet participation as well as coordinating the live broadcasts internationally at the time of the concerts. The Chinese were confronted by too many technical problems to participate. India

Scientific and humanist approaches are not competitive but supportive, and both are ultimately necessary.

—Robert C. Wood

If a little knowledge is dangerous, where is the man who has so much as to be out of danger?

—Thomas H. Huxley

185

I have a dream that one day men will rise up and come to see that they are made to live together as brothers. . . . I still have a dream today that one day justice will roll down like water, and righteousness like a mighty stream. . . . I still have a dream today that one day war will come to an end, that men will beat their swords into ploughshares and their spears into pruning hooks, that nations will no longer rise up against nations, neither will they study war any more. I still have a dream today that one day the lamb and the lion will lie down together and every man will sit under his own vine and fig tree and none shall be afraid.

—Martin Luther King

participated by taping an interview of Prime Minister Rajiv Gandhi and by airing ten hours of the concert live.

The Soviet connection turned out to be complex. Lukens traveled to Moscow and talked with many of the Gosteleradio people with whom he and Hickman had worked in producing the first two space-bridges. At the same time, Armand Hammer met with General Secretary Gorbachev and, at the request of World Wide Sports and Entertainment, raised the issue with the Soviet leader. Gorbachev agreed to participate with a 20-minute set of one of their rock bands called Autograph, and with a commentary by Vladimir Pozner. They also agreed to receive the downlink feed during the concert but made no agreement about whether they would air any of it live or at a later date.

The concerts came off almost without a hitch. The ratings for ABC were higher than at any time since the landings on the moon. Telethons were conducted in 17 countries, raising nearly $100 million. It is estimated by AT&T that over 2.1 million people tried to call the 800 number in the United States alone. Some 75,000 got through.

In their euphoria at "the whole world participating," the producers announced from the stage that the Soviet Union was showing the entire event live on Soviet television. After this information went out on the news wires, it was learned that the Soviets were indeed receiving the downlink at Gosteleradio but nothing was going out on Soviet television. This prompted Bob Geldorf to say: "It is not good enough for the second most powerful country in the world to do nothing. If the Soviet Union cannot fend for itself in terms of its own agriculture, then there is no point in them sending agricultural advisors to Africa. But they could send hoes, seeds, and drilling equipment. But they are not. It is a scandalous state of affairs!''

This statement brought angry reactions from Gosteleradio, which had never agreed to do anything more than to broadcast the Autograph/Pozner package and to receive the feed for a possible edited program at a later date. Furthermore, in fact, the Soviet government had been providing aid from the beginning of the national relief efforts to Ethiopia. The misunderstanding was eventually cleared up but the damage had been done in terms of public perception of Soviet participation.

After the concerts were over, Lukens edited a four-hour version, which included the Soviet participation. This edit was taken by the United States Information Agency, which agreed to send it to every American embassy around the world for viewing. The Hungarian and Polish governments also took the four-hour edit.

These pioneers in Soviet-American satellite communications have made a dramatic start in demonstrating possibilities. They have shown that both the United States and the Soviet Union are ready and willing to take part in this kind of exchange. They have shown that American and Soviet producers can engage in joint projects that reflect

Education is the chief defense of nations.

—Edmund Burke

We are both caught up in a vicious and dangerous cycle with suspicion on one side breeding suspicion on the other, and new weapons begetting counter-weapons.

187

In short, both the United States and its allies, and the Soviet Union and its allies, have a mutually deep interest in a just and genuine peace and in halting the arms race. Agreements to this end are in the interests of the Soviet Union as well as ours—and even the most hostile nation can be relied upon to accept and keep those treaty obligations, and only those treaty obligations, which are in their own interest. So, let us not be blind to our differences—but let us also direct attention to our common interests and the means by which those differences can be resolved. And if we cannot end now our differences, at least we can help make the world safe for diversity. For, in the final analysis, our most basic common link is that we all inhabit this small planet. We all breathe the same air. We all cherish our children's future. And we are all mortal.

—John F. Kennedy, from a 1963 speech reprinted in *Securing Our Planet*

well on both societies. They have shown, too, that the will to succeed in such projects can overcome the formidable barriers—technical, financial, bureaucratic and political—that otherwise would block them. In these critical areas, the satellite communications projects to date have been breathtaking. Despite their shortcomings, they offer hope for the future.

However, space-bridges have been isolated events with uncertain consequences. No matter how informative and moving each one has been, the telecasts have had little cumulative impact—especially since they have received scant publicity in the United States, despite garnering prime-time coverage in the Soviet Union. In the United States, where prospective producers must establish themselves in a free-market economy, no one has yet identified a consistent interest, among television stations, sponsors, or the public, that could support regular exchanges. In the Soviet Union, where such undertakings rely entirely on government support, the situation is somewhat more encouraging because responsible Soviet officials have gotten involved. They have taken part whenever they have seen a possibility that they could win for their country a better image with Americans.

Building a Space-Bridge: a Soviet Contribution

3

During the second TV space-bridge between Moscow and southern California, in 1983, a high-ranking Soviet official, Yevgeny Velikhov, quietly observed that "we're not only talking about the fact that it's *possible* to talk with one another; we're actually doing it." Appearing on the space-bridge reminded Velikhov of pictures he'd seen as a child, in 1944, when his country and the Western Allies were starting to crack the nut of Hitler's empire—pictures of "Soviet and American hands joined together, Soviet and American flags joined together." Up to this point, Velikhov's remarks fell into a diplomatic tradition that sometimes takes the form, during a "thaw," of celebrating the moment when American and Soviet troops met at Germany's Elbe River in 1945 and embraced one another as co-victors over Facism.

Then, however, Velikhov said something out of the ordinary. "At that time we conquered a very terrible enemy, but at the same time another enemy arose who is unfortunately still here with us." Watching a cassette of this space-bridge, I wondered whether Velikhov was referring to the enduring hostility between our two countries or to the existence of enormous standing armies or, perhaps, to "the bomb." It turned out to be the last of these. "Sometimes," he said of nuclear weapons, "it seems to us that these are muscles." Velikhov, however, is a physicist; he knows the effects of nuclear bombs. "But of course they aren't muscles," he continued, "this is really a cancer, and we have to perform an operation as quickly as possible to liberate ourselves from this cancer."

What made this statement so remarkable is that Velikhov is not a free-lance peacenik; he is Vice-President of the Soviet Academy of Sciences. "In order to have the courage to go through with this operation [to remove the cancer]," he said, "we have to build bridges, we have to talk with each other; each one of us has to be able to feel his own responsibility for what is happening in the world."

189

Space-bridge between Moscow and San Francisco
Drawing by Diane Schatz

Building a Space-Bridge: a Soviet Contribution

Of course it's easy to discount almost any statement from an adversary. When I've replayed Velikhov's remarks, some people have responded by saying that talk's cheap, that both sides like to pose as champions of peace until threatened with an agreement that might actually restrict their weaponry. I've heard some say that this particular speaker, in his official capacity, oversees research applicable to space-age weapons, while at the same time leading the Soviet campaign of outrage against President Reagan's "strategic defense initiative" (popularly known as Star Wars). And finally, I've been reminded that it's very convenient for the Soviets, with their enormous land army in Europe, to focus criticism solely upon nuclear weapons, as if threatening people with a bomb blast were more horrible than having the capacity to invade somebody's territory with tanks and millions of troops.

I understand all these reservations. Yet it's also clear that, just as a touchdown can result from a slight gap in the opposing team's defense, so in diplomacy a minor change of emphasis can sometimes foreshadow a major shift. If countries are caught in a system of hostility, they very seldom jump directly into a system of constructive relations. Meanwhile, an initiative that would make obvious sense if two nations were working toward a constructive system might seem disloyal or dangerously naive in the prevailing hostility. Therefore, people who want change are often led by discretion to talk in images, hints, and allusions.

What if somebody were to reply to Velikhov and his colleagues, "Yes, nuclear weaponry *is* a cancer; so are *all* weapons that menace others. And yes, we need to build bridges. Here's a particular bridge that I'd like to join in creating. What would *you* like us to build together?" In a companion book, *Securing Our Planet,* Don Carlson and I gather many specific ideas for bridges that could be built. In this section of *Citizen Summitry* we present papers about a single idea—using space-age telecommunications to introduce countries to one another, search for common ground, and share positive visions.

Chapter 9 has given a history of the early space-bridges by American writers close to the pioneers in this area. Here we do something unusual; we ask writers on the other side, from the Soviet

Union, to give their vision of this new medium. Whatever process of review may have been involved in preparing these texts, or in obtaining permission to publish them, we asked the contributors to write as individuals, not as representatives of their various organizations, whether a scientific institute, an academy, a planning office, or a theatrical company. Nonetheless, as the acknowledgements indicate, these papers have been seen by several officials, and a symposium on them has been held in the Soviet capitol, on which a report appeared in the *Moscow News*. In short, the papers are not the work of "dissidents." We assume that all contributors are loyal members of Soviet society, acting in what they believe are the best interests of that society. (Just as we make a comparable assumption about our American contributors.) However, some of their ideas may also be in the interests of our common humanity. In the tradition of free speech, Carlson and I have faith in the ability of readers to judge the worth of these proposals.

Several major American newspapers have noted that space-bridges may dupe viewers not familiar with the reality of Soviet life, that they offer the regime there a new outlet for its propaganda, reformatted as glamorous, intercontinental discussion between peace-seekers. And even if the U.S. end of the show can't be directly controlled, self-censorship can be imposed through pre-production hints about what would be considered "friendly," and the Soviets can choose to broadcast at home only what they like. (So can we.)

Also, say the critics, some early space-bridges have disadvantaged the West by presenting, as "counterparts," Soviets who actually play very different roles in their society from the ones played by the Americans who appear. Concert pianists, athletes, space explorers, ballet dancers and government-employed scientists may do similar work regardless of the country in which they perform, but who in the Soviet Union is the "counterpart" of an American entrepreneur? In what sense is a Soviet "legislator" analogous to a U.S. Congressman? When the Soviets present a state employee called a "journalist," should he be regarded as if he were Robert McNeill, Dan Rather, or Barbara Walters, or as a government public relations spokesperson?

Building a Space-Bridge: a Soviet Contribution

It's a fairly common experience of citizen diplomats visiting the U.S.S.R. to criticize some facet of their own government or society, as Americans are accustomed to do, and then be puzzled, or even feel betrayed, when their Soviet interlocutors agree with these critiques, or even amplify them, but fail to say anything negative about their own regime. The joke goes that an American visits Moscow and tells his new Russian friend, "Our system is better because we have free speech. I can stand in front of the White House and openly criticize President Reagan." The Moscovite replies, "That's nothing, I can stand in front of the Kremlin and *curse* him."

Again, disparities such as these deserve to be considered, but a judgment that a space-bridge may benefit the other side is not necessarily a valid reason to reject it. We need to consider what benefits it may offer to *us*, as against any harm it may cause. And the longer-term question is whether any particular initiative can help to shift the quality of our long-term relationship. Seen as part of a propaganda war, space-bridges remain a study in relative advantage. Seen as part of a developing relationship, however, they might help enlarge the possibilities we can envision.

For many decades, from a Western perspective, the Soviet audience has been largely insulated, on TV, from views of reality other than the Party's "line." (On the radio, of course, they have had access to broadcasts from Western Europe, to the extent that the frequencies were not being jammed by their government.) The Soviets say they simply tell their people the truth (that's what "pravda" means), while trying to protect them from what they perceive as cunning foreign propaganda. They add that in the West our minds are enslaved to the class interests of big capitalists and their allies in the government. On the other hand, in the West it's often said that the Kremlin is afraid to show its own people how prosperous the majority of people in industrial democracies are, or the way people in those societies can openly disagree with the authorities. It's a challenge to imagine how we can begin to go beyond this stalemate. Perhaps space-bridges can help.

The following papers were obtained through the initiative of Joel Schatz, a citizen diplomat who has visited the Soviet Union many times, who has experimented with "slow-scan" TV links, and who, with permission from the U.S. Commerce Department, has helped to create a computer network between the U.S. and Soviet Union. When I first met Schatz in a San Francisco Bay Area restaurant, he was typing on a lap-top computer. It turned out that he was composing a telex to Yevgeny Velikhov—would I please go through the cafeteria line and get our lunch while he finished it? When I returned with sandwiches, he was coming back from the wall-phone where, with an acoustic coupler, he had transmitted the telex to Moscow through a public space-satellite. Alluding both to the power source of his portable computer and to President Reagan's famous description of the Soviet Union, Schatz said wryly, "in and out of the 'evil empire' on four pen-light batteries."

While Schatz gathered this material, obtained permission for us to publish it, and drafted the acknowledgements that appear below, I am solely responsible for editing and arranging the texts and for writing this introduction. In the case of the major chapters, very little was cut except for passages that repeated another contributor's point or that may have strayed momentarily from our request for a positive vision. In the case of a few papers, I have chosen a brief portion that I felt made a distinctive contribution relevant to the collection as a whole. Headnotes for the chapters are restricted to biographical data obtained from one of the contributors in Moscow. Likewise, in this section we have omitted the marginal quotations found elsewhere, lest anyone think we are making oblique comments on the main texts. Within the section we want the contributors to have their say without being suppressed or "corrected." Perhaps this will help set a precedent for an exchange.

So far, most space-bridges have been American initiatives, but bridges have two ends, and by now the Soviets have about as much experience with the medium as we do. In some ways, they have more, because they have put more space-bridge material on the air than U.S. stations have. In this section, a diverse group of Soviet authors discuss the potential of this new form. In some ways they exhibit qualities that we like to regard as "American," as in the scale of their imagination, their dream of "creating humanity," expressions of peaceful intent, and belief in the power of communication. In other ways, they clearly operate in a very different culture. That is one reason we need to experiment with every means that might truly help us to understand them better, and vice versa.

—Craig Comstock

Acknowledgements

Thanks to:

Joseph Goldin, a Moscow script writer, who was responsible for compiling these essays and whose long-held vision of "creating humanity" through a network of "space-bridge" terminals is fast becoming a global reality;

Academician Yevgeny Velikhov, Vice-President, Academy of Sciences U.S.S.R., and Chairman of the Committee of Soviet Scientists Working for Peace Against the Nuclear Threat whose deep-felt sense of urgency about improving U.S./Soviet cooperation through peaceful uses of space has helped to expedite the production of these essays;

Academician Boris Rauschenbakh, Academy of Sciences U.S.S.R., whose focus on the peaceful uses of space technology began at the time he was project director for the historic first photographs of the dark side of the moon, some twenty-five years ago, and whose personal interest in this collection of papers greatly contributed to its success;

Boris Pastukhov, Chairman of the State Committee for Publication, Printing and Book Trade, who had overall responsibility for transmitting the completed material to Ark Communications Institute;

Dr. Guennady Kurganov, Editor-in-Chief, Mir Publishing House, who edited these essays for submission to Ark;

Guennady Gerasimov, Editor-in-Chief, Moscow News, who was first to announce the preparation of these essays to Soviet readers in an article published on June 23, 1985;

Yuri Sviridov, freelance Soviet translator, whose great facility with the English language has captured the spirit and essence of these essays for the benefit of Western readers; and

John Nicolopoulos and Dev Murarka, Moscow-based foreign correspondents, whose sage advice facilitated months of discussion with Soviet officials.

Building a Space-Bridge: a Soviet Contribution

A space scientist, Boris Rauschenbakh developed the Luna-3 space probe that photographed the dark side of the moon in 1959. Now 70, he is a member of the Soviet Academy of Sciences, as well as a member of the International Academy of Astronautics. Winner of the Lenin Prize for his contributions to the Soviet space program, he has written not only *The Guidance and Orientation of Space Vehicles* but also *Spatial Construction in Painting*.

An Experience of Unity

B.V. Rauschenbach

AS THEY WATCHED SHIPS SET OUT ON A LONG VOYAGE in the fairly recent past, people inevitably thought of the immensity of the Earth, of the seemingly boundless oceans and far-off lands. It was never certain that a circumnavigation would be completed. The globe seemed so immeasurably vast that if something happened "out there," it could be followed by people "here" with philosophical detachment. The great Goethe described this attitude well in his *Faust* in an episode involving a townsman chatting with his friend:

> On holidays there's hardly a better pastime
> Than chatting idly over a glass of wine,
> Just you and me,
> About that war in far-off Turkey
> Where troopers clash, and kill and flee.

The twentieth century has changed all that. The first breakthrough towards shaping man's new perception of the world came with the arrival of the aircraft. By linking the Old World with the Americas, commercial airlines made the world smaller as air travel reduced journey time from days to hours.

The arrival of the Space Age completed the process initiated by the aircraft. Indeed, all those who have flown manned space missions, cosmonauts and astronauts, brought back a very different tale

197

to tell about our home planet as compared to the yarns of the mariners of old. With remarkable unanimity they have all described the Earth as a small but beautiful blue planet. The term "beautiful" has taken on a new connotation. In the past people used to speak of the beauty of a particular locality; now we speak of the beauty of our planet as a whole. And our Earth is indeed "small" in the sense that one can orbit it in a spacecraft in ninety minutes, the duration of a stroll.

The Space Age has also brought about a major breakthrough in the field of television. It revolutionized television by converting it into a world communication medium. The transmission of the first picture of the far side of the Moon by the Soviet planetary probe *Luna-3* in October 1959 was arguably the first-ever space telecast. Although this historic event made direct planetary research possible, from the standpoint of television technology it represented the solution of a relatively simple task: transmitting a static image back to Earth. Later, the U.S. communications satellite *Telstar* (1962) and its Soviet cousin *Molniya-1* (1965) and the space orbiting relays and ground stations that followed made it possible to broadcast international and even intercontinental television programs on something like a regular basis. Today we take it for granted that the Olympic Games held on one continent are watched live by audiences in the rest of the world. Likewise, communications satellites have made intercontinental telephone communications much cheaper and consequently more readily available to the general public. Space technology has opened up and continues to open up new avenues to the peaceful unification of humanity and it would be tragic indeed if this unique opportunity were missed.

The language barrier is widely recognized as one formidable obstacle in the way of progress towards this goal. Without wishing to belittle the problems involved, I would like to describe here one ingenious solution to the problem successfully demonstrated during the first test telecast from Moscow to Paris via the *Molniya-1* communications satellite some years ago. On that occasion Soviet engineers broadcast for the enjoyment of their French counterparts a beautiful color cartoon called "The Record of a Crime" by a leading Soviet film director, Fyodor Khitruk. The characters in that movie did not speak a word. Instead they made sounds which were transmitted by a suitable set of musical instruments which simulated their voices. The French viewers, who were able to follow everything perfectly, responded with enthusiasm since the subject of the cartoon was a global problem, noise pollution in urban areas. The symbolism and the message of the amusing cartoon came across well: people everywhere are united by shared global problems which cut across the language and other barriers that divide them.

We are witnessing the rapid unfolding of a spectacular process which, as well as filling us with legitimate pride for man's powers and achievements, is carrying potential inherent dangers. We have harnessed nuclear energy, invaded space and developed industrial robots. Humanity is now technologically equipped to tackle global engineering projects and this is good news. The bad news is that the human brain does not seem to have evolved one bit from what it was in the Stone Age when humans had to rely on stone implements and wooden clubs for their survival in the daily battle against the elements. At worst, stupid or unwise actions by humans in the Stone Age resulted in the disappearance of the tribe involved, a development that hardly had any global consequences. Not so today when unwise actions resulting in a nuclear war would effectively spell the end of the human race and possibly of all life on Earth as we know it—in other words, a global catastrophe.

Some people may argue that people today are far more enlightened than their distant ancestors in the Stone Age. Educational progress of mankind is undeniable. What is disturbing, however, is that despite this progress modern man, with few exceptions, acts in the spirit of old-time, traditional views of the world, ignoring the possible global consequences of his actions. As in the Stone Age, people today often consider only the interests of "their tribe." The formidable problems of environmental pollution and the way they have been dealt with provide a good example. The management of an industrial concern, no doubt keeping the "interests of the tribe" at heart, may think nothing of poisoning with industrial effluents the waters of a river that flows not only past their own plants but across other countries as well.

It is not that the managers are insufficiently educated; some of them may hold degrees from prestigious universities. Simply their mentality is such that they are quite incapable of thinking in terms of the human race as a whole, in global terms, and then acting accordingly. It seems to me that such people still see themselves as belonging only to their own tribe, as members of a particular community, town or country; they have an extremely faint perception of their belonging to the population of our one and only home planet. Such a parochial (and, let us face it, "unenlightened") mentality generates undesirable and at times dangerous attitudes and perverted perceptions of the morality of their own behavior.

In an even more immediate sense, all this applies to the vital task of preventing a nuclear conflict. Whereas the problem of environmental protection can be tackled gradually through a combination of local and global efforts to meet local and global interests, a nuclear conflict, once it breaks out, will be short and sharp. There will simply be no time for reflection, and even the fateful decisions will be taken by automated computerized systems preprogrammed in advance of the conflict. Any idea of a gradual storing up of international experience in rational behavior under such circumstances is, of course, ludicrous, as is the idea that someone may sit serenely above or outside the nuclear battle and follow apocalyptic destruction with the philosophical detachment of Goethe's townsman. Global catastrophe, should it break out, would leave no one unscathed.

To prevent the twin menace of nuclear and ecological catastrophes threatening the very continuance of the human race, no effort should be spared to achieve, through patient negotiation conducted in good faith, political solutions leading to the elimination of the nuclear arsenals and the prevention of the militarization of outer space. Such solutions should also make provision for well-designed and efficiently managed economic activity on a global scale to reduce to a minimum, if not rule out altogether, damage to the environment. These are, of course, the most pressing first-priority challenges facing humanity today.

Wise political and economic decisions should be complemented by purposeful moves to change human attitudes in desirable ways. Positive changes in this area will help people everywhere to perceive themselves as belonging to the same family of man in which differences

200

in the form of government, state structure, ideology and the way of life are no reason or justification for war. In this "new look" humanity, these and other differences will be universally recognized as part of the legitimate and indeed desirable "unity in diversity" and will never be interpreted in the perverted sense that "life is wonderful on our side of the fence, and pretty awful on yours, so why don't you let us put things straight on your side of the fence, for your own good, too?" Every nation should be free to decide its own destiny while remaining an equal member of the world community.

A good deal is being written today about the pressing need for new thinking in the nuclear age. One effective way to encourage the emergence of the thinking required is to intensively develop people-to-people contacts in every area of human endeavor. Apart from traditional forms of contact through trade, tourism and cultural exhange, it is important to take advantage of the exciting new opportunities that the burgeoning space technology offers mankind.

I have already mentioned communications satellites capable of relaying television programs as well as telephone conversations from continent to continent. The time has come for two-way television communication not unlike telephone service. Already experimental TV contacts between mass audiences in the Soviet Union and the United States have been held, widely known as "space-bridges." This designation conveys well the essence of the experiments, as bridges do not divide, they connect.

These experiments have shown that space-bridges can be used for a wide range of purposes: from enabling scientists to hold tele-conferences to discuss topical problems, including the global consequences of nuclear war, to covering important ceremonial occasions and interactive events held in different countries. During one such "space-bridge" that linked San Francisco and Moscow, Soviet and American audiences in the two cities were able to attend simultaneously the presentation of awards to Professor Bernard Lown and Doctor Yevgeny Chazov, the co-chairmen of the International Physicians for the Prevention of Nuclear War.

Of quite a different character were space-bridges that attracted vast audiences who watched intercontinental telecasts on giant TV screens. Such space-bridges can bring together in a single happening thousands of viewers at a time, and the opportunities they offer for direct contact between mass audiences in different continents can hardly be overestimated.

To date several space-bridges, all of them linking the Soviet Union and the United States, have been held. Needless to say, as other countries join in the venture the potential of space-bridges will be enhanced.

The logistics of mounting multilateral space-bridges linking several countries at a time involve considerable difficulties. Two of these are obvious: the language barrier and the high cost. Adequate experience and techniques are already available to provide an efficient simultaneous interpretation service to deal with the first problem. The high cost could be cut in a variety of ways. As space technology and television techniques develop, the cost of space TV hook-ups is progressively reduced. Over the last fifteen years, for instance, it has dropped to one-seventh of what it was and continues to decline. On the other hand, small scientific conferences could be held using a quite inexpensive space telephone channel. Finally, mankind should sensibly divert part of the enormous amounts of money currently squandered for military purposes to support efforts contributing to the maintenance of world peace.

A free-lance script writer, Joseph Goldin, 45, is well-known to citizen diplomats who visit Moscow. He coordinates projects for the development of human potential and promotes the concept of spacebridges for the transformation of group consciousness. A brief description of his spacebridge idea appeared in the 1984 Rolex award series volume, *Spirit of Enterprise*.

A Mirror for Humanity

Joseph Goldin

ANY COMMUNITY IS ALWAYS LIMITED BY THE EXTENT TO which its information can be transmitted. From this it follows that "Humanity"—in the true sense of the word—does not yet exist. The myth of "humanity" appears in the form of political declarations, humanistic images, religious beliefs—but "humanity" has yet to emerge as a real, living community.

Our proposed conception of a network of space-bridge terminals as a new channel of direct, live, multi-lateral communication between large groups of people around the world could turn out to be the information resource with which man is at last able to transform the myth of "humanity" into reality.

A dramatic illustration of this potential was the direct, live, two-way satellite hook-up between California and Moscow that I helped to accomplish on September 5, 1982. American Robert A. Freling, research assistant on the space-bridge project, described it well. Here's an abridged version of what he said:

"On that day, using the remarkable Diamond Vision videoscreen, a landmark communications event took place. A very large screen was set up in San Bernardino, some 60 miles from Los Angeles. It was used to receive a feed, via satellite, from Moscow and relay this back to the originating Moscow studio. When the several hundred Muscovites assembled in front of the studio videoscreen saw the massive San Bernardino screen appear and then saw themselves on that screen

203

and realized that the hundreds of Californians were waving their arms to the beat of music coming from Moscow, they were affected by a new emotion of "distant proximity"—and they were happy. A true space-bridge had been created for people-to-people communication on Space Ship Earth!

"I have spoken with Soviet students who participated in this hook-up. Their accounts of what happened definitely fall into the "peak experience" category. The artificial boundaries of "me versus them" suddenly and dramatically gave way to a new feeling of unity as the Soviets were able to see themselves reflected in the eyes and smiles of their American counterparts.

"A prophet or seer I am not, but something tells me that this new form of human contact, if used wisely, could give birth to a planetary consciousness that until now has been realized only by an enlightened few. A worldwide network of satellite-linked communication centers could act as a cosmic mirror with which we, as citizens of the world, could look back at ourselves and grasp our essential unity as never before."

In a telegram sent to California on the day after the California-Moscow hook-up, I wrote:

"The world community has become the real object of natural science investigation, thanks to direct, live communication with video-feedback between large groups of people in Moscow and California. . . . Such gigantic videoscreens used for bilateral communication between thousands of people will soon become a traditional element of the environment, just like the public squares in the Greek city-states, or the forums of the Roman Empire. . . . The new feelings of "distant proximity" experienced by millions of people all over the world will create a new self-awareness and inevitably lead to a radical transformation in the way we deal with global problems. . . . The scientists who created the Bomb, and the artists who conjured up Anti-Utopia, will be challenged to find new ways of using their creative energy."

Imagine a small city connected to the network of space-bridge terminals (in the Soviet Union, "small cities" are those with under 100,000 people, and include almost 90% of our cities), with the entire population able to participate in multi-lateral communication with other cities around the world. Immediately, the temptation will emerge for truly creative scientists and artists to join forces to help ordinary inhabitants be transformed into citizens of the world. From learning languages to communicate better, to staging live theatrical events with a "global stage," ordinary people will be initiated into the zone of expanded awareness.

It can be done. Our project seeks to develop the resources and interest needed to bring such a network of space-bridge terminals into being; "humanity" in its truest sense is what we are seeking to achieve.

On August 28, 1984, I received a telex. Signed by John Naisbitt, author of the best-selling *Megatrends*, it read:

"Our 'global town meeting' earlier this month could be the beginning of something really new, linking the technology of conference calls with a growing number of radio stations. It is a technology for citizen diplomacy. It was great to hear you say, 'let us move from megatrends to megavision.' That is what the world needs, a megavision of world peace in our time."

Earlier, on August 6, an international telephone conference call was broadcast over many radio stations to mark the thirty-ninth anniversary of the atom bombing of Hiroshima. That day, a Washington radio station on which time had been obtained by Chuck Alton, President of U.S. Radio, was linked by means of telephone to people in different parts of the world, as far apart as the south of France and Hawaii, San Francisco and the Soviet Union. In Moscow, *Literaturnaya Gazeta* let us use its editorial conference room for the event. To boost the quality of the telephone signal three young engineers rewired the office phones with equipment borrowed from a disco in Moscow's fashionable Gorky Park. Upon receiving an on-the-air cue from Chuck Alton, I described to an audience of millions across half the world a project which I hoped would excite their interest. I said:

"I would personally like to invite the participants of this conference, those of you who are ready to devote your time and energies, your abilities and resources, to take part in the project called 'A Mirror for Humanity.'

"We envision this project as an alternative to the 'nuclear winter.' According to the model of a 'nuclear winter' with which we are all familiar, if a nuclear war occurs, the sun would be screened for many weeks by a thick layer of dust, smoke and soot. Thus, the fact that the sun is still in the sky from our vantage point on Earth means that not only does it remain an eternal source of cosmic energy, but a symbol of the absence of nuclear disaster as well.

"Technically, 'A Mirror for Humanity' is a project utilizing a series of gigantic video screens situated in various parts of the world, connected through a network of satellite technology called 'space-bridge.' This 'Mirror' will make it possible for millions of people to participate in the following:

"The gloomy chaos on the gigantic video screen slowly changes into a reddish glow whose intensity grows. At this moment the viewers instinctively begin to squint, as the sun rises above the horizon (the horizon line suddenly becomes distinct). The montage will take the sun up over the Earth through the network of space-bridges, switching the image from one enormous videoscreen to another in a smooth glissando, changing with the landscapes and different populations. In some countries we see yesterday's twilight, in others the dark of night, but it is, above all, people that we see everywhere: people young and old, people with their chins turned upward or their hands folded in prayer, people embracing and looking at the sun as it rises at the edge of the Earth, their eyes catching each new ray of sunlight as it streams forth. This would be the first ritual of an emerging humanity as a community.

"A wise man (St. Augustine) was asked: 'Do miracles exist?' 'They do,' he replied, 'the daily sunrise is a genuine miracle.'

"Bringing this megavision to life and realizing it technically is easier than one might think. Giant video screens are already installed on all the continents of the Earth, and they can easily be linked into a space-bridge network. All we need is a team of dedicated people committed to making this project a reality. Let's work on it together."

Two and a half months later Dr. Dannan Parry, Director of the Institute of Conflict Resolution in California, arrived in Moscow bringing with him materials for the second "global town meeting," as international radio conference calls came to be known thanks to John Naisbitt's happy touch. Looking through those materials I found a copy of a letter to Chuck Alton from Frank Lansdown of San Francisco. Lansdown wrote:

"What I wanted to say was in response to the man in Moscow who proposed the global ritual of the celebration of the miracle of a sunrise. . . . The image of people on all continents, islands, even on boats, in all the seas, in a twenty-four hour celebration of one sunrise all over the earth, that daily miracle, that universal . . . eternal event caught me—such an easy global participation, which made all the wordy abstracts and generalities that followed seem banal. I listened for a response to that proposal. None came as discussion turned to other topics. I thank you for having heard that proposal. I thought of Ikhnaton's sun rituals in Egypt's XVIIIth dynasty."

After reading this I thought that perhaps there were other people elsewhere who might believe the project worth implementing. Having transcribed the text of my remarks from a compact cassette recording of the broadcast, I xeroxed quite a few copies and proceeded to circulate them to a broad cross-section of people.

The result was that during the second global town meeting held on December 9, 1984, the composer Paul Winter told the listeners of fifty radio stations in thirty U.S. cities that he was willing to write a music score for the ritual of the daily sunrise using themes from his *Missa Gaia* (Earth Mass). Producer Rick Lukens, with whom I had worked on the first Moscow-California space-bridge which linked the participants in the San Bernardino U.S. festival in California with their age-mates in Moscow, promised that he would try to get China to join the 'Mirror.' In the remaining minutes allotted to me by Chuck Alton I just had time to say that employees of the Moscow office of the Mitsubishi Company had made available to me a map of the location of its Diamond Vision videoscreens, those marvels of twentieth century electronics. I did not see why Ted Turner, of Cable News Network, should not link those screens together via communications satellite to turn the "Mirror" into a working tool of self-knowledge for mankind, not unlike the radio telescope used by astrophysicists to study the cosmic objects of the Milky Way.

Academician V.I. Vernadsky, who fathered the concept of a biosphere, believed that there are discoveries which contribute to the growth of a scientific world view in contrast to other achievements which have significance only in the context of the history of specific disciplines. The discovery of America, for example, had an immense impact on the scientific world view. By contrast, attempts to reach the North and South Poles did not have much of an impact on the development of the scientific world view although they were of great interest to geographers.

In assessing the progress of modern communications technology this analogy seems applicable. We can use this analogy in the evaluation of a new channel of communication represented by over-size, high-resolution videoscreens which, in conjunction with communications satellites, offer the possibility of creating a network of space-bridge terminals for direct live contacts between large groups of people on all continents. This could offer unprecedented opportunities for important studies in comparative typology of cultures and international relations at a critical juncture in history.

The Eyes of People Talking

The new communication channel may become a vehicle for fostering the planet's collective reason. This is of special importance now that the proximity of the notions "not us" and "enemy" serves as a platform for confrontation between countries having different political systems, different social and cultural traditions. A collective awareness of the path we are all following and of the possible consequences which must be avoided calls for informal contacts—not among machines, no matter how clever, rapid, and efficient in computer analysis—but among people who can rejoice and suffer, think and feel. People who have been drawn to each other in face-to-face contacts will hardly become enemies. The eyes of people talking to each other are a living mirror capable of changing its parameters, a feedback capable of multiple transformation. Thereby the transformation process becomes self-catalyzing, enabling rapid progress toward truth.

—G. Ivanitsky

A biophysicist, Genrikh Ivanitsky, 50, is a corresponding member of the Soviet Academy of Sciences and Director of the Academy's Biological Research Center. He holds the Lenin Prize in recognition of his cell research.

An architect, Alexei Gutnov, 47, is a department chief at the Moscow Institute of City Planning, dealing with the master plan for the development of the Soviet capital. Author of books and articles, he has won international awards for his contributions to planning.

Frame for a Mirror: an Architect's View

Alexei Gutnov

GLOBAL TELEVISION LINK-UPS VIA COMMUNICATIONS satellite will enable mankind for the first time ever to take a look at itself in a mirror. Looking into this mirror, everyone will feel himself part of one human family and see the world at large as part of his private world. The universe of human existence expanded to cover the whole of the planet Earth will add a new meaning to one's sense of loyalty to one's country and one's compatriots as an integral and unique part of the Universe.

Space-bridges are not just another form of telecast. Many of the negative effects of mass culture stem from the fact that its more than dubious values insinuate themselves imperceptibly as people stare at the television screen in the privacy of their homes. A man frozen in his chair with his eyes fixed on the "idiot box," a passive and pitiable being lost from contact even with his immediate family, has become the stock butt of ridicule in countless cartoons.

Space-bridges add an entirely new dimension to television as we know it by offering not only long-distance transmission of information but also direct, person-to-person contact through the medium of giant videoscreens. The impact of the shared experience as produced by the legitimate theater or a mass rally can be amplified severalfold thanks to the global scale of a space television network. The resultant new sense of "distant proximity" experienced by the participants

Building a Space-Bridge: a Soviet Contribution

in world-wide "megavision" sessions will give rise to a new self-awareness and possibly a new sense of global fellowship.

With "megavision" links in the form of global space-bridges, not only a philosopher or a poet of genius, as happened in the past, but the proverbial man in the street may feel himself a citizen of the world, a tenant of our common home, a passenger on our one and only spacecraft, the planet Earth. Space-bridges, thus, may induce a new sense of responsibility in us all for the survival of the human race and reinforce our ability to act. Eventually the new medium of intercultural communication may transform the historically established procedures for decision-making on a wide range of problems facing the human race as a whole.

We should not forget, on the other hand, that technology gone mad has spawned the monstrous Bomb, and called into being the hideous phantoms of anti-Utopia. The new channel of mass communication must therefore be placed, from the outset, under the control of the international community and remain reliably insulated from contamination by the perilous spirit of enmity, chauvinism and unhealthy rivalry.

As I see it the proposed "mirror for humanity" will help bring the future closer. As an architect and urban developer I am naturally primarily concerned with its implications for architecture, for the city. What kind of architectural "frame" should we create for the "mirror for humanity"?

The video screens of the first space-bridges were set up in television studios and at sports stadiums that had not been adapted for global video link-ups. The translation of the "mirror for humanity" project into reality will require the erection of space-television theaters specially equipped for the purpose. Let us call them space-television terminals. A typical terminal will have, as its basic components, a large video screen (or rather, a system of video screens) and a video arena—a hall or some other enclosed space specially equipped for communication sessions between large groups of people, with their messages received and transmitted via space satellite.

In due course the whole planet will be covered with a network of space-television terminals. Initially these will be few in number—

only one or two, perhaps, on each continent. As time passes their number will steadily grow.

The major terminals will serve as continental, regional, interstate and national centers for international communication, information exchanges, education and experience exchange in the field of space television communication. These will be large complexes incorporating, apart from video screens, also display rooms, data banks, and convention facilities for holding international symposia and workshops for specialists. Most of the ordinary terminals, rather modest in size, will serve as a vehicle for human communication in its most universal, democratic, and technically perfect form, which will stimulate creative thinking, imaginative approaches and social activity. Apart from this, it will also become a monumental symbol, at once memorable and clear to the mind, of the dawning era of global intercultural communication.

In terms of its social implications, the space-television terminal has a valid claim to becoming the dominant structure of the coming age. For a long time now, architecture has lacked a really democratic, culturally significant structure that might give expression to the spirit of the times, in the way the ancient Greek and Roman temples and forums, the Gothic cathedral, or the market place did in the past. Both the church and (to a greater extent, perhaps) the theater have lost their universal character, and inexorable time has ousted both to the outlying periphery of cultural consciousness.

Combining as it does the supreme achievements of civilization in science, technology and the arts, the space-television terminal deserves to become a shrine of the dawning new age of intercultural communication by satellite. It will serve as a kind of temple for a new social movement on which the peoples of the world will pin their hopes for peace, unity, and balanced economic and cultural development.

The outlines of the terminal will dominate the cityscape of the twenty-first century rather like the cathedral or the town hall did in the medieval city. Perhaps the only structure which can lay some claim to this role today is the television tower, if it were not for its strictly functional, "dehumanized" character. A space television terminal will be different. Its value for the city will not be confined to pure technology. As a center for human communication, a window on the world,

211

and as a school for international cooperation, the terminal will introduce a new organizing dimension into the city's spatial structure. It will become a symbolic starting point in the process of humanitarian renovation of the urban environment.

Theater and Space Technology

Any alternative artistic project begins with a search for adequate expression, a suitable language. The trend towards an inter-media idiom must have influenced that specific kind of activity that has come to be known as "space-bridge" (or space video technology). At one time not so long ago the theater tried to give up technology—it declared itself "poor" and settled down in "no man's land." The actor got rid of all the paraphernalia and appeared in the "stark nakedness" of his soul and in an abiding faith in the miracle of gesture, elan, and rhythm. In contrast, the inter-media idiom was a response to the scientific and technological revolution: disco shows and gala performances with multiscreen projection, laser, holography, quite a slew of wonders conceived by man's mind and wrought by his hands. The space-bridge seems well suited to link these two counter trends (or rather, avert their collision), a sophisticated technology designed to secure direct people-to-people contacts.

—S. Volynets

An art critic, Sergei Volnyets, 32, is a researcher at the Moscow Institute of Theatrical Design and author of several publications on the experimental theater movement in the U.S.

212

A Byelorussian writer and dramatist, Ales Adamovich, 58, has written books on World War II such as *Blockade Book*, and *I am From a Burning Village*, which has been translated into English. He is also author of the scenario for the film, "Go and See," the Soviet gold-medal-winning entry at the 1985 Moscow Film Festival.

One Billion

Ales Adamovich

FOR A MOMENT I WAS AGHAST WITH AMAZEMENT (AS were, apparently, many others) when the Soviet nuclear scientist Yevgeny Velikhov, sitting in a Moscow TV studio and looking at his own image reflected on a huge videoscreen under a California night sky, spoke words that became common coinage overnight: "We must not delude ourselves: nuclear weapons are not muscles, they are a cancerous tumor. . . . " I recall the surprise coupled with joy and the powerful surge of unanimity that we read on the faces of thousands of distant Americans watching that videoscreen in San Bernardino, California, where they had converged for a "festival of unity," attracted by music and promised electronic miracles at a "happening" organized and funded by Stephen Wozniak of Apple Computers.

A crowd of an estimated 300,000 Americans saw not only Velikhov but also other Russians who, according to all the hackneyed stereotypes of official propaganda, were supposed to be up to no good, cooking up mischief, deceptions and intrigues while naive, carefree and fun-loving Americans were having a good time. They saw Soviet students, then a leading Soviet pop star and, finally, Soviet children. And suddenly it hit them that the smile of trust and concord was possible; was, in fact, long overdue on the faces of both Americans and Soviets, who were so tired of a long period of unnatural and artificially stimulated alienation and fear.

The first space-bridge between Moscow and California was fol-

213

lowed by six others over the past three years. These meetings via space TV had something of the spirit of that memorable linkup between American and Soviet soldiers at the Elbe River in the spring of 1945. Watching the space-bridges we felt we must move across time, overcoming the sterile wastes of the cold war, back to the voices, the embraces and the smiles of our wartime allies against Hitler.

The experience of seven space-bridges demonstrates that there is a real chance now to counter the massive, well orchestrated media effort to distort the true image of the neighbor-nation across the Bering Strait by using the same Space Age technology as the mass media, for direct contact and communication—for citizen counter-propaganda, so to say. The point is that the same sophisticated level of technology used to maintain the combat readiness of nuclear missiles with their elaborate guidance systems can be used, instead, to enable one billion people around the globe to talk to one another, direct via communications satellites.

The participants in the first space-bridges later confessed to completely inexpressible, incomparable sensations they all experienced under the impact of "direct vision." You seem to be omnipresent, flying from continent to continent at the speed of light, coming into direct contact with people whose existence you did not even suspect a moment ago—people so distant and yet so close appear before you with magical ease. The separating walls of space and distance crumble down, and with them many other walls.

Just picture the scene. You talk to your fellow men at the other end of the world and, as you do, you can see yourself on a huge videoscreen "out there" among members of your audience.

In the future, space-bridges will instantly link up meeting with meeting across the globe, festival with festival, a peace march on one continent with a space march on another, and you will be able to watch it all "as it happens." A veritable mirror for humanity! You will have a unique opportunity to grasp the profound meaning and implications of this unprecedented "megavision" and experience a sense of belonging to one human family. The participants in the Global Town Meeting will see the planet Earth, our common home, the way Yuri Gagarin saw it from outer space, the way the Soviet and U.S. astronauts saw

it when they linked up in mid-orbit in a symbolic gesture of friendship during the Soyuz-Apollo joint mission in 1975.

Intensive work is under way in Moscow to explore the potential
of the new communication channel so powerful and comprehensive
in its impact. The technology for it is there and will be improved as
time goes by. No less important is to explore the humanitarian implications. In a bold move the Department of Art-related Problems
of the Mass Media at Moscow's prestigious Institute for the Advanced
Studies of the Arts has held a seminar to discuss in depth and formulate in specific and realistic terms a project unprecedented in the
history of culture—the logistics of a Global Town Meeting bringing
together one billion people. Participants included the Soviet contributors to this book.

Among others who spoke, philosopher U.F. Koryakin sounded
a warning note that, incredible as it may sound, the danger of nuclear
holocaust is equally capable of uniting people in a fight for peace and
of dividing them through fear and distrust. But there is yet another
danger of planetary proportions which, though frightening people, also
stimulates them to make concerted efforts to avert it. We refer to the
danger of ecological destruction. Thus far we have been aware of the
nuclear and ecological threats in isolation, as it were. The only sound
approach is to attack both in combination, by concerted efforts of all
the nations.

Indeed, it would be good to put across to the one-billion-strong
audience of the proposed Global Town Meeting the simple and yet
poignant message that it is crazy to contemplate "star wars" at a time
when mankind is in danger of losing the planet Earth, ecologically;
that the human race, if the present perilous policies are not reversed,
will destroy the very basis of its existence, the air we breathe, and
the water we drink. We are at a critical juncture in history. Now is
not the time for arguing back and forth; what we need is action to
save what is left, and ourselves.

Academician B.V. Raushenbakh, whose talents as a space scientist in 1959 helped mankind to photograph the far side of the moon,
perhaps has the right to cast this sad reproach in the teeth of a guilty
humanity: modern man, says he, still acts (with very few exceptions)

215

in the same way his ancient predecessors did, considering the short-term interests of "his own tribe." But as Raushenbakh adds, "space technology has opened up paths which can lead to a peaceful unity of the nations of the world and it would be a tragic mistake to miss this unique opportunity."

The need for a Global Town Meeting cannot be overemphasized. It could be opposed only by those who fear that after seeing and hearing the "other side," their own people may ask angrily, "Now wait a minute, are these the people we are being told to atom bomb? Who says we cannot reach agreement with them? Are we supposed to risk sliding towards nuclear suicide instead of sharing the common burden of our similar concerns and problems? Are we supposed to believe that?"

A wise man once said that mankind is made up of the living and the dead with the latter in the vast majority. In this day and age we have every reason to qualify this maxim by adding that mankind also includes billions yet unborn. These potential human beings will outnumber both the living and the dead. They are the future of the human race. We know now that one of the avenues leading to this future lies through outer space. Not through the outer space of "star wars" but through a peaceful outer space, criss-crossed by the beautiful rainbows of spacebridges that unite friendly nations.

All contributors to this section live in the U.S.S.R., but one is not a Soviet citizen. Correspondent for the Athens daily *Eleutherotypiy* and the weekly *Tachydromos*, John Nicolopoulos is a Greek specialist on the Soviet Union. Trained at the University of London School of Slavonic and East European Studies, the Sorbonne, and Columbia University, he taught Russian history at the State University of New York. He is 50 and has lived in Moscow since 1980.

Citizen Tele-diplomacy

John Nicolopoulos

THE PERIOD SINCE RONALD REAGAN'S REELECTION HAS been marked, here in Moscow, by a veritable flurry of U.S.-Soviet citizen diplomacy. More and more Americans, apparently, feel compelled to make some kind of personal contact with the "other side"— especially since they don't expect with any confidence that official relations between the two countries are in for any quick improvement. The Soviets have welcomed these private overtures not only because they accept American political realities, but also because they would like to take President Reagan at his pre-electoral word to meet the Soviet Union halfway in a renewed disarmament dialogue, and make him stick to it. In this pursuit, the presence of American "witnesses" and a direct appeal to the American hinterland—Reagan's political base—can certainly be helpful.

Among the various constituencies represented in this stream of visits, the one that impresses most is the one connected with the on-going technological revolution in the field of telecommunications. We are dealing here with two distinct trends: two-way television links by satellite, the so-called "space-bridges," and the combination of existing telephone service with the world's computer network, a trend that is less spectacular but vastly more intriguing as to its future development and consequences.

The use of personal computers as versatile telecommunications

217

terminals is already an established trend and may be said to represent one of the most important keys to the future. As the complexity and sophistication of the equipment increases, its actual size and cost fall. This is the well known revolutionary essence of microelectronics, which has captivated the average Soviet citizen no less than the average American. Hardly a day goes by without a lengthy account in the Soviet press in praise of the personal computer. The notion that a box no larger or heavier than a desk dictionary can replace traditional methods of communication and research, thus making all users equal regardless of surrounding inequalities, cannot but exercise a profound appeal to the Russian mind.

"Global Town Meetings," normal telephone links with the addition of the computer factor in the form of slow-scan TV, beckon as the gate to this communication utopia. I am sure that certain elements in the Soviet power structure, on one hand, and in the U.S. Administration, on the other, will not greet this development with great enthusiasm. And yet, an information explosion of this magnitude is probably the only alternative we have to the politico-military explosion we have lived in dread of since World War II.

A Radio Shack personal computer was the appropriate centerpiece at the Moscow end of a recent Global Town Meeting, the second. It was not connected to anything this time: it merely played the modest, for its capacities, role of "personal secretary" to one of the organizers, Joel Schatz, a benevolent, bearded, denim-clad, patriarchal figure from San Francisco. The small slow-scan video connection originally planned had fallen through, and the only things linking us with producer Chuck Alton in Los Angeles were two telephone lines—our host's phone and an extension from the neighboring apartment. The first phone was used by the participants in the encounter as they took their turns talking with their American counterparts. The other, the back line, was firmly in the grip of that omnipresent and omniscient Moscow intellectual Joseph Goldin, whose contribution to Soviet-American unofficial peace-making will one day, I am sure, provide the subject for more than one doctoral dissertation. It was Goldin's idea to anchor the Moscow end of the international conference call in the apartment of his friend Djuna Davitashvili.

Building a Space-Bridge: a Soviet Contribution

Goldin's friendship with Djuna, the legendary Assyrian healer from the Caucasus who is said to have treated some senior Soviet figures, harks back to his involvement with the study of "hidden human reserves," including parapsychological phenomena, particularly in the area of perception and learning, by a special commission set up under the auspices of the Soviet Academy of Sciences. Goldin's thoroughly unorthodox style of operating, however, relying on spontaneous and informal contacts with Soviet and foreign colleagues, could not be easily accommodated in institutional surroundings. The upshot of it all was that Goldin himself was briefly "institutionalized" in a mental clinic, where he organized seminars on Lozanov's suggestological theory of learning and wrote the scenario for his anti-nuclear-war production "A Mirror for Humanity." The briefness of this sequence, by the way, testifies to an increasing toleration of the unorthodox creative impulse here.

Be that as it may, Global Town Meeting #2 was offered Djuna's Caucasian hospitality on December 9, 1984, from 5:30 to 7:00 a.m., Moscow time. (Global Town Meeting #1 had been held on the anniversary of the Hiroshima bombing, on August 6, 1984, from the offices of the weekly *Literaturnaya Gazeta*, which has always had a weakness for Goldin's "happenings." The American end had featured Betty Bumpers of "Peacelinks"; Don Carlson, Chairman of Consolidated Capital of San Francisco and peace activist; George Leonard, author of *Human Potential*; John Marks of "Search for Common Ground"; John Naisbitt, author of *Megatrends*; Carol Rosin, founder of the Institute for Security and Cooperation in Outer Space; and others.)

As far as the early morning guests sipping their cups of Turkish coffee in Djuna's apartment were concerned, the main features of Global Town Meeting #2 would be the dialogue between the directors of the suicide crisis centers of Moscow and Los Angeles, Professor Aina Ambrumova and Dr. Norman Farberow; Djuna's discussion of a series of experiments conducted between her in Moscow and Professor Russell Targ in San Francisco; all this to be topped by a literary exchange between Norman Mailer and the Soviet poet Evgeni Yevtushenko.

Building a Space-Bridge: a Soviet Contribution

The sequence was of a compelling character: first, the megalo-politan suicide syndrome due to stress, loneliness, isolation; then, an instance of the human spirit soaring above physical obstacles, in a way that could be termed "supernatural"; and, finally, human inventiveness and ingenuity making this special "gift" the common heritage of all mankind. And so back to the little magic box that can be linked with the telephone receiver of any apartment, from L.A. to Moscow. As it turned out, the line was cut off due to switching problems before Mailer and Yevtushenko could exchange their lines—but that did not seem to make much difference: the event spoke for itself.

So with the feeling that our Symposium had assumed such dimensions of Platonic perfection that we could afford to run our poets out of town, we turned to the hearty breakfast that Djuna had all ready on the table for us in the next room. Hot tea spiked with various exotic brandies, black bread, sausages, cheese, fruit. The talk was of future conference calls with or without image, possible participants, topics. It slowly dawned on us, as the very day itself that was beginning in Moscow, that our choice was unlimited, and at our fingertips.

Another source of this euphoria had been a short exchange in the course of the intercontinental dialogue, which had gone almost unnoticed at the time: a few words from Ted Turner, owner of the Cable News Network, who was at the Los Angeles studio with Chuck Alton, to Joseph Goldin in Moscow. It was an expression of support from someone who had it in his power to turn a marginal happening into a mainstream event.

A week after the international conference call from Djuna's apartment, I found myself at a similarly early hour in the palatial concert hall of "Gosteleradio"—Soviet State Radio and Television—in Ostankino, an aristocratic estate on what was, in the eighteenth century, the edge of Moscow. (Now the city stretches quite a few miles beyond, enveloping Ostankino and its English-type park in a forest of high-rise apartment buildings.)

The occasion was quasi-identical to the Global Town Meeting, but in a different key: to begin with, we had before us the wide TV screen used in simultaneous telecommunication links, the so-called "space-bridges." This immediately infuses an aura of large crowds and

Building a Space-Bridge: a Soviet Contribution

big money, Hollywood-style show business and plain American business procedures—a touch of Rotary Club function with overtones of a church service on Sunday, in an upper-middle-class Sunbelt suburb. . . . A California peace group called "Beyond War" was about to give an award over a space-bridge linking Moscow with San Francisco.

Beyond War is an organization of successful businessmen, early-retired young millionaires of the hard-working self-made Puritan-ethic stripe, who have become peace activists and are determined to succeed in this pursuit in the same short order as in their business ventures. Recipients of the prize, the "Beyond War Award," were the two co-presidents of International Physicians for the Prevention of Nuclear War—Dr. Bernard Lown, the Harvard cardiologist, accepting his award in San Francisco, and Professor Evgueni Chazov, top Soviet cardiologist, in Moscow. This was the second "Beyond War Award" (like Global Town Meetings, the award got under way in 1983). The first award was appropriately given to the Catholic Bishops of the United States for their pastoral letter, "The Challenge of Peace: God's Promise and Our Response."

The show was slowly getting under way. On the Moscow end, Winston Boone, Beyond War representative, looking like a Marlborough cowboy in an expensive business suit, was recounting at length how he met the Russians on the Elbe as an American infantryman in World War II. "It was a very joyous occasion," he said, and the 2000-strong Soviet audience in the studio, consisting of professionals and administrators, cheered. Then the Soviet master of ceremonies, TV commentator Vladimir Pozner, put the crowd through a rehearsal of the greeting: "Good *Eve*-ning San Fran-*cis*-co!"—to be met from the other side with an equally jovial "Dobroye *Utro*, Mosk*va!*"

From San Francisco, Richard Rathbun, President of Beyond War, blue-eyed, trim-mustached and square-jawed, launched the meeting. There was optimism: "Can the American People and the Soviet People work together? The obvious answer is *yes!*" There was pride in the affirmation that "we are the two most powerful nations that ever existed." The pain of the readjustment from one to two superpowers was acknowledged: "If we really look at the world, we will suffer. Suffering has always been the price of seeing . . . [But] the human spirit

221

has never known boundaries . . . The development of nuclear weapons has changed our environment forever . . . We must turn away from mutual suicide, to new global mutual respect."

Dr. Lown got up to receive his award. "The enemy is neither capitalism nor communism, but these genocidal nuclear weapons," he said. "The struggle is between catastrophe and survival. Either we live together or we die together: there is no other alternative." He pointed out that the availability of absolute weapons makes it psychologically necessary to believe in an absolute enemy. This is why the public must be educated in a new way of thinking. "Although not a single weapons system has been dismantled as a result of our activity, we have had a definite influence in the political process: there is no more talk now of a limited nuclear exchange or of winning a nuclear war."

It was now Chazov's turn. His main point was that human reason will prevail. It could have been a spinoff of one of Chernienko's key slogans, addressed to the domestic as well as to the international scene: "Let's be rational." It is a popular slogan, because it hits the surrealistic atmosphere brought about by excessively bureaucratic management, particularly in the economy. It could be translated, for the American ear, "Let's lay off Catch-22." And we all know how apt this is in describing the military mentality. "I can conceive of no higher award," Chazov concluded, "than recognition of my contribution to the struggle for Peace." Then he chatted with Lown over the space-bridge—but they had little to say since, as they explained to the audience, they had spent seven hours talking together less than a week ago.

There was an audible change of gears, and the program went into the concert part, like a washing machine entering a new cycle. Zhanna Bitchevskaya, a popular Russian folk singer, did a bilingual version of "Where have all the flowers gone" which did not fail to bring tears to her eyes—they shone like diamonds in the studio lights. Etta James joined in from San Francisco, then children's choirs were added and finally the combined audiences sang along on a specially composed peace song entitled "The Blue-Green Hills of the Earth." A catchy tune by Paul Winter, it went over fine.

At a little champagne reception afterwards, after congratulating

222

Building a Space-Bridge: a Soviet Contribution

Dr. Chazov and picking up a few compliments regarding Andreas Papandreou for my Greek readers, I had a chance to talk with one of the Beyond War leaders, Donald R. Wurtz, who was standing nearby, head and shoulders above the crowd, quietly pouring himself some black coffee. He explained Beyond War strategy: ten states in the West, the Sunbelt and New England, including California, Oregon, Washington, Arizona, Colorado, Georgia, Massachusetts and one Mid-Western state, Iowa, were selected for special attention in the first year, on the basis of *Megatrends*. After establishing a solid base in these states, Beyond War would be ready to spread out nationwide. The tactical aspects of the operation are highly reminiscent of corporate or even military PR campaigns. The approach is educational—large presentations on the nuclear issue are coupled with "Interest Evenings"; "Orientation Packages" are put together; a three-evening course on "How To Deal with the Intellectual Issues of the Beyond War Movement" is offered, all aimed at a broad section of middle class professionals, scientists, administrators, businessmen.

The result is a powerful organization of educated, talented and dedicated men, coordinated by a full-time staff of eighty from its national office in Palo Alto, of whom only two people are paid salaries. The rest are either on leave of absence through some kind of sabbatical arrangement with their firms, which is becoming a general practice, or are successful people who have chosen to retire early. Forty of the eighty full-time workers in the national headquarters belong to this latter category.

"Our biggest problem," said Don Wurtz, "is training people fast enough—training them to lead." I asked him to what extent he sees his organization as a political lobby. "No," he said. "Lobbies, including the Peace movement, have gone after individual items. They haven't changed a thing. We believe that we must hit at the base. This doesn't mean, of course, that we are not willing to cooperate with other organizations."

It is definitely a new type of activism, with probably far-reaching consequences. Don Wurtz's own story is a good case in point: Don was a partner in Arthur Anderson and Co., the international accounting firm. About three years ago he was invited to a talk by Paul Warnke,

Building a Space-Bridge: a Soviet Contribution

at a lunch for forty people hosted by concerned Republican businessmen in San Francisco. After the talk they were shown the film "The Last Epidemic." At this point, said Don, he realized he had to do something. He got together with a few others and founded Beyond War. Last July he retired early. His firm has a policy of making a substantial severance payment to partners who leave to enter public service. From then on he began to give all his time to the movement.

"We've got all kinds of professionals, including top-notch media people—and with their expertise we have brought the words Beyond War, according to our calculations, before seventeen million people in the last two years," said Don. "This award is our first major international action. We have also set up a U.S.-U.S.S.R. task force to answer the question: What's possible?"

Fascinating talk, particularly when we consider that it comes from the heart of what has been traditionally ultra-conservative territory. We mentioned the importance of the new technological revolution in communications. If a revolutionary change in political attitudes of such an influential stratum of the American middle class can be considered to be the other side of that coin, then we are really in business. The world will have something other than continuous crisis to look forward to.

I ate another caviar sandwich, washed it down with a glass of champagne, and skipped out of Ostankino into the roadside snowdrifts in a much better mood than the early hour warranted. A small yellow bus, moonlighting as a taxi, drew up and we were soon swallowed up by the Moscow morning rush hour.

Later, my guess that citizen "telediplomacy" will become a familiar feature of the second half of the 1980s was confirmed in talks with Kim Spencer, producer of the Beyond War space-bridge; Sheryl Mendosa, aide to Congressman Brown, of California, who takes a special interest in space-bridges; David Howard, editor of *Evolutionary Blues*, who is also getting interested in U.S.-Soviet communication projects; and finally Joel Schatz and Joseph Goldin, both deeply involved in the "Global Town Meeting" conference calls.

Space-bridges will certainly proliferate. As for the "Global Town Meetings," the plan is to make them a regular monthly 90-minute radio (and possibly TV) event, aimed at a world-wide audience. The latter aspect is a truly positive contribution, since the whole world is an interested party to the outcome of the U.S.-Soviet confrontation—a confrontation which the overwhelming majority of mankind would like to see taking the form of a peaceful dialogue.

Peace Be Within Thy Walls

Are we humans or wild beasts? We should ask ourselves this question more often. Peace be within thy walls, man, where there is always a war on between conscience and cowardice, kindness and ignorance. Peace be within thy walls, where there is still a lot of injustice, for it is not always that good triumphs over evil, and the human over the wolfish. We know this is a see-sawing battle in real life. That's why we in the theater want good to win in our shows. Not just on the stage. We want it to win in the hall, among the audience, in your hearts. This is why we show many things that are evil for our common home.

Now that a "mirror for humanity" has been invented, we can, right from the stage of our theater in Moscow's Olympic Village, communicate with audiences in New York, San Francisco, or any other city. The entire arsenal of the satiric shop will have to be mustered for this unprecedented battle against the forces of evil threatening our common home. We shall expose evil, and we shall mock it, you and I. A mocked evil loses its fangs. A mocked evil is a victory of good. May this good fill our hearts and seethe in righteous anger at all that is not worthy of a human being. May it challenge whatever spoils life in our common home. We believe in you, man, and we shall stand up for you! Peace be within thy walls.

—Arkady Raikin

One of the most daring and popular performers on the Soviet stage, Arkady Raikin, 74, is a comedian. A Hero of Socialist Labor (the highest civilian distinction) and winner of the Lenin Prize, he founded the Theater of Miniatures, which he has directed for 45 years. Among his theater's recent hits is "May Your Home Be At Peace, Man."

With a Ph.D. in the history of cinematography, Alexander Lipkov, 45, is an art critic. Senior Research Associate at the Moscow Institute for Advanced Study of the Arts, he is the author of more than 300 articles and several books pulished in the U.S.S.R. and elsewhere.

A Planetary Attraction

Alexander Lipkov

THE PROCESS OF ACQUIRING NEW KNOWLEDGE NORMALLY begins when one becomes intrigued by a mystery to be unravelled or when one is faced with the challenge of crossing a frontier into the unknown.

We live in a world of boundaries of all kinds. There are political, legal, moral and class borders and demarcations set by man's physical potential and by the limits of his psyche. But no member of civilized society, nor indeed mankind as a whole, can exist without being sustained by an abiding faith in his ability to push these boundaries outwards, often at the price of a supreme physical or mental effort.

In this sense the very idea of "space-bridges" to help people of different countries to communicate directly and feel themselves more keenly as part of one global human family seems to have a good future. It is a bold new project in intercultural communication which is what we all need now that the situation in the world is so dangerously complicated.

Any of the communication media already available or just emerging may sooner or later give rise to a new art form. Oversize videoscreens are as large as, if not larger than, the biggest of the movie screens which until fairly recently were only used at drive-ins. Such videoscreens, situated thousands of miles apart, can bring together, in a single "happening," audiences of hundreds of thousands across the world. This capacity would have been the envy of the magicians of classic fairy tales with their magic mirrors. And yet for all its innovative features the new-born mass entertainment-cum-news medium represented by the "mirror for humanity" rests on the solid foundation of what has gone before it.

Back in 1923 the magazine *Lef* in Soviet Russia carried an article by Sergei Eisenstein, a young theater director who would leap into fame two years later as the creator of a film classic, *The Battleship Potemkin*. The article introduced a new term for the film director's vocabulary, "attraction." Later, explaining his reason for introducing the new term, Eisenstein wrote, "We had to find a unit for measuring the impact made on audiences by different art forms. Science had its 'ions,' 'electrons' and 'neutrons,' so what was wrong with 'attractions' for the world of art?" "Attraction" as a unit of expressiveness is an integral element of a work of art designed to produce an intense effect on the senses whether it should take the form of laughter or terror, admiration or anger. Originally trained as an engineer, Eisenstein seemed to have fallen in with the general enthusiasm for what was known at the time as *technicism*, a trend which was to influence his subsequent career as film director. Eisenstein later incorporated attractions of enormous impact in his films. Examples included the close-up of ugly meat worms crawling in the rotten beef intended for the crew of *The Battleship Potemkin*, the stroke of a Cossack's whip slicing in two a woman's eye, or that baby carriage rolling down Odessa's famous staircase which seemed to epitomize police brutality wreaked on a scattering crowd of defenseless, terrified people.

The term "attraction" traces its genealogy back to the early days of the circus. In 1835 Phineas Barnum, the great American showman and circus impressario, purchased Joice Heth, the reputed colored nurse of George Washington who allegedly lived to a ripe old age of 161. Barnum publicized her widely and took in $1,500 a week exhibiting her in a highly successful hoax. Thus it was that Barnum, with the slave woman as his central attraction, introduced the term "attraction" into the language of the circus.

Almost a hundred years later Sergei Eisenstein borrowed the term, lending to it a different and more significant connotation. For all the difference between the two interpretations of the term given by a great circus showman and a great film director, the two shared the same

227

psychological mechanism for affecting the audience.

Curiously enough, the majority of those who, down the centuries, have used "attraction" in different areas of human endeavor to influence people for various ends did not even realize that they were actually using the technique.

This was the case in science, in art, in religion, in politics and in the military field. In each of these areas people with imagination found ample scope for the application of attraction-type mechanisms.

We all remember Thor Heyerdahl's epic crossing of the Pacific on the *Kon-Tiki*, a primitive balsawood raft, to prove his theory of the migration of people across the Pacific in ancient times. Heyerdahl needed to attract the attention of the world in part to challenge the long-established theories prevailing in the field at the time and to introduce his theory into academic currency.

Examples of ingenious "attractions" are to be found in the realm of art as well. Thus Fyodor Tolstoy, a Russian water colorist of the nineteenth century, once painted a fly with such uncanny realism that anyone looking at it instinctively tried to flick it off to enjoy the painting without its vexing presence. In music we have Haydn's Symphony No. 6 in which the placid flow of melody at first lulls the listener into a pleasant drowsy reverie until he is shocked out of it by a crashing hammer crack of kettle-drums.

The church has extensively used its own particular kind of "attractions" in the form of "miracles." Even the magic lantern, that precursor of the cinema, was invented by a Jesuit monk, Rudolph Kirchner, to induce the local congregation to entrust their souls to God with greater fervor by working on their imagination through the "miraculous" effects of the magic lantern.

Attractions have been an invariable concomitant of politics, of course. Our twentieth century has seen two notable examples, one sinister, the Reichstag fire engineered by the Nazis, and one hilarious, staged in China and starring Chairman Mao leading a collective swim down the Yangtze River. In more distant times public executions designed to put fear of God into the hearts of the public before the chastising long arm of the law and the power of the sovereign were essentially popular political "attractions" that pulled huge crowds.

Building a Space-Bridge: a Soviet Contribution

In the department of military "attractions," our generation has had the misfortune to witness one that was quite unprecedented in human history: the atom bombing of Hiroshima. It was not so much the destruction of that ill-starred Japanese city that the U.S. command was after (any other city of comparable size within the A-bomb's effective radius could have become the victim) as psychological impact on the world.

The morality of using attraction-type techniques clearly poses a problem in every area of human endeavor. Witness the tenacious grip on "attractions" secured by mass culture which has been exploiting violence, crudity, sex and all manner of psychic deviations, in short everything that is abnormal, freaky and bizarre. Most attractions cannot be blamed for the way they are used, or rather abused, by the mass media. There are, however, attractions with a built-in potential for abuse. Indeed, any attraction tends to exploit critical, threshold or borderline states and qualities. All attractions advertized as representing the "ultimate" in their particular fields, the most beautiful and the ugliest, the biggest and the smallest, the loftiest and the meanest, the sublime and the ridiculous, put our ideas of the possible and the impossible, the allowed and the forbidden, to the test. In the realm of art, "attractions" often lie dangerously close to the aesthetic outer limit, sometimes crossing it and compelling a reappraisal of erstwhile canons and standards.

As I see it the "attraction" potential of "space-bridge" communication springs from its adding an important new dimension to our traditional ideas of what constitutes borderlines and frontiers. Space-bridges may eventually overturn conventional ideas of the possible and the impossible in the family of man, and thus make direct contact between great masses of people divided by the barriers of vast distances, political systems and different ideologies possible. Without abolishing the barriers separating their countries, space-bridge linkups will help people to forget about them for a while. Like the carnivals of the Middle Ages, space-bridges may relieve most of us in our fast-moving world of the often crushing burden of daily preoccupations and responsibilities, with their inevitable rules, regimentation and red tape, and usher their participants into the happy new world of untrammelled freedom, at least for a time.

I believe that the script writers of future "space-bridge" hook-ups would do well to draw on the experience of those open-air popular entertainments that were staged in Soviet Russia in the immediate post-revolutionary years. Such spectacular productions as "The Over-throw of the Autocracy," "Hymn to Emancipated Labor," and "Towards a World-Wide Commune" involved tens of thousands of people and presented reenactments of the storming of the Bastille and the Winter Palace, and the fierce battles of the rebellious slaves led by Spartacus against the legions of Rome. In reliving the history of world revolutions the participants of those pageants felt themselves to be the makers of history.

To be sure, the directors and cast of those spectacular productions were in many ways naive people who, fired by revolutionary enthusiasm, expected the imminent dawn of the golden age of a just society on earth. The historical experience of the generations since then has often been rather bitter and disappointing. Even so it has failed to extinguish the flame of ordinary people's utopian dream of a planetary human com-munity based on freedom, equality, the brotherhood of man, and hap-piness. It is to be hoped that "space-bridges" will contribute to the realization of this age-old dream. On the other hand, they may well reveal the essential inadequacy of the intercultural communication technology available to us today, and equally the sadly low level of human consciousness. Even if this dream does not become a reality within the lifetime of the present generation, in any event "space-bridge" link-ups will certainly contribute to progress towards this goal.

When Joseph Goldin, the dynamic Moscow intellectual who has been at the center of the "space-bridge" project in Moscow since its inception, outlined his "mirror for humanity" during an international telephone conference call on August 6, 1984, among those who responded to it was a listener in Menlo Park, California. He phoned into the radio studio in Washington, D.C. which anchored the space-bridge in the U.S. and asked what one should do to induce the mass media to shift the focus onto positive developments in their report-ing instead of keeping the public on a diet of crime, violence and natural disasters.

230

Building a Space-Bridge: a Soviet Contribution

Paraphrasing this question we might say that since the news media which churn out a daily torrent of bad news are unthinkable without "attractions" and sensationalism, the task facing us today is to try to get the mass media to move away from exploiting attractions that scare people and make them fear the future, and towards attractions that will help them look to the future with optimism and hope.

Transforming
Our Consciousness

4

Say that space-bridges become common, citizen diplomacy expands, and widespread student exchanges occur between the U.S. and the Soviet Union: what will we talk about? What values will guide us? Simply to put people in front of one another, whether electronically or in the flesh, is only the first step. Out of what vision will we converse?

Photograph by Dave Bohn

If we remain within the usual way of thinking, the ability to exchange messages more easily may only confirm our distress with one another and our bleak feelings about the future. As it is, sixty-eight percent of Americans agree that "if we and the Soviets keep building more and more missiles instead of negotiating to get rid of them, it's only a matter of time before they are used."* However, many of us sense that if we learned to meet on a different level than we generally have, something positive could occur. If we reach that level, would we be talking in order to try to prevent war, or what?

In college, and for some years after, I thought mostly in terms of preventing war rather than of creating peace. I was excited about many ideas for lessening the risk of war. For example, around 1960 I met a psychologist named Charles Osgood who had an approach to reducing international tensions. One side would take a peaceful initiative on its own, announce it as part of a major policy shift, invite the other side to reciprocate and, as tension began decreasing, would repeat the cycle with a larger step. Dr. Osgood described this process as "graduated reciprocation in tension-reduction," which he called GRIT for short and which is fully described in *Securing Our Planet*, a companion to this book. Ideas such as this can be misapplied or even abused for propaganda value, but I continue to believe they offer much potential.

I gradually realized, however, that even the most ingenious methods can take us only as far as we are willing to go. For example, arms control has been intended to reduce the enormous danger inherent in the deployment, by two antagonistic powers, of nuclear weapons and various "delivery vehicles." Arms control has undoubtedly been successful in such areas as limiting environmental contamination by nuclear tests, forbidding weapons that both sides had decided not to deploy anyway, and limiting the total number of delivery vehicles. However, the number of warheads that could easily be delivered any afternoon, in perfect compliance with the SALT treaties, is catastrophic.

*The Public Agenda Foundation in collaboration with The Center for Foreign Policy Development at Brown University, *Voter Options on Nuclear Arms Policy*, 1984, page 40.

So, what to do? Even if we became less irrational in the ways we threaten one another, would this be peace?

Avoiding the worst forms of "crisis instability" is certainly crucial, but making peace springs from a consciousness different than the one evidenced in arms control. Ultimately it springs from a personal experience of compassion for the Self and for the Other.

Developing and exercising this compassion is the great adventure of our time. As compassion moves outward to learn how to live with (and to adopt parts of) what is strange and foreign to us, so it moves inward to come to terms with the "shadow" parts of ourselves. As a result of this outer and inner work, we are more and more capable of recognizing the higher self that all people potentially have in common, of transforming ourselves in the image of this higher self, and thus of going beyond the boundaries that ordinarily divide people from one another.

As a program of development, this may sound, to some, like hopeless romanticism or even total nonsense. To those who are drawn to the spiritual traditions of humankind, however, it may instead remind them of what Aldous Huxley called the "perennial philosophy."

Somebody may be able to propose a path to outer peace that does not involve a development of the inner spirit. I have been unable to find one. Whenever I have tried to "fight war," I have eventually felt that I was becoming part of the problem. Whenever I have imagined profound rearrangements within the tradition of "realism," I have been left wondering what could possibly motivate the adoption of them. It seems to me, as to a growing number of others, that a change in consciousness must precede any conclusive reordering of relations in the outer world.

I once heard a very funny discussion in a restaurant along the California coast. The people at the next table were imagining a ritual that would have the effect, if enough people took part, of transforming all the world's uranium and plutonium into harmless lead. They called it "reverse alchemy." During a routine check of aging warheads, an inspector would discover the absence of radiation and realize that the missile was topped by what amounted to an over-sized fishing sinker. (The larger missiles would have "multiple independently targeted" fishing sinkers.) Imagine the panic this could create on both sides, as each suspected sabotage by the other.

In order to prevent panic, said the folks at the next table, they would quickly announce to an astonished and grateful world that all nuclear bombs on earth had been transformed out of existence, and that the former nuclear powers might as well celebrate. When I asked them what it would take, in their view, for reverse alchemy to occur, they talked about "changing the thought-forms."

Today, in most quarters, alchemy is remembered only as an expression of ineffectual greed for precious metal and as the ludicrous precursor of modern chemistry. It was Carl Jung who, as much as anyone, recovered alchemy's inner essence. On the surface, it's true, alchemy claimed to change base metals into gold. Its hidden meaning, however, was that the human spirit could, through certain techniques of inner work, be transformed to a higher stage of evolution. In this view, the outer paraphernalia of alchemy was only a symbol—misleading to a materialist—of these profound inner practices.

In a similar spirit, the people whom I overheard in the restaurant clearly knew that their ritual would not physically transform the nuclear material in the world's 50,000 warheads. Playfully, wistfully, they were searching for a method to change the consciousness of the societies that build warheads and threaten mayhem with them. In a more circumspect way, the contributors to this section are engaged in a similar search.

It's often observed, especially by ecologists, that problem A can't be solved in isolation from problem B; that everything's related. Here I want to stress a different point—that a problem often can't be solved at all on the level on which it's presented. We must approach it on another level. For example, if an arms race becomes grotesquely dangerous, it's natural to respond by trying to "control arms." If the arms race nonetheless continues, for a quarter century, maybe it's time to shift to a different level and deal, say, with the hostility that's expressed by deploying the weapons.

Let me illustrate how crazy things can get if we fail to shift levels. Years ago in Berkeley I was having lunch with a very bright man who had written superbly about deterrence and who had friends in the Pentagon. With my best poker face, I asked whether he'd heard about the Soviet plot to manufacture mechanical cows covered with real hide, fitted with soulful glass eyes, and with space for thermonuclear bombs in their bellies. After smuggling the bombs into the U.S., Soviet agents would don their Stetsons, get in their pick-up trucks, and deliver these deadly critters to specified pastures in the mid-West. Guided by radio, the cattle would munch their way to the perimeter fences of the various missile silos. Once they were all in place, a signal would be given . . . .

I intended this as a light-hearted burlesque of the arms race, but before my colleague caught on, he told me, quite seriously, that he had the phone number of a Pentagon colonel who should hear about this at once. I should call him collect. I declined, however, on the ground that, after the usual cost overruns, the U.S. would soon have thermonuclear polar bears, pale as Moby Dick, swimming toward the northern coast of the Soviet Union. Since the relatively happy era of this lunch, of course, we have developed the cruise missile, which renders my fantasy quite superfluous.

A wholly different kind of thinking is necessary. If transformation were a game, we could speak of a few simple rules: (1) shift to a new level, or put the problem in a new context, (2) look inside to discover what is sustaining the outer action, (3) instead of trying only to resist these negative impulses, allow positive alternatives to emerge that can replace the merely defensive response, and (4) develop an exercise called "creating common ground."

A friend recently told me about a workshop called the "enlightenment intensive." The group pairs off and one partner asks the other, "Who are you?" After listening in a neutral way to the reply, without commenting, he or she then inquires again, "Who are you?" And this continues through an entire day, with periodic changes of partners. Obviously the respondent soon runs through the ordinary stories we tell about who we are. In the next layer, maybe, responses are anxious, confused, angry, sad, or guilt-ridden; but eventually, I am told, participants discover that the truth is better, simpler, and more profound than they had dared to hope.

I often think of this exercise when I read, in the *New York Times*, about the dreary course of some inconclusive negotiation in Geneva. Regardless of the personal qualities of the diplomats, these rituals are often programmed to fail, because they reflect the same style of official thought that got us into the trouble from which they're meant to extricate us.

As all of this futile summitry is being played out, however, currents of transformation are appearing in many places, among ordinary citizens. There's a new consciousness about peace, a new set of thought-forms or, if you prefer, a new paradigm. In this section, some people who are living this transformation describe how it feels, and show how others can share in it.

—Craig Comstock

One evening a few of us from Ark were dining with a well-known actress who had supported anti-war and other progressive causes. When we mentioned somebody's proposal to make a movie on peace, she burst out, "How boring—there's no tension in peace—drama's built on conflict." Clearly, to judge from her autobiographical writings, this actress has enjoyed the adventures of a seeker. We were reminded of Bob Fuller, who proposes "a better game than war"—for him it's the challenge of completing the Self by encounter with the Other. In a similar spirit, Michael Nagler questions the common view of peace as the absence of war, which he calls the negative definition and which, according to him, leads to all manner of conceptual mischief. A professor at the University of California in Berkeley and a follower of Gandhi's spirit of "satyagraha" or truth-power, Nagler seeks a positive definition of peace.

A Positive Vision in a Cynical Age

Michael Nagler

A BASIC DISPARITY IN MODERN civilization came into stark relief two summers ago when Mother Teresa of Calcutta rushed into the rubble of West Beirut to rescue orphaned children. Mother Teresa had recently received the Nobel Peace Prize. So had Israeli Prime Minister Begin, whose operation had reduced the city to rubble and orphaned those children.

What is peace? Two contradictory definitions seem to have coexisted since antiquity without causing confusion, until recent times. Modern peace science—a fledgling discipline— knows them as *negative* peace, adequately defined as the absence of war, and *positive* peace.

Positive peace has yet to be adequately defined at all.

Futurist Willis Harman reminds us that "we human beings have an awesome ability to deceive ourselves," and the question of peace, with its emotional urgency and denotational vagueness, is where this capacity is most devastatingly exercised.

A May 25, 1984 letter to the highly conservative *Washington Times* complains that Rudolph Hess, "prisoner of peace," is being deprived of his freedom "all because he tried to stop a large scale war." The writer might be dismissed as a crank, but in fact his negative definition of peace is unquestioned throughout society. The corrugated iron barricades between Protestant and Catholic neighborhoods of Belfast are called "peace lines." They are now being rebuilt permanently in brick. The artillery barrage of Beirut was part of an operation called "Peace for Galilee." And of course, one of the most dangerous first-strike nuclear weapons has been dubbed "Peacemaker."

My aim is not to stigmatize adherents of the negative definition who are found in many lands and at all levels of officialdom. Rather, it is in the spirit of Freeman Dyson's attempt to bring the "two worlds" of pro-defense and anti-nuclear thinking into contact—worlds sundered largely by their unexamined adherence to negative and positive peace ideals. I would show that the thinking of each group is perfectly logical, given its assumption about the nature of peace, and that a clearer articulation of the positive side could help bring about an open and fruitful debate.

Our greatest obligation to our children is to prepare them to understand and to deal effectively with the world in which they will live and not with the world we have known or the world we would prefer to have.

—Grayson Kirk

*One of the most common
uses of the word "peace"
is to denote the absence
of war. But if this is the
meaning of peace, then
most of the world is at
peace most of the time.
This does not seem to be
an adequate definition.
Would a violently enforced
occupation of one country
by another be described
as a state of peace? Is a
well-ordered but violently
oppressive government
"at peace"? Is New York
City, with its high
murder, rape, and robbery
rates at peace because it
is not at war with
Chicago? Perhaps, then,
peace is the absence of
violence. But can we say
that there is peace in a
country where the reins
of power are held so tightly
and tyrannically by the
government that protest is
impossible? Do we want
to say that there is peace
in countries where*

At present, all operational terms in the debate mean opposite things, depending on whether one's overriding definition of peace is negative or positive: Is "security" dominating one's enemies, or learning to live so that one does not have enemies? Is "strength" the power to hurt others, or to make appropriate sacrifices and undertake necessary corrections in one's own course?

It is not possible—fortunately—to reduce the emotional charge carried by the concept of peace. But though we cannot, and should not, make the term less emotional, we should certainly be able to make it less confusing.

About twelve years ago Heinrich Schneider, co-director of the Vienna Institute for Peace Research, summarized much of what recent peace research has gained by stating that if we must have a definition by negatives, the opposite of peace is not war, but violence. "Non-war" would be achieved in the Middle East if the enemies of Israel were driven out, in the East-West confrontation if the Soviets would accept perpetual inferiority; in Central America if the peasant population were completely subdued and terrorized. But none of these conditions would be peace, because all of them contain violence of body, mind and spirit.

"Violence" itself, however, requires definition. The well-known Norwegian peace research scholar, Johann Galtung, has defined violence as, simply, that which inhibits the fulfillment of a human being.

Perhaps this only brings us to a third unknown: what is a human being? How is he or she to be fulfilled? But in fact we gain much clarity by taking on these two logical questions, because they rescue the ancient problem of war and peace from the technosphere and reground the contemporary debate in human realities. Beneath the technological face of our civilization and its dilemmas lie unresolved human problems which have changed only in appearance over many thousands of years. This is particularly poignant in the area of arms control and the larger task of building a stable peace system, for it is here that attempts at technical and scientific solutions have most dishearteningly eluded us.

For the technologically minded, it may be self-evident that the job of science is, as Edward Teller says, to determine how the forces of nature can "serve the human will." But more than a thousand years ago St. Augustine, in his *Confessions*, exposed the fallacy of this argument: "My will was captured by the Enemy." By "Enemy" Augustine meant the dark, chaotic forces of hatred, fear and greed that then as now lurk beneath the surface of human consciousness. Teller is thus cavalierly declaring it the job of science to place the catastrophic powers of nature at the disposal of these psychic forces. The relationship between a negative definition of peace and a non-human sense of how to achieve peace are not coincidental, nor is the policy result.

Johann Galtung argues that there is something essential about the value of *each* human life which cannot be violated if we are to speak of peace. Thus the challenge is to

governments and ruling elites allow people to suffer in poverty and die of starvation? Is acquiring such an aggregation of force so that no country is tempted to breach the peace, real peace? Taking this line of thought further, does even the threat of violence shatter peace? For thirty-five years the U.S. and U.S.S.R. have had no major violent confrontations. Yet they have thousands of nuclear weapons pointed at each other. Many citizens of both countries have been profoundly affected by the threat of nuclear war. Is this peace? What impact does the threat of destruction have on the quality of our lives?

—Educators for Social Responsibility

241

No matter how valiantly we are fighting against war, we may by this very act push the world closer to the brink. Fighting against anything is war, no matter how noble the cause. But even the absence of war is not peace. We know this by our own day-to-day lives. Lack of open conflict with a person does not mean we are filled with an inner peace. Only a compassionate heart connects us to the reality that contains new visions—those of true peace. Every time we experience a single day of inner stillness and joy, we are empowered to expand it into a second and a third day. A space opens in our hearts, and when two hearts recognize and acknowledge each other, a connection happens. It happens again and again as other hearts are joined in this stillness. Dances of inner joy begin to merge into one harmonious movement upon the stage of the earth.

the entire notion of sacrificing the few for the many, as well as that of terrorizing one group for the advantage of another—cornerstones of every peace edifice civilization has built down the centuries. In this spirit Gandhi himself, in a rare comment on international peace, defined it as that state in which every person is fully realized.

Peace in its own right; peace, not the absence of something else; peace, a system in which no one need be sacrificed—the concept may strike us as rather visionary. But it should be. "Where there is no vision," runs the rediscovered text of Proverbs 29:18, "the people perish." Without the vision of a remote condition like peace how can we know which steps would lead us there?

I accept Gandhi's definition, and one of St. Augustine in *The City of God*—"Peace is the ordered tranquility of all parts of a system." But I have also been experimenting with another: that state in which all parties spontaneously desire one another's welfare. Any truly positive definition tells us immediately not only that the "Peacemaker missile" cannot bring positive peace—if it is not, indeed, some kind of grotesque joke—but that the deterrent concept itself cannot be equated with building peace.

Until we have such a positive definition, "arms control" is doomed to remain, as experienced negotiators have learned, a euphemism for creating conditions in which the numbers of arms in fact increase and are more swiftly deployed. Conversely, the potential of many good ideas, doomed to remain muffled in the present confusion, could suddenly emerge in a positive peace perspective. Nonviolent "social defense" comes immediately to mind, or interventionary "peace brigades," like those having unheralded successes against severe violence right now in Guatemala, Costa Rica and Nicaragua.

These methods of conflict resolution are completely victimless. They do not mortgage society to the services, and ultimately the values, of a military cadre. They could be safely instituted as long- and short-term measures. Because they call upon values and social skills out of which a distant order of stable peace could grow, even where there are no more overt conflicts to resolve, they are not desperate holding measures but seeds of the future. Because they are entirely non-threatening to the true well-being—as opposed to the malevolent purposes—of any adversary, they can be classified, without irony, as peace measures.

Before the scientific community today is the idea of an "oath of Pythagoras," like the Hippocratic oath of physicians, under which its members could pledge to refrain from working on clearly destructive projects. Initiated fifteen years ago by a Berkeley-Stanford group, it has recently been embraced by International Student Pugwash and has gained moral support in the Pope's remarkable address to the Pontifical Academy of Sciences in November 1983.

From a positive peace perspective this is an excellent but incomplete idea. Scientists and engineers should, of course, have the op-

The dance is one of tremendous joy and power. Steadily this foundation of peace begins to charge the atmosphere itself and becomes a stabilized reality for everyone who desires it.

—LaUna Huffines

243

Unfortunately, neither our society nor our instruction dramatizes or acclaims the peaceful dimensions of our everyday activities. For the most part—be it in the stories on the evening news, the accounts in our history books, the competition in the marketplace and the sports arena, or the cops and robbers TV shows—our attention is focused on violence, confrontation, competing interests, and winners and losers. In fact, we experience peace on many levels and in many areas of our lives. These experiences are usually active, positive, and among the most meaningful in our lives. For instance, when we

tion of non-participation in the design, testing or development of destructive weapons, without facing sanctions or being professionally disadvantaged. But they should also pledge to become engaged in constructive works badly needed for human survival in many parts of the world. This would replace whatever loss might accrue to national defense from such abstention, since severe underdevelopment problems are not only an active cause of conflict, but such problems are inherently forms of violence. Pope Paul VI once said that "development is the new name for peace." (I would say, "appropriate development.")

Most importantly for the future of science and society, scientists and engineers should pledge part of their time to learning and teaching the structure of stable peace. In the eloquent words of Carl Von Weizsäcker, the real job of science "does not lie in abandoning research or suppressing scientific information but in transforming the political order of the world, which in its present form makes the misuse of scientific knowledge almost inevitable."

Like the drawings used in perception tests, where figure and ground keep switching back and forth as the perceiver stares at them, how we look at the whole world can be turned inside out between two ways of viewing. In the old way, history always unfolds as "between two wars." In the new, as Gandhi said, peace is the even process of history and wars are its breakdowns. In the old way, as Richard Barnet put it, "nuclear war is unthinkable, but tens of thousands of people are paid to think about it every day." In the new way, at least as many people will be employed to work out the structure of peace, in at least as enthusiastic detail.

In a sense, either view is perfectly valid. But in a tragic and immediate sense, they are terribly unequal. The idealistic response and emotional charge released by the word "peace" will always be strong and this is as it should be. "Peace" awakens one of the deepest aspirations of the human spirit. Again to cite St. Augustine, "Man by the very laws of his nature seems, so to speak, forced into fellowship and, as far as in him lies, into peace with every man." In our own world, in Gallup polls taken from 1947 on, most Americans have consistently listed peace—whatever they understood by it—as the issue most important to them.

Yet most human energy today is mobilized by negative peace—often, as with "Peace for Galilee," a concept hardly distinguishable from war. That energy belongs by right of idealism to the positive peace vision and program. It should be repossessed by those of us who hold this vision, for the benefit of mankind.

This will require the moral courage to cling to a positive vision of peace, unsentimentally, in a cynical age. It will also require that we define clearly and work out in reasonable detail the emotional, political, economic and social structure of such a peace.

recall personal moments of peace we remember a sublime moment with nature, an experience of a deep sense of meaning and inner harmony, a time of inspiration, profound joy, or even exhiliration. On an interpersonal level, we recount moments when fear and destructive conflict are absent in our relationships with family and friends. We recall times of abundance and joy, shared struggle and commitment. We remember the pleasures of giving and receiving, of creating and celebrating together.

—Educators for Social Responsibility

Author of *The Tao of Physics,* *The Turning Point,* and a book on the "Greens" in West Germany, Fritjof Capra teaches that what seem like problems to be solved are actually limitations built deeply into a certain way of regarding and dealing with the world. What's needed is a "paradigm shift" from a mechanistic view to a systems view. Director of the Elmwood Institute in Berkeley, Capra shows in this chapter how the shift applies to peace in much the same way it applies to health.

As in Health, So in Peace

Fritjof Capra

THE THREAT OF NUCLEAR WAR IS THE most dramatic symptom of a multifaceted, global crisis that touches every aspect of our lives: our health and livelihood, the quality of our environment and our social relationships, our economy, technology, our politics— our very survival on this planet. Conventional politicians no longer know where to turn to minimize the damage. They argue about priorities and about the relative merits of short-term technological and economic "fixes" without realizing that the major problems of our time are simply different facets of a single systematic crisis. They are closely interconnected and interdependent and cannot be understood through the fragmented approaches pursued by our academic disciplines and government agencies. Rather than solving any of the difficulties, such approaches merely shift them around in the complex web of social and ecological relations. A resolution can be found only if the structure of the web itself is changed, and this will involve profound transformations of our social and political institutions, values, and ideas.

The first step in overcoming the crisis, in my view, is to recognize that the required profound cultural transformation is, in fact, already beginning to take place. This transformation has many aspects. At its core is a dramatic shift of world views; a shift from a mechanistic to a holistic and ecological vision of reality. The paradigm that is now beginning to recede has dominated our culture for several hundred years, during which it has significantly influenced the rest of the world. This world view consists of a number of ideas and values, among them the belief that the universe is a mechanical system composed of elementary material building blocks, the view of the human body as a machine, the view of life in a society as a competitive struggle for existence, the belief in unlimited material progress to be achieved through economic and technological growth, and the belief that a society in which the female is everywhere subsumed under the male is one that follows a basic law of nature. During recent decades all of these assumptions have been found severely limited and in need of radical revision.

The mechanistic world view was formulated most succinctly in seventeenth-century science by Galileo, Descartes, Newton, Bacon, and several others. During the subsequent three hundred years it was extremely successful and dominated all scientific thought. Today, however, its limitations have become clearly visible, and scientists and nonscientists alike

The earth does not belong to man; man belongs to the earth. This we know. All things are connected like the blood which unites one family. All things are connected. Whatever befalls the earth befalls the sons of the earth. Man did not weave the web of life; he is merely a strand in it. Whatever he does to the web, he does to himself.

—Chief Seattle,
a Native American

There will one day spring from the brain of science a machine or force so fearful in its potentialities, so absolutely terrifying that even man, the fighter, who will dare torture and death in order to inflict torture and death, will be appalled, and so abandon war forever. What man's mind can create, man's character can control.

—Thomas Alva Edison

247

will have to change their underlying philosophies in profound ways in order to participate in the current cultural transformation.

Mechanistic Views of Health and Peace

I would like to illustrate the limitations of Cartesian-Newtonian thinking with two examples—health and peace—examples that will turn out to show some striking parallels. The mechanistic view of health still dominates our medical institutions and the mechanistic view of peace dominates the thinking of our politicians and the military. In both cases we have to realize, of course, that the mechanistic view and the "engineering approach," as I shall call it, are of great value. But they are limited and must be integrated into a larger holistic framework.

Descartes compared the human organism to a clockwork. "I consider the human body as a machine," he wrote. "My thought compares a sick man and an ill-made clock with my idea of a healthy man and a well-made clock." Many characteristics of current medical theory and practice can be traced back to this Cartesian imagery. Health is often defined as the absence of disease, and disease is seen as a malfunctioning of biological mechanisms which are studied from the points of view of cellular and molecular biology. The doctor's role is to intervene, using medical technology, to correct the malfunctioning of a specific mechanism, different parts of the body being treated by different specialists.

As medical scientists define health as the absence of disease, so military strategists define

The trouble concerns the fact that the 'truths' of the modern scientific world view, though they can be demonstrated in mathematical formulas and proved technologically, will no longer lend themselves to normal expression in speech and thought. . . . We do not know whether this situation is final. But it could be that we, who are earth-bound creatures and have begun to act as though we were dwellers of the universe, will forever be unable to understand, that is to think and speak about, the things which nevertheless we are able to do. In this case, it would be as though our brain, which constitutes the physical,

peace as the absence of war, and the engineering approach to health has its counterpart in the engineering approach to peace. Politicians and military men tend to perceive all problems of defense as problems of technology. The idea that social and psychological considerations—let alone philosophy or poetry—could also be relevant is not entertained. Moreover, questions of security and defense are analyzed predominantly in Newtonian terms—"power blocks," "action and reaction," the "political vacuum," and so on.

In contemporary health care the human organism is generally disassociated from the natural and social environment in which it is embedded, and the large network of phenomena that influence health is reduced to its physiological and biochemical aspects. In very similar ways, the conventional approach to defense reduces the large network of phenomena that influence peace to its strategic and technological aspects. And even those aspects are further reduced as politicians and the military continue to talk about national security without recognizing the dangerous fallacy of this simplistic and fragmented notion. Most of our politicians still seem to think that we can increase our own security by making others feel insecure. Since the threats made with today's nuclear weapons threaten to extinguish life on the entire planet, the new thinking about peace must necessarily be global thinking. In the nuclear age, the entire concept of national security has become outdated; there can only be global security.

In conventional medical thinking, the

material condition of our thoughts, were unable to follow what we do, so that from now on we would indeed need artificial machines to do our thinking and speaking. If it should turn out to be true that knowledge (in the modern sense of know-how) and thought have parted company for good, then we would indeed become the helpless slaves, not so much of our machines as of our know-how, thoughtless creatures at the mercy of every gadget which is technologically possible, no matter how murderous it is.

—Hannah Arendt

*At present, we think
of national defense and
domestic development as
two separate activities.
National defense is
regarded as the building
of arms and armies, and
the formation of military
coalitions between nations
with mutual interests. In
truth, genuine national
defense is intertwined
with social and human
needs. The decentraliza-
tion of energy, food, and
industrial production not
only returns a measure
of control to people and
their communities, it also
makes the nation less vulnerable to disruption and
attack. The development
and use of renewable
resources—combined with
conservation—lowers
household energy budgets,
keeps more of the nation's
wealth from leaking away
to mineral-producing
nations, creates new
industries and jobs,
reduces pollution, and
eliminates most types of
environmental damage.
At the same time,
renewables decrease our
dependence on foreign
governments so that we
are not easily crippled
by supply cutoffs or*

therapy involves technological intervention. The self-organizing and self-healing potential of the patient is not taken into account. Similarly, conventional military thinking holds that conflicts are best resolved by technological intervention and does not take into account the self-organizing potential of people, communities, and nations—see Afghanistan, Grenada, Poland, Nicaragua, and many other examples.

The conceptual problem at the center of contemporary health care is the confusion between disease processes and disease origins. Instead of asking why an illness occurs and trying to remove the conditions that lead to it, medical researchers try to understand the mechanisms through which the disease operates, so that they can then interfere with them. Very often, their research is guided by the idea of a single mechanism that dominates all the others and can be corrected by technological intervention. Similarly, politicians tend to be blind to the origins of conflict and concentrate instead on the external processes; for example, on the visible acts of individual violence rather than the hidden structural and institutional violence.

Patriarchal Values

The mechanistic world view has been complemented by a value system that is much older than Cartesian-Newtonian science. The values, attitudes, and behavior patterns which dominate our culture and are embodied in our social institutions are typical traits of patriarchal culture. Like all patriarchal societies, our society tends to favor self-assertion over integration, analysis over synthesis, rational knowledge over intuitive wisdom, competition over cooperation, expansion over conservation.

None of these values and attitudes is intrinsically good or bad, but the imbalance that is characteristic of our society today is unhealthy and dangerous. The most severe consequence of this imbalance is the ever-increasing threat of nuclear war, brought about by an overemphasis on self-assertion, control and power, excessive competition, and a pathological obsession with "winning" in a situation where the whole concept of winning has lost its meaning, because there can be no winners in a nuclear war.

There is now a rich feminist literature on the roots of militarism and war in patriarchal values and patriarchal thinking. Patriarchy, these authors point out, operates within the context of dominance/submission. Thus parity of nuclear weapons is not enough for American generals; they want superiority. This "macho" competition in the arms race extends to the size of missiles. During one administration, military lobbyists persuaded politicians to spend more money on defense by showing them upright models of Soviet and American missiles, in which the Soviet missiles were larger, although it was known that the larger missiles were technically inferior. The phallic shape of these missiles makes the sexual connotation of this competition in missile size obvious. Patriarchy equates aggression and dominance with masculinity, and warfare is held to be the ultimate initiation into true manhood.

drawn into resource wars. Weaned from imported oil and minerals, we do not require a substantial military presence in far-off corners of the globe. The job of national security becomes much less complicated and expensive. In a society of this kind, conservation, solar technology, environmental protection, recycling, and small-scale food production become our key defense industries. The national landscape is sprinkled not with nuclear weapons systems, mammoth factories, and big, vulnerable power plants, but with low-technology energy systems, a multitude of local power plants using largely renewable fuels, and small facilities producing goods close to their ultimate markets.

—William Becker

What are our images of peace? The most common visual images in our culture are doves, or sunsets, or fields of flowers. Sometimes we are offered children playing in the breeze, boats lazily anchored in quiet

251

coves, or the soft sounds of caressing violins, lutes, and harps. The feelings these images elicit are the same—calm, quiet, serenity, bliss. Contrast this to images of war— noise, guns, blood, tears, action, drama, courage, heroics, romance, Dynamic Generals, Heroic Nurses, Shining Guns. The images of war are vivid, varied, and plentiful. They are exciting. Peace seems boring by contrast, especially if experienced for more than an hour or two. Barbara Stanford, in her book Peacemaking, *quotes a high school student, "Dead people are peaceful." Is it any surprise then that recent research by Educators for Social Responsibility indicates that many of our young people have clear conceptions of war, while their conceptions of peace are vague? Often they see peace as dull, passive, or as merely the absence of war.*

—Educators for Social Responsibility

To conclude my illustration of the parallels between concepts of health and concepts of peace within the old paradigm, I should mention that in both areas the mechanistic views are perpetrated not only by scientists, politicians, and generals, but also—and perhaps even more forcefully—by the pharmaceutical and military industries, which have invested heavily in the old paradigm. The scientific establishment and the corporate community match each other perfectly, since the outdated Cartesian world view underlies both the theoretical framework of the former and the technologies and economic motives of the latter. To change this situation is now absolutely vital for our well-being and survival, and change is possible if we are able, as a society, to shift to the new holistic and ecological models.

The systems view of living organisms seems to provide an ideal basis for a holistic approach to health, an approach that is profoundly ecological and thus in harmony with the Hippocratic tradition which lies at the roots of Western medicine. At the same time, the parallels between health and peace can be carried further: corresponding to the systems view of health there is also a systems view of peace.

At the core of the systems view of health lies the notion of dynamic balance. Health is an experience of well-being resulting from a dynamic balance that involves the physical and psychological aspects of the organism, as well as its interactions with its natural and social environment. The natural balance of living organisms includes, in particular, the balance between their self-assertive and integrative tendencies. To be healthy, an organism has to preserve its individual autonomy, but at the same time it has to be able to integrate itself harmoniously into larger systems. Imbalance manifests itself as stress, and excessive stress is harmful and will often lead to illness.

A holistic approach to peace will consist largely in finding healthy, nonviolent ways of conflict resolution. This will mean, first of all, developing a holistic view of the network of economic, social, and political patterns out of which conflicts arise. Once these patterns have been understood, a wide range of methods may be used to resolve the conflicts. Humanistic psychologists, family therapists, and social workers have spent the last two decades studying group dynamics and have developed a whole spectrum of techniques of stress management and conflict resolution. It is now time to apply these techniques at the political level—nationally, between nations, and globally.

As everyone concerned about nuclear war knows, no longer can a person or nation do anything to enhance its own security separate from stabilizing the whole system (community, planet) of which it is a part. The World Peace Corps would encourage that larger perspective. Behind this proposal lies the observation that wars in general, and the present arms race in particular, are made possible by the support and participation of citizens who fear the difference of the "other" (the "enemy"), and are led to fear his intentions. This distrust operates consistently in the justification of military activity.... [We need to] provide a counterbalance to one of the conditions necessary for sustaining wars and the preparations for war: excessive fear born of ignorance.

—Robert Fuller, "Proposal for a World Peace Corps," in *Securing Our Planet*

Celebrated as author of *The Aquarian Conspiracy* (1980), Marilyn Ferguson persuasively illustrates how change occurs, gathering examples around a set of basic ideas in a way that liberates energy, much as Betty Edwards did in *Drawing on the Right Side of the Brain* (1979). In effect, both of these women told readers, "You can do it—you have been prevented from developing more fully only by a self-defeating culture—go beyond it and your natural goodness and skill will lead you into a new world." In this chapter, drawn from her book, Ferguson shows how the world appears to a global citizen, to someone who sees it as a whole. Like Capra, she is a Marco Polo returning with treasures from the "New Age." As there were some in Venice who disbelieved in China, so skeptics today scoff at any silks, bells, or spices from the new paradigm. It's reminiscent of the 19th-century Boston lady, who, upon returning from the wild West, was asked how she had traveled. "By way of Braintree," she replied, naming the Boston suburb through which she had left town. Ferguson offers a guide-book to outposts far beyond Braintree.

Switching on the Light

Marilyn Ferguson

VICTOR HUGO PROPHESIED THAT IN the twentieth century war would die, frontier boundaries would die, dogma would die—and man would live. "He will possess something higher than these—a great country, the whole earth . . . and a great hope, the whole heaven."

Today there are millions of residents of that "great country, the whole earth." In their hearts and minds, war and boundaries and dogma have indeed already died. And they possess that large hope of which Hugo wrote.

They know each other as countrymen.

The Whole Earth is a borderless country, a paradigm of humanity with room enough for outsiders and traditionalists, for all our ways of human knowing, for all mysteries and all cultures. A family therapist says she urges her clients to discover not who is right or wrong but *what they have as a family*. We are beginning to make such an inventory of the Whole Earth. Every time one culture finds and appreciates the discovery of another, every time an individual relishes the talents or unique insights of another, every time we welcome the unexpected knowledge emerging from inside the self, we add to that inventory.

Rich as we are—together—we can do anything. We have it within our power to make peace within our torn selves and with each other, to heal our homeland, the Whole Earth.

We look around at all the reasons for saying No: the failed social schemes, the broken treaties, the lost chances. And yet there is the Yes, the same stubborn questing that brought us from the cave to the moon in a flicker of cosmic time.

A fresh generation grows up into a larger paradigm; thus it has always been. In many science fiction tales the adults are barred from the transformation experienced by a new generation. Their children grow irrevocably beyond them, into a larger reality.

Those of us born into the "broken-earth" paradigm have two choices: we can go to our graves with the old view, like the generations of die-hard scientists who insisted there were no such things as meteorites, or germs, or brainwaves, or vitamins—or, we can consign our old beliefs unsentimentally to the past and

[Alexis de] Tocqueville said it may happen that people abandon an idea that has stood dominant over their culture for a long time, but they abandon it quietly, one by one, and they don't tell each other that they no longer believe in this idea, so everyone continues to assume that everyone else still believes it. Because they're timid and they're not expressing their change of mind, this (in a sense) dead idea continues to have power over the society. It was interesting the expression that Tocqueville used was, "and it chilled innovation"—that is, you can't do anything new because nobody has admitted that the old isn't working.

—Marilyn Ferguson on audio cassette, "Beyond the Boundaries"

255

take up the truer, stronger perspective.

We can be our own children.

New Mind, New World

Not even the Renaissance has promised such a radical renewal; as we have seen, we are linked by our travels and technology, increasingly aware of each other, open to each other. In growing numbers we are finding how people can enrich and empower one another; we are more sensitive to our place in nature; we are learning how the brain transforms pain and conflict; and we have more respect for the wholeness of the self as the matrix of health. From science and from the spiritual experience of millions, we are discovering our capacity for endless awakenings in a universe of endless surprises.

At first glance, it may seem hopelessly utopian to imagine that the world can resolve its desperate problems. Each year fifteen million die in starvation and many more live in unrelenting hunger; every ninety seconds the nations of the world spend one million dollars on armaments; every peace is an uneasy peace; the planet has been plundered of many of its nonrenewable resources. Yet there have been remarkable advances as well. Just since the end of World War II, thirty-two countries with forty per cent of the world's population have overcome their problems of food scarcity; China is becoming essentially self-sufficient and has controlled its once-overwhelming population growth; there is a net gain in world literacy and in populist governments; concern for human rights has become a stubborn international issue.

Defending oneself has traditionally been viewed as a kill-or-be-killed proposition in which all outcomes are either victory or defeat and only one can win. That understanding may have been appropriate enough, though fearfully destructive, in prior centuries, but the advent of nuclear weapons annuls victory and makes everyone a loser. Thus we must either stretch our consideration of the defense of the realm to include our adversaries or move to a naturally more inclusive concept that considers the fate of each party to the conflict and seeks to preserve all from harm. We extend this concern to our adversaries not from sympathy but from self-interest. We know well enough that if we do not look to their safety, we will have none ourselves. We can no

We have had a profound paradigm shift about the Whole Earth. We know it now as a jewel in space, a fragile water planet. And we have seen that it has no natural borders. It is not the globe of our school days with its many-colored nations.

We have discovered our interdependence in other ways, too. An insurrection or crop failure in a distant country can signal change in our daily lives. The old ways are untenable. All countries are economically and ecologically involved with each other, politically enmeshed. The old gods of isolationism and nationalism are tumbling, artifacts like the stone deities of Easter Island.

We are learning to approach problems differently, knowing that most of the world's crises grew out of the old paradigm—the forms, structures, and beliefs of an obsolete understanding of reality. Now we can seek answers outside the old frameworks, ask new questions, synthesize, and imagine. Science has given us insights into wholes and systems, stress and transformation. We are learning to read tendencies, to recognize the early signs of another, more promising, paradigm.

We create alternative scenarios of the future. We communicate about the failures of old systems, forcing new frameworks for problem-solving in every area. Sensitive to our ecological crisis, we are cooperating across oceans and borders. Awake and alarmed, we are looking to each other for answers.

And this may be the most important paradigm shift of all. *Individuals are learning to trust—and to communicate their change of*

longer gain security at their expense. This is a subtle but significant step beyond defensive thinking and opens the possibility of developing strategies that transcend polarities instead of reinforcing them. It is also a step beyond relinquishing threats (a necessary and laudable move, but insufficient in itself) in that it does not simply block the illegitimate use of one's own armed forces but indicates an alternative direction for assertive and independent action. Mutually protective strategies must thus replace bids for unilateral advantage. The defense of one must include the defense of the other. What in the pre-nuclear age was a moral imperative has in the nuclear age become a practical necessity.

—Mark Sommer, "Alternative Security Systems," in *Securing Our Planet*

257

mind. Our most viable hope for a new world lies in asking whether a new world is possible. Our very question, our anxiety, says that we care. If we care, we can infer that others care, too.

The greatest single obstacle to the resolution of great problems in the past was thinking they could not be solved—a conviction based on mutual distrust. Psychologists and sociologists have found that most of us are more highly motivated than we think each other to be! For instance, most Americans polled favor gun control but believe themselves in the minority. We are like David Riesman's college students, who all said they did not believe advertising but thought everyone else did. Research has shown that most people believe themselves more high-minded than "most people." Others are presumed to be less open and concerned, less willing to sacrifice, more rigid. Here is the supreme irony: our misreading of each other. Poet William Stafford wrote:

If you don't know the kind of person I am
and I don't know the kind of person you are
a pattern that others made may prevail in
     the world,
and following the wrong god home, we may
     miss our star.

Following the wrong god home, we have seen all of those we did not understand as alien, the enemy. Failing to comprehend each other's politics, cultures, and subcultures, which often are based on a different world view, we questioned each other's motives . . . denied each other's humanity. We have failed

No government or social system is so evil that its people must be considered as lacking in virtue.
As Americans, we find Communism profoundly repugnant as a negation of personal freedom and dignity. But we can still hail the Russian people for their many achievements—in science and space, in economic and industrial growth, in culture, and in acts of courage. Among the many traits the peoples of our two countries have in common, none is stronger than our mutual abhorrence of war. Almost unique among the major world powers, we have never been at war with each other. And no nation in the history of battle ever suffered more than the Soviet Union in the Second World War.

258

to see the obvious: "most people," whatever their philosophy about how to get there, want a warless society in which we are all fed, productive, fulfilled.

If we see each other as obstacles to progress, our assumption is the first and greatest obstacle. Mistrust is a self-fulfilling prophecy. Our old-paradigm consciousness has guaranteed its own dark expectations; it is our collective negative self-image.

Now, as we are learning to communicate, as ever-increasing numbers of people are transforming their fear and finding their bonds with the rest of humanity, sensing our common yearnings, many of the planet's oldest, deepest problems show promise of breaking and yielding. The shift for which we have waited, a revolution of appropriate trust, is beginning. Instead of enemies, we are looking for allies everywhere.

When an international conference, "The Future of the West," convened at the University of Southern California, the authorities agreed firmly on one point: the conference had been misnamed. The West, they said, can have no future apart from the East. This awareness may signal what Martin Heidegger called "the still unspoken gathering of the whole of Western fate . . . the gathering from which alone the Occident can go forth to meet its coming decisions—to become, perhaps, and in a wholly other mode, a land of dawn, an Orient."

Beneath the trappings of culture, anthropologists have said, lies a whole other world. When we understand it, our view of human

At least 20,000,000 lost their lives. Countless millions of homes and families were burned or sacked. A third of the nation's territory, including two-thirds of its industrial base, was turned into a wasteland—a loss equivalent to the destruction of this country east of Chicago. Today, should total war ever break out again—no matter how—our two countries will be the primary targets. It is an ironic but accurate fact that the two strongest powers are the two in the most danger of devastation.

—John F. Kennedy, from a 1963 speech reprinted in *Securing Our Planet*

259

Nonviolence is by no means a universal panacea, but it is one of the instruments of human betterment which deserves to be more clearly understood and prepared for, with regard to both its limits and its potentialities. There is now a large and serious literature on this subject. It can no longer be regarded as an eccentricity of saints. It should be part of the curriculum of every military academy. There should be institutes for its study and organizations to teach it. It represents an expansion of the agenda or repertory of the decision maker in many different types of social systems. It may be, as a high official in the Indian defense establishment once said to me, that it is much more suitable for aggression than for defense, more suitable for instance to create wanted social change than to defend against unwanted social

nature will change radically. Now we confront an array of possible ways to be. The global village is a reality. We are joined by satellite, supersonic travel, four thousand international meetings each year, tens of thousands of multinational companies, international organizations and newsletters and journals, even an emergent pan-culture of music, movies, art, humor. Lewis Thomas observed:

"Effortlessly, without giving it a moment's thought, we are capable of changing our language, music, manners, morals, entertainment, even the way we dress, all around the earth in a year's turning. We seem to do this by general agreement, without voting or even polling. We simply think our way along, pass information around, exchange codes disguised as art, change our minds, transform ourselves. . . . Joined together, the great mass of human minds around the earth seems to behave like a coherent living system."

The proliferating small groups and networks arising all over the world operate much like the coalitional networks in the human brain. Just as a few cells can set up a resonant effect in the brain, ordering the activity of the whole, these cooperating individuals can help create the coherence and order to crystalize a wider transformation.

Movements, networks, and publications are gathering people around the world in common cause, trafficking in transformative ideas, spreading messages of hope without the sanction of any government. Transformation has no country.

These self-organizing groups are very little

like old political structures; they overlap, form coalitions, and support each other without generating a conventional power structure. There are environmental groups like Les Vertes in France and the Green Alliance in Great Britain, women's groups, peace groups, human rights groups, groups battling world hunger; thousands of centers and networks supporting "new consciousness," like Nexus in Stockholm; publications like *Alterna* in Denmark, *New Humanities* and *New Life* in Great Britain, linking many groups; symposia on consciousness in Finland, Brazil, South Africa, Iceland, Chile, Mexico, Rumania, Italy, Japan, the USSR.

The Future in Our Hands, a movement launched in Norway in 1974 and inspired by a book of that title by Erik Damman, now numbers twenty thousand of that country's total population of four million. The rapidly growing movement promotes "a new lifestyle and a fair distribution of the world's resources." It emphasizes the need for industrialized nations to curb their consumption patterns and seeks ways to boost the living standard of Third World countries. According to a national survey, fifty per cent of the Norwegian population supports the goals of the movement, seventy-five per cent believe that their nation's standard of living is too high, and eighty per cent fear that continued economic growth will lead to an increasingly stressful, materialistic lifestyle.

The movement is fueled by grassroots power. Small local groups determine their own course in furthering the collective goals. A

change. This, however, needs to be investigated. What is most urgent is that nonviolence should be taken seriously.

—Kenneth Boulding, "Seven Planks for a Platform," in *Securing Our Planet*

I am merely pointing out that women, whether subtly or vociferously, have always been a tremendous power in the destiny of the world and with so many of them now holding important positions and receiving recognition and earning the respect of the men as well as the members of their own sex, it seems more than ever that in this crisis, "It's Up to the Women!"

—Eleanor Roosevelt

261

related movement started in Sweden in 1978 and another is now under way in Denmark.

These social movements transcend traditional national borders, with Germans joining French demonstrators to protest nuclear power plants. Johann Quanier, British publisher of *The New Humanity* journal, said, "The strands of free thinking within Europe are now being drawn together; despite the conflicts, the tension, and the differences, that territory is preeminently suitable for the emergence of the new political-spiritual framework."

To Aurelio Peccei, founder of the Club of Rome, such groups represent "the yeast of change . . . scattered, myriad spontaneous groupings of people springing up here and there like antibodies in a sick organism." An organizer of a peace group remarked on his discovery of these networks and their sense of "imminent world transformation." Many brilliant, creative thinkers have affiliated internationally to help synthesize the intellectual support for an emergent vision for the planet. To them it is more than a mere scenario, one of many possible futures, but rather a responsibility; the alternatives seem to them to be unimaginable.

The Threshold Foundation, based in Switzerland, stated its intent to help ease the transition into a planetary culture, "foster a paradigm shift, a new model of the universe in which art, religion, philosophy, and science converge," and promote a wider understanding that "we exist in a cosmos whose many levels of reality form a single sacred whole."

Afterward when we talked about our demon ritual, we realized that it had provided us with a model for a process whereby we might live with and at the same time work to change our prospects in the Nuclear Age. In naming our demon we had identified the ways we, as individuals and a society, participate in perpetuating the arms race. Just as we could only devise and enact ways to change the world situation cooperatively, so we had invented our ritual together and we had literally put our heads together to make it happen. In its creation and performance we had each spoken our mind, yet

262

From Power To Peace

We are changing because we must.

Historically, peace efforts have been aimed at ending or preventing wars. Just as we have defined health in negative terms, as the absence of disease, we have defined peace as nonconflict. But peace is more fundamental than that. Peace is a state of mind, not a state of the nation. Without personal transformation, the people of the world will be forever locked in conflict.

If we limit ourselves to the old-paradigm concept of averting war, we are trying to overpower darkness rather than switching on the light. If we reframe the problem—if we think of fostering community, health, innovation, self-discovery, purpose—we are already engaged in waging peace. In a rich, creative, meaningful environment there is no room for hostility.

War is unthinkable in a society of autonomous people who have discovered the connectedness of all humanity, who are unafraid of alien ideas and alien cultures, who know that all revolutions begin within and that you cannot impose your brand of enlightenment on anyone else. . . .

After a recent congress in Vienna on the role of women in world peace, Patricia Mische wrote of "the transformation already slowly in process among individuals and groups who, in a deep probing of their own humanness, are discovering the bonds they have with people everywhere."

Can the arms race be reversed? "A prior

singing together had brought our separate awarenesses into a collective presence, a unified aliveness, a sense of shared vulnerability and shared power. We had realized the interconnection and caring among us. The insight brought us to the issue of taking action. We knew that the act of future visioning could not be complete if we did not work to make our visions real, and we realized that our remembrance of our interconnection and caring must be the basis for any actions we take to bring them about.

—Chellis Glendinning

263

My earliest arms-control proposal dealt with the president's remoteness from reality when facing a decision about nuclear war. A young officer follows the president with a black attaché case containing the codes needed to fire nuclear weapons. I envisioned the president at a staff meeting considering nuclear war as an abstract option. He might conclude, "On SIOP Plan One, the decision is affirmative. Communicate the alpha line XYZ." Such jargon holds reality at a distance. My suggestion was quite simple. I proposed to place the code number in a little capsule that would then be implanted right next to the heart of a volunteer. The volunteer would carry a big, heavy butcher knife as he or she accompanied the president. If ever the president wanted to fire nuclear weapons, he would have to kill one human being personally and realize what an innocent death is. Blood on the White House carpet— it's reality brought home.

question," Mische said, "would be, '*Can people—and nations—change their hearts and minds?*'" The Vienna participants seemed living testimony that the answer is Yes. At the close of the congress one participant asked, to tumultuous applause, that at future conferences speakers not be required to identify themselves by nationality. "I am here as a *planetary* citizen," she said, "and these problems belong to all of us."

In *The Whole Earth Papers*, a series of monographs, James Baines described a "power paradigm" and a "peace paradigm." For millennia, he said, we have lived under the power paradigm, a belief system based on independence and domination. Yet it has always existed alongside the components for a peace paradigm: a society based on creativity, freedom, democracy, spirituality. To foster a global shift, Baines said, we can now create "a web of reinforcement": leadership comfortable with uncertainty, heightened public awareness of the contradictions in the power paradigm, exciting models of new lifestyles, appropriate technology, techniques for expanded consciousness and spiritual awakening. Once these ideas coalesce into a coherent new paradigm grounded in transformation, we will see that humanity is both a part of creation and its steward as well, "a product of evolution and an *instrument* of evolution."

We need not wait for a leadership. We can begin to effect change at any point in a complex system: a human life, a family, a nation. One person can create a transformative environment for others through trust and friendship. A warm family or community can make a stranger feel at ease. A society can encourage growth and renewal in its members.

We can begin anywhere—everywhere. "Let there be peace," says a bumper sticker, "and let it begin with me." Let there be health, learning, relationship, right uses of power, meaningful work. . . . *Let there be transformation, and let it begin with me.*

All beginnings are invisible, an inward movement, a revolution in consciousness. Because human choice remains sacrosanct and mysterious, none of us can guarantee a transformation of society. Yet there is reason to trust the process. Transformation is powerful, rewarding, natural. It promises what most people want.

Perhaps that is why the transformed society exists already as a premonition in the minds of millions. It is the "someday" of our myths. The word "new" so freely used (new medicine, new politics, new spirituality) does not refer so much to something modern as to something imminent and long awaited.

The new world is the old—transformed.

When I suggested this to friends in the Pentagon they said, "My God, that's terrible. Having to kill someone would distort his judgment. The president might never push the button."

—Roger Fisher, "To Gain a Peace in the Nuclear Age," in *Securing Our Planet*

Peace is not the elimination of the causes of war. Rather it is a mastery of great human forces and the creation of an environment in which human aims may be pursued constructively.

—James H. Case, Jr.

A professor of engineering at Stanford, a Regent of the University of California, and president of the Institute of Noetic Sciences, Willis Harman writes about "the power of the images we hold." It's as if his credo were "Credo, ergo sum"—I believe, therefore I am. Like many contributors, he cautions that "being against war is not at all the same as affirming peace," but he goes much further, arguing that reality is somehow affected by the beliefs we hold about it. For example, he says that dwelling upon fear that a nuclear war will occur actually contributes to the very result we fear. To the extent that we get what we affirm, we should take care what we believe, just as, if prayers are answered, we should pause before asking. It's easier perhaps to reflect in the case of requests, which are specific acts, than of beliefs, which tend to form unconsciously and to persist. Harman asks us to consider the effect of the unconscious beliefs we hold about other societies, and the benefits of changing those beliefs.

Nuclear Weapons and The Expansion of Consciousness

Willis W. Harman

Since wars are born in the minds of men, it is in the minds of men where we have to erect the ramparts of peace.
—UNESCO Charter (Preamble)

Problems such as nuclear weapons, pollution, and ecological imbalance stem directly from our own behavior and hence are fundamentally psychological in origin. . . . The current threats to human survival are actually symptoms of our individual and shared psychological dysfunctions.
—Roger Walsh, M.D., Ph.D.

TWO SCIENTIFIC DEVELOPMENTS OF the past half-century stand out as not only profoundly affecting history but also being in an important relationship to one another. One is the unleashing of the power of the atom; the other is major progress toward the unfettering of the human mind. The first, which led to the development of nuclear weapons, almost demands the second, advances in the understanding of human consciousness. For the fantastic destructive power of modern weaponry, posing as it does a threat to the survival of civilization, calls for a far more thorough understanding of deeper human motivations and aspirations, values and perceptions, perversities and potentialities than any society has ever achieved—an understanding which has indeed been in the making in the fields of consciousness research and the modern psychologies.

Probably the most consequential single finding in the field of human consciousness research is the discovery of the startling extent to which our perceptions, motivations, values, and behaviors are shaped by *unconscious beliefs* which we acquire from our early experiences and from the cultural milieu. These unconsciously held beliefs (for example, "I am inadequate," "The world is hostile") amount to an "inner map" of reality which influences how we perceive the world about us—the perceptions in turn tend to reinforce the "inner map." These unconscious beliefs determine where we experience limits to our own powers, and they block us from fuller use of the inner resources available to us.

The discussion below briefly reviews the profound shift in outlook which this psychological insight brings to the global problems,

I'm reminded of the short poem that runs, "Let's stop hurting each other. You go first." This is between husband and wife. That shows how hard it is to interrupt a cycle of fear. It almost can't be done by trying to do it. You can't resolve, "I'm not going to be afraid." It doesn't work that way. All you can do is very, very slowly and incrementally build a little more trust. You can't by an act of will become unafraid. You can, just maybe, over the course of time, learn how not to scare the other person. So I can't learn to be unafraid of the Russians, but I can learn how not to threaten them and then, if they like that, they can learn how not to threaten me and then fear will be out of fashion. It won't have been generated as much as over (say) the last 5 or 10 years.

—Robert Fuller on audio cassette, "A Better Game Than War"

267

I have spent my life in the study of military strength as a deterrent to war, and in the character of military armaments necessary to win a war. The study of the first of these questions is still profitable, but we are rapidly getting to the point that no war can be won. War implies a contest; when you get to the point that contest is no longer involved and the outlook comes close to destruction of the enemy and suicide for ourselves—an outlook that neither side can ignore—then arguments as to the exact amount of available strength as compared to somebody else's are no longer the vital issues. When we get to the point, as we one day will, that both sides know that in any outbreak of general hostilities, regardless of the element of surprise, destruction will be both reciprocal and complete, possibly we will have sense enough to meet at the conference table with the understanding that the era of armaments has ended and the human race must conform its actions to this truth or die. The fullness of this

and then suggests an answer to the ever-present nuclear-age question, "What can I do? What can I do to help bring sustainable global peace?"

Two Contrasting Perceptions

There is a familiar and influential perception of the world in which the present massive confrontation of nuclear weapons is a regrettable but inescapable consequence of technological progress. From this perspective, attempts to negotiate arms limitation agreements are certainly worthwhile, but realistically the only assurance of stability and of continuing non-use of the weapons lies in a balance of strength. The assumption that military and political decision-makers will behave rationally, in keeping with their awareness that a nuclear holocaust would indeed mean the end to civilization, is our sole insurance against a nuclear exchange. In this perception of the world, a call for peace seems either a romantic dream or a failure of nerve.

In sharp contrast to this is an alternative perception of reality, which both is more hopeful than the first and involves a more positive image of human potentialities. In it, the global problems of war, urban slums, rural poverty, hunger, over-population, progressive desertification, pollution, unemployment, and all the rest, are seen to be solvable with the necessary resources being available. This alternative perception tends to lead away from feelings of despair, fear, distrust, and hostility; it tends to lead the individual to make a healthy, creative response to the nuclear issue.

It is no less "human nature" to see the world the second way than the first. It is no less realistic, although it is likely to seem so to many. However, one's first reaction is most likely to be one of skepticism. The global problems seem real; the alternatives that would lead us out of the nuclear impasse seem nonexistent.

We humans have an awesome ability to deceive ourselves. Once we have settled on one perception of "reality," all evidence to the contrary tends to become invisible; all hints that our picture might be seriously incomplete or even wrong are warded off like flies on a summer day. Examples are legion. For instance, anthropologists find that individuals who are raised in different tribes literally perceive different realities—and each one finds that his experience bears out *his* tribe's traditional view. The hypnotized subject who has accepted the suggestion that a pencil is a hot soldering iron will not be swayed by arguments to the contrary, and in fact will respond with all the physical signs of a burn if the pencil is placed on the back of his hand. The annals of history and of psychotherapy are full of examples of "resistance" and "denial," which are in essence ways of warding off evidence that challenges the person's "inner map" of reality.

We do not necessarily perceive the world in a way that in fact would be most in our self interest. For example, the paranoid sees the environment in a way that causes much self anguish, and rational argument or even contradictory experience may fail to change

potentiality has not yet been attained, and I do not, by any means, decry the need for strength. That strength must be spiritual, economic, and military. All three are important and they are not mutually exclusive. They are all part of and the product of the American genius, the American will. But already we have come to the point where safety cannot be assumed by arms alone. But I repeat that their usefulness becomes concentrated more and more in their characteristics as deterrents than as instruments with which to obtain victory over opponents as in 1945. In this regard, today we are further separated from the end of World War II than the beginning of the century was separated from the beginning of the sixteenth century.

—Dwight D. Eisenhower, letter of 4/4/56

When negotiators bargain over positions, they tend to lock themselves into those positions. The more you clarify your position and defend it against attack, the more committed you become to it. The more you try to convince the other side of the impossibility of changing your opening position, the more difficult it becomes to do so. Your ego becomes identified with your position. You now have a new interest in "saving face"—in reconciling future action with past positions—making it less and less likely that any agreement will wisely reconcile the parties' original interests. The danger that positional bargaining will impede a negotiation was well illustrated by the breakdown of the talks under President Kennedy for a comprehensive ban on nuclear testing. A critical question arose:

that perception. The business executive whose stressful existence has brought about serious cardiovascular disease will often continue this risking of life rather than perceiving work in such a way that it is less stress-producing. It would not seem to serve us well to perceive the world in such a way that there is no viable alternative to the nuclear impasse, yet that is the all-too-common perception.

It does not come easily, of course, to recognize that the view of reality which we have held most of our lives, and which is also held by most of those around us, is a parochial view which has been shaped by all the suggestions we have absorbed along the way, just as the perceived world of the hypnotized subject has been shaped by the suggestions he has accepted. In fact, this is such an unpalatable recognition that it appears a vast number of persons would risk the destruction of civilization rather than fundamentally change their perceptions of the world—so fundamentally that the nuclear dilemma appears solvable and each of us can make a direct and significant contribution to that solution.

A Provocative Analogy

There is a parallel at the individual level that may make it more plausible that the second, alternative perception of the global situation might turn out to be at least as valid—and as possible—as the first. This is what might be called "the fundamental lesson of psychotherapy." Many, many people have undergone a fundamental reorganization of their "inner maps of reality." Typically, this change was brought about by life's crises.

Sometimes it was characterized by trauma and breakdown; sometimes the passage was aided by formal psychotherapy or a spontaneous spiritual awakening. However diverse their individual experiences, person after person has learned the same basic lesson: no matter how insoluble and overwhelming may seem the problems faced—emotional, financial, in relationships, at work, or in the family—*perceived another way, they are all solvable* and, furthermore, *all the resources necessary for their solution were available all along!*

No one could have persuaded the person, before his or her transformation, that such a conclusion was possible. Similarly, rational arguments alone are not very likely to convince that a similar conclusion holds with regard to global problems.

In the widely acclaimed work of Alcoholics Anonymous, the so-called "Twelve Steps" describe the essential process of change. The first two of these are:

1. We admitted we were powerless over alcohol—that our lives had become unmanageable.

2. We came to believe that a power greater than ourselves could restore us to sanity.

The first step is typically very strongly resisted, but the cure cannot proceed without it. The second step is the answer to the argument that "I don't know what I can do." There is a part of our minds that *does* know—a part not always directly accessible to conscious awareness.

How many on-site inspections per year should the Soviet Union and the United States be permitted to make within the other's territory to investigate suspicious seismic events? The Soviet Union finally agreed to three inspections. The United States insisted on no less than ten. And there the talks broke down—over positions—despite the fact that no one understood whether an "inspection" would involve one person looking around for one day, or a hundred people prying indiscriminately for a month. The parties had made little attempt to design an inspection procedure that would reconcile the United States's interest in verification with the desire of both countries for minimal intrusion.

—Roger Fisher and William Ury, "Getting to Yes," in *Securing Our Planet*

271

Now is the time for the United States to take independent initiatives that will break the arms control deadlock and accelerate the arms reduction process. As the leader of the free world and the leader in the nuclear weapons race, we should take action that is in our self-interest and made possible by our democratic system of government. We can demonstrate to the world our resourcefulness and imagination, our willingness to experiment and take a carefully calculated risk that is minimal when compared to the enormous risk of nuclear war. There is a powerful precedent for this kind of leadership and American independent action. Twenty years ago President John F. Kennedy, speaking at the American University commencement, made the bold declaration that the United States would not conduct any further atmospheric nuclear testing as long as other nations would also refrain from testing. . . . Once again it is time for the United States to exercise leadership and take bold action.

It may be that something like this applies in a collective sense with regard to the global problems. The "first step" is to recognize that global society has indeed become unmanageable. We may expect that step to be strongly resisted, as in the case of the alcoholic. The "second step" is to recognize that when we say "I don't know what to do," we are lying to ourselves. *At a deeper level, we do know what to do.* If this is indeed true with regard to the global dilemmas, we should not expect that to be a provable proposition. It might, however, be a *discoverable* truth. (It was St. Exupery who said, "Truth is not that which is demonstrable; it is that which is ineluctable"—inescapable.)

Realizing something like the above, what can an individual do to help? I think the question is answerable.

Some argue that we need to agree on disarmament; others dismiss that as impractical. Some argue for nonviolent conflict resolution—which is, of course, what the United Nations was set up to provide. Some say if we would just learn to love one another, and speak peace around the globe, we would have peace; others dismiss that as simplistic. Some speak up for political action; others for meditation and inner peace. Many sound confused, or despairing.

It turns out, I believe, that there are four things that one can do—and they must all be done to make a balanced contribution. These are:

1. *Say no!* Say no to the insanity of tolerating an intolerable condition.

2. *Say yes!* Say yes to the evolutionary transformation that alone can bring us sustained peace and common security.

3. *Do your inner work.* Discover that it is possible to shift to a more positive perception of the world, no less realistic than the previous perception and far more likely to lead to a constructive response.

4. *Do your outer work.* It is important to be involved with some work in the world. It will keep the inner work from becoming too introspective, and the outer work will be increasingly effective as it is informed by progress in the inner work.

Say no to the prospect that our children and our children's children must grow up in fear that the world will have destroyed itself before they can have a chance to live their lives. Say no to the continued legitimacy and glorification of war as an instrument of national policy—for any nation. And spread the word.

The nineteenth century Prussian strategist von Clausewitz defined war as "an extension of state policy by other means." To move from this rational argument for war to a complete delegitimating of war would be one of the most profound shifts in the history of humankind. Yet it can come about when the people of the world change their minds and demand it. It *must* happen, because the alternative is the suicide of the human species.

The really fundamental changes in human history—such as the ending of the Roman era or of the Middle Ages—have come about not through the arbitrary decisions of a few

We should begin immediately a step-by-step program of American initiatives aimed at slowing, stopping, and reversing the Soviet-American nuclear arms race.

—Harold Willens, "Taking the Next Steps," in *Securing Our Planet*

The fatalistic view of the war-function is to me nonsense, for I know that war-making is due to definite motives and subject to prudential checks and reasonable criticisms, just like any other form of enterprise. And when whole nations are the armies, and the science of destruction vies in intellectual refinement with the sciences of production, I see that war becomes absurd and impossible from its own monstrosity. Extravagant ambitions will have to be replaced by reasonable claims, and nations must make common cause against them.

—William James, "The Moral Equivalent of War," in *Securing Our Planet*

A vast history exists of people who, refusing to be convinced that the apparent "powers that be" were omnipotent, defied and resisted powerful rulers, foreign conquerers, domestic tyrants, oppressive systems, internal usurpers, and economic masters. Contrary to usual perceptions, these means of struggle by protest, non-cooperation, and disruptive intervention have played major historical roles in all parts of the world, even in cases in which attention is usually concentrated on parallel or later political violence. These unrefined forms of non-violent struggle have been used as major or predominant means of defense against foreign invaders or internal usurpers for the most part without preparation, training, or planning.

leaders, but because vast numbers of people changed their minds a little bit. People give the legitimacy to all social institutions, no matter how powerful these institutions may seem to be. But on occasion, people remember they also have the power to withdraw legitimacy. In the past, legitimacy has been withdrawn from slavery, cruel and unusual punishment, officially sanctioned torture, dueling, subjugation and mutilation of women, female infanticide. The legitimacy can be removed from war when people's consciousness changes —and their will to act (particularly women's)— is awakened. (The characteristics of a few female world leaders notwithstanding, the feminine consciousness tends to be life-revering and nurturing, and war has always been almost entirely a man's game.)

Since World War II, war is no longer a contest between trained armies; it is the desolation of civilian populations. Its legitimacy must be removed; there is no other way.

Say yes to the evolutionary transformation that alone can bring us sustained peace and common security. Affirm the positive image of a world in which war as a deliberate policy instrument is unthinkable; in which the knowledge to create nuclear weapons, to devastate cities, to poison whole populations, and to desolate the environment, is not feared because it would not be misapplied. A world in which every planetary citizen has a reasonable chance to create through his or her own efforts a decent life for self and family; in which men and women live in harmony with the earth and its creatures, cooperating to create and maintain a wholesome environment for all; in which there is an ecology of different cultures, the diversity of which is appreciated and supported; in which there is a deep and shared sense of meaning in life itself—meaning that does not have to be sought in mindless acquisition and consumption.

Recognize, understand the implications of, and affirm that war can be outlawed only through a total change in the beliefs that separate nation from nation, persons from nature, and each of us from our deeper selves. No technical solution will suffice to remove the peril of the nuclear weapons—no nuclear freeze, no multilateral arms limitation agreements, no "Star Wars" beam technologies to shoot down enemy missiles. Affirm that this change in the world mindset can be accomplished. The change will spread mainly person-to-person, and every individual's efforts count.

Recognize the power of the images we hold. Holding a negative image—dwelling on the fear that a nuclear exchange might come about, or on the anger toward our leaders who continue to escalate the numbers of missiles—contributes very directly to bringing about that which is feared or hated. Being against war is not at all the same thing as affirming peace. Holding a positive image, vividly imagining a desired state, contributes to that state coming about—in ways that may seem quite mysterious if we have too limited a belief about the capabilities of the human mind.

We are not talking about a simplistic "power of positive thinking." To hold and

These situations include: German strikes and political non-cooperation with the 1920 Kapp Putsch against the Weimar Republic; German government-sponsored non-cooperation in the Ruhr in 1923 with the French and Belgian occupation; major aspects of the Dutch anti-Nazi resistance, including several large strikes, 1940–1945; major aspects of the Danish resistance to the German occupation, including the 1944 Copenhagen general strike, 1940–1945; major parts of the Norwegian resistance to the Quisling regime and the occupation; and the Czechoslovak resistance to the Soviet invasion and occupation, 1963–1969.

—Gene Sharp, "Shifting to a Non-Military Defense," in *Securing Our Planet*

affirm a positive image of a world that works for almost everyone; in which there is harmony between peoples, and between people and the earth; in which the scourge of war is banished forever—is not simplistic. Because of the interconnectedness of all minds, affirming a positive vision may be about the most sophisticated action any one of us can take.

It is true that it may be simplistic to believe that if we just all love one another and speak peace, peace will come into the world. It may be simplistic beause powerful unconscious forces make our love ambivalent, and our peace tinged with hidden conflict. Collectively held unconscious beliefs shape the world's institutions, and are at the root of institutionalized oppression and inequity. "Peace" will always be no more than a temporary truce if there exist widespread perceptions of basic injustice, needs unmet, and wrongs unrighted. But if one affirms the positive image regularly and persistently, eventually this seems to modify the unconscious beliefs, thereby changing the perception of the world—and even the world itself.

The inner work comprises at least three aspects: (1) discovering the potentialities of the "deep intuition" as guide and resource; (2) changing the inner beliefs that bring about individual non-peace and limited capacities; and (3) changing the inner beliefs that, collectively held, shape national and global institutions which perpetuate conditions of non-peace in the world.

The state of publicly accessible knowledge regarding this inner work has improved

Most people consider themselves to be somewhat impotent to stop things. Even people who are actively working toward disarmament, I think, frequently feel helpless. They're doing it but they don't really expect it to work. This is ironic, but nobody can empower us but ourselves. People, if they think it's within the realm of the possible, want to see a different kind of life. We have all had experiences when the warmth and the creativity and the energy of human dynamics was so exciting that we hated to see it end. Maybe it was a project we were working on

276

dramatically in recent decades. Half a century ago, a reductionistic and positivistic science seemed to be making a very effective argument that only the sense-perceived and measurable world was real, and that the capabilities of mind were limited by the physical dimensions of the brain. It seemed that the more science one learned, the less plausible was any sort of religious or spiritual story, and the more education one had, the more skeptical one became regarding the further reaches of the mind and intuitive powers. In this regard, there has been a remarkable turnaround. Scientists of note like David Bohm and Roger Sperry and Rupert Sheldrake speak openly of nonmeasurable but inferrable (and perhaps intuitable) aspects of reality. It now seems that with further scientific advance some sort of spiritual accounting of humankind becomes increasingly plausible, and less in conflict with scientific findings. Age-old meditative exercises and spiritual practices are being reassessed. From a variety of scientific and scholarly disciplines—experimental psychology, psychotherapy, cultural anthropology, parapsychology, comparative religion—come evidences that the main if not the only limits to the human mind are in the inner beliefs. There is a gradually unfolding realization of the powers and profound wisdom of the hidden mind.

For the discovery and appropriation of the hidden inner resources, a variety of meditative approaches are easily accessible. Through these, one learns to be conscious of oneself in new and transcending ways, and to discover

with a group of people; maybe it was a play that we were in; people even organizing a surprise party for somebody at the office. There is an everyday kind of magic. On the other hand, if we allow ourselves to fall into the kind of pattern that most of us have spent a good part of our lives in, of remembering the negative more than we remember the positive, then even though we might desire another world we won't believe that other people could or do.

—Marilyn Ferguson
on audio cassette, "A Better Game Than War"

277

potentialities for inner peace that seem ultimately authentic and universal.

In addition to the meditative approaches, some other techniques are useful in dealing with the kinds of unconscious beliefs that generate conditions of individual non-peace—of fear, distrust, and hostility. These unconscious beliefs we pick up, presumably, from childhood socialization and through the "hypnotic" suggestions of the surrounding culture. They sometimes change spontaneously or through traumatic life experiences—coming close to death, or a great grief, for example. Many people are led to one or another kind of psychotherapy because the "inner maps" are disadvantageous in terms of causing pain and feelings of separation. Approaches involving guided imagery and positive affirmation (autosuggestion) can be very powerful.

The idea that collectively held beliefs create world conditions for non-peace is much less widely appreciated than the relationship between individual beliefs and personal problems. Yet the dynamic is much the same. Just as it proves to be true that the fundamental cause of individual non-peace is to be found in the person's unconscious beliefs, so a similar conclusion turns out to hold for non-peace on a global scale. *The fundamental causes of non-peace on the planet are to be found mainly in the collective beliefs of the various societies—beliefs which are partly consciously held, but are in great measure unconscious.*

It is by no means apparent that this is the case. In fact, on first reading, the above statement may seem not only wrong but non-

Is it also possible that the way in which the two superpowers choose to respond to the challenge presented by outer space may lead either to their ultimate self-destruction or to their redemption? The capacities for both good and evil dwell in each of us, and we can choose whether and how we will use those capacities to shape history. In deciding the fate of outer space, we can choose to allow the triumph of violence in our psyches and souls, imposing our darkness on the earth and on the universe. Or we can

278

sensical. We are used to seeking explanations of the state of global non-peace in the ambitions and frustrations of leaders in countries; in the flaws of past treaties; in the competition for "lebensraum," natural resources, and foreign markets; in religious and economic ideological conflicts. No doubt these explanations are partially accurate. But underlying them, as a more fundamental breeding ground of non-peace, are the largely collective beliefs that so subtly create barriers, separations, tensions, and collisions. These beliefs are difficult even to become aware of, and certainly to test, mainly because the people around us tend to share the same beliefs and tacitly to take them for granted.

Imagine, for example, what beliefs and priorities are implied by the "defense" policies of the U.S. and the U.S.S.R., and by the fact that the separate goals of the two superpowers are for each so compelling that no alternative can be found to massive nuclear confrontation. Imagine, too, the beliefs implied by the enormously expensive and unprecedented worldwide arms race in "conventional" weapons which is assumed to be unavoidable—regrettable as it is that the diversion of resources into arms is thwarting satisfaction of the most basic human needs in many of the poorer countries. What can one infer from the fact that Western industrial society, which exerts such a powerful influence over the rest of the world, lauds consumption of goods and services—approvingly referring to citizens as "consumers"—even though frugality would clearly be preferable from the standpoints of

choose to recognize and act on the knowledge of our indwelling in one another and in the earth. We can choose to utilize our creative capacities and technological genius for leading the human community in the cooperative development of outer space for the advancement of peace and human well-being on earth.

—Patricia M. Mische, "Star Wars and the State of Our Souls," in *Securing Our Planet*

279

There is another element, more important than all, without which there can not be the slightest hope of a permanent peace. That element lies in the heart of humanity. Unless the desire for peace be cherished there, unless this fundamental and only natural source of brotherly love be cultivated to its highest degree, all artificial efforts will be in vain. Peace will come when there is realization that only under a reign of law, based on righteousness and supported by the religious conviction of the brotherhood of man, can there be any hope of a complete and satisfying life. Parchment will fail, the sword will fail, it is only the spiritual nature of man that can be triumphant.

—Calvin Coolidge

resource depletion and environmental impact? Far-reaching decisions are based on economic criteria and the financial bottom line, even when the social and ecological consequences of those decisions are disastrous. (One consequence of this is a formalized disregard for the welfare of future generations—overuse and depletion of agricultural lands, profligate consumption of fossil fuels, discounting the future, all are justified by "sound economic logic.") The competitive and materialistically acquisitive drives observed in persons' economic behavior are considered "normal"; however, the currently prevailing scientific understandings tend to deny or explain away the noblest of human motivations because altruism, love, and spiritual yearnings are "unscientific" concepts. These examples but hint at the underlying irrationalities which an objective observer might deduce from our collective behavior. To such an observer, the solution to our vexing problems would lie quite apparently in a change of beliefs.

It can be anticipated that a strong resistance may develop toward the challengers of tacit collectively held beliefs. Recall the church fathers who refused to look through Galileo's telescope because the moons that he claimed to have discovered traveling around Jupiter couldn't exist. Recall the pronouncement of the influential Lavoisier committee to investigate objects supposedly flying in from outer space—that there could be no such thing as meteorites because "there are no stones in the sky to fall." Recall how reports of operations performed using hypnotic suggestion as an anaesthetic were denied publication in medical journals of three continents, because there was no "mechanism" to explain the absence of pain; patients must have been "pretending" not to feel pain as legs were amputated and abdominal surgery performed! We are in a similar position when we seek to unveil our ill-serving collective beliefs. The changes will not be easily accepted. Societies have never been overly kind to heretics.

This inner work is unsettling at first—both the work with self-image and the uncovering of pathogenic collective beliefs. Yet as it progresses, it becomes exhilarating. As the negative, separating beliefs are brought to light, the positive vision of a world that could be will strengthen, and the actions to help bring it about will become more sure-footed.

Each one of us has his or her own unique outer role to be discovered and played. It may be a significant public role, or it may be a small quiet one. It may be a role of social activism, of patient healing, of lecturing to great crowds, or of parenting at home. Whatever it is, it is important to do it as well as possible, with both the nature of the role itself, and the way it is carried out, being progressively informed by ongoing inner work.

It is critical that we have an adequately comprehensive picture of the interconnected aspects of global non-peace, for they must be understood together. Global non-peace includes at least the following:

the ever-present threat of triggering a nuclear exhange, with massive loss of life and mass creation of human desolation;

Shall Tongue be mute,
when deeds are wrought
which well might shame
extremist hell?
Shall freeman lock the
indignant thought?
Shall Pity's bosom cease
to swell?
Shall Honor bleed?—Shall
Truth succumb?
Shall pen, and press, and
son be dumb?

—John Greenleaf Whittier

281

persistent "local" wars with "conventional" weapons leaving a steady wake of human misery;

a global arms race involving expenditures of over a billion dollars a day, with some of the poorer countries spending more on military preparation than on health care, education, and human welfare together;

widespread poverty, with accompanying disease, malnutrition, and starvation, and with strains on the natural environment that include overgrazing, deforestation, soil erosion, and surface water pollution;

environmental degradation and resource exploitation stemming from the economic activites of the industrialized societies; and

increasing tensions between the industrialized, mass-consuming North and the poverty-stricken South.

It is important to keep in mind these broader dimensions of non-peace, because many of them are much longer-lived than the U.S.-U.S.S.R. enmity. Sixty years ago it was the Germans who were inhuman monsters (as we were taught to perceive them); forty years ago the Japanese were subhuman devils. Now it is the Russians who are the personification of evil, but in historical terms that perception is also likely to be a relatively transient one.

Our enemy is not the Russians, but a mind-set. Behind all the components of global non-peace are the tacitly held premises, conscious and unconscious, that shape the institutions and the policies and the "laws" of economics, and yes, even the sciences and technologies. And each one of us has complicity

What are some of these opportunities? If everyone with any significant power made the right decision every time, that would be as close to utopia as we could get. There are only three reasons people don't make the right decisions. One is that they are bad decision makers. Our job is to find better ones— that is what politics is about. Second, they are operating on bad assumptions. Our job is to correct their assumptions. And third, they are subject to constraints such as misguided public opinion. Our job is to remove those constraints. To get a wise decision, we need to tackle every aspect of

282

in the non-peace, to the extent that we un-critically buy into the prevailing belief system.

Doing one's outer work is important, not just because the work itself, on any aspect of the non-peace, contributes to a more workable society, but also because the work is sensitizing. It keeps the inner work from going sterile. It preserves one from indifference.

The Soviet novelist Bruno Yasensky wrote: "Be not afraid of your enemy; the worst he can do is kill you. Be not afraid of your friends; the worst they can do is betray you. But beware of indifferent people. They do not kill and do not betray, but it is with their tacit consent the assassinations and betrayals are perpetrated on this earth."

A Parting Thought

Modern weaponry with its fantastic de-structive power is the ultimate achievement of the industrial era. No other product of the industrial paradigm so clearly demonstrates on the one hand its awesome technological power, and on the other hand its anomic in-difference to the human consequences of the products it generates. The nuclear warhead, symbol of man's "conquest" of the secrets of the atom, now holds us all hostage. Yet it may ultimately be our salvation, in somewhat the same way that a near brush with death, or an emotional breakdown, may turn out to be the trigger that results in a life being reshaped. There are many other aspects of global non-peace besides the nuclear threat that have needed attention for some time. There are serious flaws in our present materialistic, com-

a problem in every way possible. No amount of useful research will overcome poor decision makers, no number of good decision makers will overcome bad assumptions or harmful constraints. Somebody has to propose a solution. Somebody has to put it on a decision maker's agenda. Some-body has to persuade others that it is a good idea, and somebody has to carry out the idea. There is enough to keep us all busy.

—Roger Fisher, "To Gain a Peace in the Nuclear Age," in *Securing Our Planet*

Transforming Our Consciousness

Peace is at hand! As a thought, a desire, a suggestion, as a power working in silence, it is everywhere, in every heart. If each one of us opens his heart to it, if each one of us firmly resolves to serve the cause of peace, to communicate his thought and intimations of peace—if every man of good will decides to devote himself exclusively for a little while to clearing away the obstacles, the barriers to peace, then we shall have peace.

—Hermann Hesse

petitive, achievement-oriented Western industrial paradigm that called for a reperception of reality, for a better vision of the planetary future. Because the nuclear impasse presents us with a situation which is so obviously insane, it may also furnish the incentive to break through our own resistances and reperceive our own destiny.

Are there grounds for optimism? Do we have enough time? Those are probably unprofitable questions. The one question that matters is: how am I investing my life?

It matters what we think about peace (Nagler and Capra), about social change (Ferguson), and about adversaries (Harman). It also matters what we believe about the nature of human evolution. Is it simply mechanistic, or is there, in the words of William James, a "cosmic consciousness . . . into which our several minds plunge as into a mother sea"? A leading figure in transpersonal psychology, Roger Walsh here shows how the goal of self-awareness set by the "perennial philosophy" can help us not only to survive the present world crisis but also to find a satisfying, enlivening purpose. Those who think mainly in terms of "crisis control centers" and a new round of "arms control" negotiations may find it irrelevant to consider cosmic consciousness. They may bring up the old line, "If you intend to wait till human nature changes, you will need a soft cushion." But this retort rests upon a very narrow view of what human nature has shown itself capable of. Recently two members of Ark were hooked up to state-of-the-art biofeedback equipment programmed to distinguish alpha waves. In the brain, alpha is associated with creativity, intuition, and bliss. In a single week, trainees can use the feedback to teach themselves to increase sharply the incidence of alpha waves—to control a basic aspect of the electrical activity in their brains. Soon a highly sensitive unit may become available to the same market that made a runaway success of the Sony Walkman. It's a long jump from alpha waves to world peace but we should not be too quick to limit our definition of human nature.

An Evolutionary View

Roger Walsh

A human being is part of the whole called by us universe, a part limited in time and space. He experiences himself, his thoughts and feelings as something separated from the rest, a kind of optical delusion of his consciousness. This delusion is a kind of prison for us, restricting us to our personal desires and to affection for a few persons nearest to us. Our task must be to free ourselves from this prison by widening our circle of compassion to embrace all living creatures and the whole of nature in its beauty.
—Albert Einstein

285

Transforming Our Consciousness

The farther back you can look, the farther forward you are likely to see.

—Winston Churchill

FOR THE FIRST TIME IN MILLIONS OF years of evolution, all the major threats to our survival are human-caused. Problems such as the population explosion, starvation, resource depletion, ecological imbalances, and nuclear weapons all stem directly from our behavior and can therefore be traced largely to psychological origins. This means that the current global threats to human survival and wellbeing are actually *symptoms* of our individual and shared states of mind. These "symptoms" reflect and express the faulty beliefs and perceptions, fears and fantasies, defenses and denials which shape and misshape our individual and collective behavior. The state of the world, in other words, reflects the state of our minds; our collective crises mirror our collective consciousness. That same consciousness which both created and was created by our millions of years of evolution now stands threatened by its own remarkable, though incomplete, success.

Clearly we have created a world situation which appears to demand unprecedented psychological and social maturation for our survival. Until now we have been able to cover or compensate for our psychological shortcomings. We've been able to consume without fear of depletion, discard wastes without fear of pollution, bear children without fear of overpopulation, and fight without fear of extinction. We have been able to act out our psychological immaturities rather than having to understand and outgrow them, to indulge our addictions rather than resolve them, and to revolve through the same neurotic patterns rather than evolve out of them. But if all the world is a stage, it is no longer a big enough one for us to continue playing out our psychological immaturities. It is time for us to grow up, and we ourselves have created the situation which may force us to do so.

This growing up which is demanded of us, this psychological maturation, this development of consciousness, is a form of evolution. For evolution is of both bodies and minds, of matter and consciousness.[1] "Evolution is an ascent towards consciousness," wrote Teilhard de Chardin, a view which has been echoed by Eastern thinkers such as Aurobindo, who thought that "evolution of consciousness is the central motive of terrestrial existence" and that our next evolutionary step would be "a change of consciousness."

Moreover, this evolution is of a new kind. For it is conscious evolution; a conscious choosing of our future, driven by necessity but steered by choice. "Man occupies the crest of the evolutionary wave," said Aurobindo. "With him occurs the passage from an unconscious to a conscious evolution."[2] This is not only evolution but the evolution of evolution.

Because it demands greater development and maturation of us, our global crisis may therefore function as an evolutionary catalyst. Necessity may be the mother not only of invention but also of evolution. This gives us a very, very different view of our situation. For from this perspective our current crisis can be seen not as an unmitigated disaster but as an evolutionary challenge, not just as a pull to regression and extinction but as a push to

We're not going to get rid of the knowledge of how to create nuclear weapons and so we then have to take the legitimacy away, not only from war, but even from preparation for war, because otherwise the nuclear weapons are always there in the background; when somebody gets desperate enough they will be rebuilt. We now are in a period in which it's fashionable to be very cynical about this and say, "Well, you know, human nature is what it is and we will never get rid of war, and so the best we can do is to try to reduce the number of nuclear weapons and to control them as best we can." Well, that won't do. That won't do for my children, my grandchildren; it won't do at all.

—Willis Harman on audio cassette, "Beyond the Boundaries"

new evolutionary heights. It can be seen as a call to each and every one of us, both individually and collectively, to become and contribute as much as we can. This perspective gives us both a vision of the future and a motive for working toward it.

But, it might be argued, isn't this image idealistic? Yes, indeed it is! But this is by no means bad. For on one hand our situation seems to demand nothing less than this, and on the other, idealistic images can be very helpful if used skillfully.

Unfortunately, our usual use of ideals is far from skillful. On one hand we tend to regard them as hopelessly unattainable and either scoff or give up in despair. On the other, we use them as excuses for punishing ourselves whenever we don't attain them. Either approach is a good way of ensuring ourselves more pain.

But there is a more skillful way of using ideals. This is to see them not just as goals which must be reached, but as guiding images or visions which provide signposts and directions for our lives and decisions. Such images attract us to actualize them and ourselves.

This is the way in which we need to view the evolutionary image of our current situation and the developmental advances it might elicit. It is crucial that we not automatically dismiss them as hopelessly idealistic. Rather, we need to see them as possibilities offering guidance and direction for escaping our current quandary and for realizing our potentials as both individuals and as a species.

This challenge of individual maturation

It would seem as though common sense and reason ought to find a way to reach agreement in every conflict of honest interests. I myself think it our bounden duty to believe in such international rationality as possible. But, as things stand, I see how desperately hard it is to bring the peace-party and the war-party together, and I believe that the difficulty is due to certain deficiencies in the program of pacificism which set the militarist imagination strongly, and to a certain extent justifiably, against it. In the whole discussion both sides are on imaginative and sentimental ground. It is but one utopia against another, and everything one says must be abstract and hypothetical.

—William James,
"The Moral Equivalent of War," in *Securing Our Planet*

288

and evolutionary advance may be one of the most fulfilling tasks we can undertake. For this pull to greater awareness, to actualize our full potential, and to transcend our present limits may be a major human motive. At least humanistic, transpersonal, Jungian, Eastern, and certain existential psychologists think so. "The basic actualizing tendency is the only motive which is postulated in this system," said the great humanistic psychologist Carl Rogers.[3]

To fulfill this desire may therefore be deeply rewarding. Failing to fulfill it, on the other hand, may result not only in a failure of growth, but in a particular kind of psychological suffering, a kind which often goes unrecognized. For when these actualizing needs go ungratified their effects are subtle, existential, and therefore less easily identified. "In general, they have been discussed through the centuries by religionists, historians, and philosophers under the rubric of spiritual or religious shortcomings, rather than by physicians, scientists, or psychologists," said Abraham Maslow.[4] He called them "metapathologies" and described such examples as alienation, meaninglessness, and cynicism, as well as various existential, philosophical, and religious crises. Yet these are the very symptoms which have plagued Western societies increasingly in recent decades[5] and which contribute to the growing sense of social unrest. In other words, the very immaturities and failures of psychological growth from which stem our global crises may also be central to the prevailing psychological malaise of our time.

A perspective which sees our global cri-

As we fall asleep tonight, we can envision tomorrow lived in such a spirit of aliveness. This spirit will be expressed by reaching out and connecting from the heart with everyone possible, in an appropriate way. Our hearts thus will expand until we actually experience a magnificent space within. At that moment we can join our hearts with all hearts around the globe offered in the same way. Soon we will be able to contain the entire planet within the chambers of our hearts, for compassion extends beyond space and time. Through this act of practical compassion for ourselves and for others, the habit of struggle will fade into vague memories as the new spirit of living compassion gains momentum. It begins with me and with you.

—LaUna Huffines

ses as potential evolutionary catalysts may therefore help in several ways. Research shows that when people face a life-threatening crisis they feel a desperate need to restore their self-esteem by attempting to regain mastery of the situation and finding some sense of meaning in it.[6]

An evolutionary view meets these needs well. It provides a sense of meaning on a grand scale; a scale which encompasses the totality of contemporary threats, includes individuals and the entire species, and transcends all traditional national and political boundaries. It enhances self-esteem by seeing our current situation, not as final proof of human inadequacy and futility, but rather as a self-created challenge speeding us on our evolutionary journey. It motivates us to regain mastery of the situation and in the process demands that we fulfill our individual and collective potential far more than at any time in history. It also provides an antidote to the metapathologies of purposelessness and alienation which have been growing in developed countries during recent decades.

"By their own theories of human nature, psychologists have the power of elevating or degrading that same nature," wrote Allport. "Debasing assumptions debase human beings; generous assumptions exalt them."[7] An evolutionary perspective appears to provide a meaningful and inspiring view of our contemporary predicament and to exalt human nature at the same time.

Such a perspective is also similar to those which have occurred at other times of great

Perhaps we can all agree that peace means the absence of war. However, is it the absence of conflict? Is a peaceful world one in which there is no conflict? If so, is such a world possible? Earth is made up of a wonderful diversity of different forms of life. Must this diversity be reduced so that any conflicts due to differences are also eliminated? A world without difference, though, is a world that has no life at all, no interaction, no change or growth. It is a world of death. Perhaps the peaceful world is by necessity the dead one? Few would think so. Peace cannot be equated with sterility and an unchanging passivity. Peace cannot be such a fragile quality that the least amount of challenge can shatter it. Rather, it is a robust power that

290

transformation. Analyses of the few truly major transformations of human self-image throughout history suggest that they have all included a broad-ranging synthesis of knowledge and an evolutionary view of humankind.[8] The first order of business for humanity, said the great thinkers such as Plato and Thomas Aquinas who sparked these transformations, is to align ourselves with this evolution.

But where is this evolution taking us? What is our destiny in the universe? To answer this is to go beyond objective facts and to state our personal philosophy, our faith, and our worldview.

The two extremes are probably represented by materialism and "the perennial philosophy," the central core of understanding common to the great religions. To the materialist perspective, life and consciousness are accidental by-products of matter, and their evolution is driven by the interplay of random events and the instinct for survival. The purpose of human life and evolution is solely what humanity decides it is.

The perennial philosophy, which lies at the heart of the great religions and is increasingly said to represent their deepest thinking,[9] suggests a very different view. It views consciousness as central and its development as the primary goal of existence. This development is said to culminate in the condition variously known in different traditions as enlightenment, liberation, salvation, *moksha*, or *satori*.

The descriptions of this condition show remarkable similarities across cultures and cen-

embraces conflict and transforms it into fuel for...growth, unfoldment, life. It does not ask that we eliminate differences nor even tolerate them but that we use them creatively, willingly, zestfully in celebration of the richness of creation and the presence of new potentials. In this context, I would offer my image of peace: peace is the resolution of conflict in ways that are mutually empowering to all concerned. Violence or war, in whatever form it takes, whether physical or psychological, is the perpetuation of conflict in the guise of resolving it. Peace is the ability to accept and embrace conflict and not be threatened by it and thereby to use it in the interests of life.

—David Spangler

291

Peace is a state of heart. When we live in the familiar reality of struggle, frustration, and resulting anger, we have grave difficulty imagining a reality of stability, strength, and joyful feeling. Yet we have had this experience too, and when we do, we know that it is as real as struggle. And we want others to enjoy it. Each moment we live in this world of reality we are creating a new level of peace. When we awaken with delight for our lives, everything and everyone around us appear to have changed. We feel grateful to be connected once again to our self and to the world. Our state of

turies.[10] Its essence is said to be the recognition that the distortions of our usual state of mind are such that we have been suffering from a case of mistaken identity. Our true nature is said to be something much greater, an aspect of a universal consciousness, Self, Being, Mind, or God. The awakening to this true nature, claimed a Zen master, is "the direct awareness that you are more than this puny body or limited mind. Stated negatively, it is the realization that the universe is not external to you. Positively, it is experiencing the universe as yourself."[11]

Similar descriptions could be found in almost any culture. Typical is the claim by an Englishman that to realize our true identity is to "find that the I, one's real, most intimate self, pervades the universe and all other beings. That the mountains, and the sea, and the stars are a part of one's body, and that one's soul is in touch with the souls of all creatures."[12] Nor are such descriptions the exclusive province of mystics. They have been echoed by philosophers, psychologists, and physicists.[13] "Out of my experience . . . one final conclusion dogmatically emerges," said the great American philosopher William James.[14] "There is a continuum of cosmic consciousness against which our individuality builds but accidental forces, and into which our several minds plunge as into a mother sea."

From this perspective evolution is a vast journey of growing self-awareness and return to our true identity.[15] Our current crises are seen as expressions of the mistaken desires, fears, and perceptions which arise from our mistaken identity. But they can also be seen as self-created challenges which may speed us on our evolutionary journey toward ultimate self-recognition.

Which worldview is correct? Are we solely survival-driven animals or are we also awakening Gods? How can we decide? Both worldviews give answers which are similar and different: similar in that they both tell us to research and explore, different in what they tell us to explore. For the worldview of materialism says to explore the physical universe and thereby ourselves; the perennial philosophy says to explore our own minds and consciousness and thereby the universe. In practical terms it seems crucial that we do both. Our survival and evolution require no less than that we deepen our understanding of both the universe within and the universe without.[16]

Whichever worldview we adopt, then, still allows us to see our contemporary crossroads as an evolutionary challenge calling us to choose and create our destiny. That challenge asks of us that we relinquish our former limits, and be and become and contribute all that we can. It calls us to play our full part in the unfolding human drama which we ourselves have created and asks that we choose, both individually and collectively, something entirely new: conscious evolution.

In the words of Duane Elgin, "hard material necessity and human evolutionary possibility now seem to converge to create a situation where, in the long run, we will be obliged to do no less than realize our greatest possibilities. We are engaged in a race between self-

appreciation simultaneously connects us to others as well. Opportunities to bridge the gap that separated us were there the day before, but through our focus upon fears and struggle, we didn't see them. Every time we experience gratitude, it rapidly spreads into new directions. We're building a framework for true peace in the world as this gratitude becomes constant in our lives.

—LaUna Huffines, author of *Connecting With All the People in Your Life*

discovery and self-destruction. The forces that may converge to destroy us are the same forces that may foster societal and self-discovery."[17]

1. Wilber, K. *Up from Eden*. New York: Doubleday, 1981.
2. Aurobindo, A. *The Future Evolution of Man*. India: All India Press, 1963.
3. Rogers, C. "A Theory of Therapy, Personality, and Interpersonal Relationships as Developed in the Client-Centered Framework," in S. Koch (Ed.), *Psychology: the Study of a Science: Formulations of the Person and the Social Context: Vol. 3* (pp. 184–256), New York: McGraw-Hill, 1959.
4. Maslow, A.H. *The Farther Reaches of Human Nature*. New York: Viking Press, 1971 (pp.316–317).
5. Yalom, I. *Existential Psychotherapy*. New York: Basic Books, 1980.
6. Taylor, S. "Adjustment to Threatening Events: A Theory of Cognitive Events," *American Psychologist*, 1983, *38*, 1161–1173.
7. Allport, G.W. "The Fruits of Eclecticism: Bitter or Sweet," *Acta Psychologica*, 1964, *23*, 27–44.
8. Mumford, L. *The Transformations of Man*. New York: Harper Brothers, 1956.
9. Huxley, A. *The Perennial Philosophy*. New York: Harper & Row, 1944; Smith, H. *Forgotten Truth*. New York: Harper & Row, 1976; Wilber, K. *Up from Eden*. New York: Doubleday, 1981; Wilber, K. *A Sociable God: A Brief Introduction to a Transcendental Sociology*. New York: McGraw-Hill, 1983.
10. Walsh, R. and Vaughan, F. (Eds.). *Beyond Ego: Transpersonal Dimensions in Psychology*, Los Angeles: J.P. Tarcher, 1980; Walsh, R. and Shapiro, D. (Eds.). *Beyond Health and Normality: Explorations of Exceptional Psychological Well-being*. New York: Van Nostrand, 1983; Shapiro, D. and Walsh, R. (Eds.). *Meditation: Classic and Contemporary Perspectives*. New York: Aldine, 1984; Wilber, K. *The Spectrum of Consciousness*. Wheaton, Ill.: Quest, 1977; Wilber, K. *The Atman Project*. Wheaton, Ill.: Quest, 1980.
11. Kapleau, P. *The Three Pillars of Zen*. Boston: Beacon Press, 1965 (p.143).
12. Harman, W. "An Evolving Society to Fit an Evolving Consciousness," *Integral View*, 1979, *14*.

13. Wilber, K. *Up from Eden*, 1984; and K. Wilber (Ed.). *Quantum Questions: The Mystical Writings of the World's Great Physicists*. Boulder, Colo.: New Science Library/Shambhala.
14. James, W., in G. Murphy and R. Ballou (Eds.). *Psychical Research*. New York: Viking, 1960 (p.324).
15. Wilber, K. *Up from Eden*. New York: Doubleday, 1981.
16. Walsh, R. *Staying Alive: The Psychology of Human Survival*. Boulder, Colo.: Shambhala, 1984.
17. Elgin, D. "The Tao of Personal and Social Transformation," in R. Walsh and F. Vaughan (Eds.). *Beyond Ego: Transpersonal Dimensions in Psychology*. Los Angeles: J.P. Tarcher, 1980 (pp. 248–256).

296   **Detail of "Peace Trek" image created by Diane and Joel Schatz**

Jumping Ahead and Looking Back at the Future

5

There's a well-known story I've always loved, about a Maine farmer who, when asked by a tourist how to get to Boston, says simply, "Can't get there from here." Trying to work for peace, many of us have felt the gap implied by the hayseed's rebuff. If he'd ever *been* to Boston he could tell the way, of course, but to him it's no-place—literally a "utopia." Unless he's just spoofing the tourist, the farmer has never ever *imagined* his way to Boston. If he had, the tourist might craftily seek help by saying, "Well, pretend that you were *in* Boston: how would you get back here to the farm?"

That's the strategy of the contributors to this section. First they imagine the utopia they wish to reach: they pretend it already exists, and that we've somehow reached it. They pause to enjoy it. The place seems real. Instead of restricting themselves to the barnyard of our present reality, they walk in their minds along Beacon Street. Then they make the second move: given that the city exists, they say, "How did we get here?" They discover a route. The more serious they are, the more care they take to work out the way in detail.

I call this "jumping ahead and looking back at the future." It's usually difficult to imagine what to do tomorrow—or even worse, today—in order to move toward an abstract goal, especially if you have doubts about its practicality. A journey of a hundred miles *does* begin with a single step, but often the motivation arises from, and the direction is likewise set by, imagining the goal.

Vividly imagining a favorable future, as if you were already living in it, has several benefits. You have an opportunity to discover what you most desire, in the way you enjoy the plot of a novel rather than in the way you may admire an abstract proposal. And since you feel as if you're already living there, instead of worrying about its possibility, your mind automatically acts as if a way exists from where you actually are to the place you're imagining. "Of course you can get here from there," it says.

297

Jumping Ahead and Looking Back at the Future

As a methodology of hope, jumping ahead and looking back at the future runs the risk of febrile utopianism. I was reminded of this in the summer of 1985 in Berlin at the annual meeting of the International Institute of Strategic Studies, which brings together academics, government officials, think-tank analysts, and journalists concerned with the defense of Western Europe. Instead of imagining how peace could be brought to the heart of Europe, they were quite properly discussing such unpleasant questions as what would happen if the Soviets were to launch a blitzkrieg toward the Rhine. The answer according to the commander of NATO, who has made the same point in public, is that the U.S. would very soon be reduced to either surrendering the territory or using nuclear weapons.

At that conference I was reading a book called *Hawks, Doves, & Owls: An Agenda for Avoiding Nuclear War*, written by three professors at Harvard University's John F. Kennedy School of Government.* They make many excellent suggestions, but at the end, after discussing alternatives to nuclear deterrence, they throw up their hands, saying "these observations offer only a little comfort." Avoiding the trap of unchecked utopianism, they warn that "well-intentioned efforts to escape [some reliance on nuclear deterrence] before conditions are appropriate could make nuclear war more likely." In short, you *can* get there from here but you very well might crash on the way and die horribly.

Since this is really not enough hope to sustain a vibrant civilization, the professors call for "bold, creative approaches," warning that "the community of defense and foreign policy specialists must resist cynicism toward nontraditional concepts, misplaced confidence that all of the important ideas have been examined, and condescension to newcomers from other fields." In fact, the authors go so far as to counsel that the beginning of wisdom is "humility," which in Cambridge is strong medicine.

---

*Graham T. Allison, Albert Carnesale, and Joseph S. Nye, Jr., editors, *Hawks, Doves, & Owls: An Agenda for Avoiding Nuclear War* (W. W. Norton & Co., 1985), page 246.

Jumping Ahead and Looking Back at the Future

In this section, contributors give at least a rough draft of an alternative to all the "scenarios" common to the field of national security. In general, the latter scripts are driven by fear, follow a route laid out by extrapolation, and never leave the paradigm where they began. To get anywhere that we really want to go is going to require all the data, analytical skills, and ingenuity of the specialists— inspired, however, by an imagination that's able to jump ahead and look back at the future.

Seldom are the requisite faculties of mind found in a single person. A methodology needs to be developed in which ways of thinking that usually devalue one another can, instead, inspire and discipline one another.

At college I had an experience of both the difficulties and rewards of this process. From various sources, I happened to hear about a number of different programs that sent young Americans to work in "underdeveloped" countries, as they were still being called. Typically, the participants were college-age, willing to learn an exotic language and work in simple (not to say primitive) surroundings, all for very little financial reward. What they *did* get was experience of a radically different culture and the satisfaction of helping share something they knew how to do, whether it was speaking English, teaching sanitation, planting hybrid seed, or whatever.

It occured to me that the U.S. government could create a similar program, on a vastly larger scale. This was in 1960. John F. Kennedy was making a bid for the Presidency, and I was then filling the same editorial post on the *Harvard Crimson* that JFK had reportedly held years before. After meeting through this connection, we had worked together successfully on a piece of Federal legislation. I made use of this acquaintance to urge that he propose, in his campaign, what soon became the Peace Corps.

The story is germane here because, in developing the idea, I encountered considerable scepticism among friends and among some of the experts whom I interviewed. They said young people liked idealistic gestures but would pull back when asked to spend a few years in an isolated village. They said the cultural gap would be too wide to allow Americans who had come of age in Eisenhower's suburbs to contribute anything useful to people in Columbia, Kenya, or Thailand, where annual family cash income wouldn't pay for the stereos enjoyed by the American kids. They said the Soviets would accuse the volunteers of being spies and thus would wreck the entire program. They said Americans are so bad at learning foreign languages that communication would be next to impossible. They said many things.

I felt discouraged. At that point, I decided to set aside all the objections for a while and to imagine how the program, in a particular place, might ideally work. I jumped ahead, and nourished by the vision, I was confident enough to think of ways to start dealing with the intermediary steps. Later, as I met others who contributed to the idea of the Peace Corps, I found several using a similar technique.

Of course the arms race and chronic enmity between the U.S. and Soviet Union are difficulties on a scale vastly greater than anything faced by the founders of the Peace Corps. In many ways the superpowers are stuck. It's obvious that the problem will not be solved primarily be extrapolation from where we are. In the absence of a larger vision, any steps seem to involve risk and confusion greater than the benefits they promise in the short run.

It's not enough for the superpowers to be toying with the idea of "arms control." In some respects they'd obviously be much better off if they'd both stopped at the level of minimal deterrence, such as the U.S. achieved more than 20 years ago. But the terrible threat of arms can't be approached solely, or even mainly, in terms of hardware. Peace is a political question. It's a system-shift. As long as the superpowers relate mainly in terms of "arms control," crucial as it is, they will continue to be caught within the same dynamic of mutual menace.

In personal life a system-shift occurs, for example, when two people decide to stop a feud, to bury the past instead of each other. Usually the "reasons" that had so entangled them are then left behind in the relief of stopping the hostilities; they may even become friends. In intellectual life it's a system-shift when you always thought one way, and now you see things in a different light. In international life, it's a system-shift when two countries—such as France and

Germany or the U.S. and Japan—decide to compete economically instead of bombing one another.

A systems-shift has the quality of a leap. It crosses old boundaries. It calls for a decision, accompanied often by the question, "Why not?" All of us have done this in some way, to some degree. It does not always work out well. But whenever it does, a new world is created.

In our relations with the Soviet Union, a systems-shift is needed. Instead of our best minds restricting themselves to the question of how to threaten the other side more convincingly, gain marginal advantages, and perhaps restrain the worst effects of the arms race, we need a new image of what we could build together. The national security elites on both sides tend to reject this suggestion. The Soviets may dismiss it as "utopianism," totally divorced from the concrete reality created by economic interests and the correlation of military forces. Western thinkers may scorn it as "sentimentalism" or as "flakiness" (induced, perhaps, by proximity to the San Andreas fault).

In the face of such responses, we must recall the warning of the Harvard authors about "cynicism toward nontraditional approaches" and "condescension to newcomers from other fields." Can the present system truly assure our security over the long run? Data gathered by researchers at Brown University show that nuclear war is predicted by a much smaller percentage of "experts" than of the general public. I suspect that analysts dependent solely upon rational analysis assume the world will behave reasonably; it's their bias. Another war that couldn't possibly have started was World War I. In contrast, ordinary citizens live in the world of Murphy's Law: "If something can go wrong, it eventually will."

The contributors to this section are all saying, "If something can be clearly imagined as going right, it might."

—Craig Comstock

While an undergraduate at Harvard, one of the Ark staff recalls sneaking into a graduate seminar conducted by Henry Kissinger. A roly-poly guest was addressing the class, recounting what he called "scenarios" to illustrate the outcomes of nuclear strategy. As he spoke rapidly and with blackly lambent wit about "acceptable" levels of death and destruction, he appeared as a kind of stand-up comedian of the apocalypse. His name was Herman Kahn. Part of his genius lay in accustoming listeners to "think about the unthinkable," to stop acting as if nuclear war could never happen. In this regard, his scenarios were an aid to the imagination. Now the world dramatized by Kahn is easily "thinkable." What some of us find harder to imagine is long-term survival, much less a better world. Author of *Beyond the Bomb* (Expro Press/The Talman Company, 1985), Mark Sommer proposes a form of "political science fiction" in which scenarios would describe not Kahn's "ladder of escalation," but various pathways to peace.

Spinning Peace Scenarios

Mark Sommer

WHEN I WAS FIRST LEARNING TO SPLIT wood fifteen years ago in British Columbia, I used to have a devilish time breaking open the two-foot rounds of alder and oak in my woodpile. The axe would prance across the surface of the dense green wood without the slightest inclination to enter and divide. Sometimes it would simply glance off the round and land on my boot, where it did indeed threaten to enter and divide. There were times during that first frigid winter's apprenticeship when I thought I'd simply expire before splitting enough wood to warm myself and my food. After many a humiliating hour of ebbing energy and eroding confidence, I approached Jim Campbell, the farmer on whose land I was living, to ask his advice.

Jumping Ahead and Looking Back at the Future

"How in God's name do you get your axe through this impenetrable stuff?" I pleaded.

He smiled, amused at my frustration. "Easy," he said. "The reason you can't do it is because you don't *think* you can. Stand with the axe in your hand and the round in front of you. Now, gazing at the wood, imagine your axe head not at the top of the round, glancing off, but all the way down at the bottom, having already split it. If your imagination is good enough, you'll strike it hard enough to do the job."

I tried his advice, and to my surprise it worked. My strength grew and my aim improved with my rising confidence, all fueled by a sturdy, positive imagination. In the years since, I've gained enough skill in the art of wood-splitting that I no longer need to boost my strength with my imagination, but I have applied Jim Campbell's advice to a variety of other challenges I've faced and have found it effective in every instance. It is more than an exercise in fantasy, a mental sleight-of-hand, or a different kind of confidence game. If done well, it becomes a means of clearing space, in yourself and in the world around you, for new and hitherto seemingly impossible things to happen. It is a means of stretching beyond your known capabilities by overleaping your self-doubts and placing yourself in the circumstances of imagined success. Confident that the feat is indeed possible, you find yourself acting with sufficient resolution to overcome all obstacles.

It seems to me that this technique has more than a little to offer us in the challeng-

The wild places are where we began. When they end, so do we.

—David Brower

In this world the one thing supremely worth having is the opportunity to do well and worthily a piece of work of vital consequence to the welfare of mankind.

—Theodore Roosevelt

303

ing process of inventing alternatives to the war system. The general public is not alone in wondering whether peace is actually possible. Even professional peace researchers, surveying the drift of recent events, find it difficult to muster much confidence that our proposals will be adopted anytime soon. So prevalent is despair in the profession of peace work that many of us may be unaware of the degree to which we doubt the very possibilities we strive to create.

This skepticism communicates itself in a great many ways—in an overdeveloped capacity for critical analysis and an underdeveloped capacity for generating alternatives, in an overused intellect and an underused imagination, in reactive rather than initiatory politics. Like the public at large, we tend to view peace as the poor orphaned sister of war, a state of being without substance or reality of its own, a merely hypothetical possibility. We are so certain of failure that we hobble our imaginations at the very moment when we most need to unfetter them.

It seems to me that at this point, something more than linear and logical thinking is in order, something more on the order of what Edward de Bono calls "lateral thinking." The only means by which we can overcome the debilitating despair brought on by a sober appraisal of the odds against us is to engage in a deliberate overleaping of the obstacles between "here" and "there," to place ourselves in the territory of peace itself—or, in the case of the wood-splitting, to imagine the axe head resting in the chopping block, having travelled

People are always blaming their circumstances for what they are. I don't believe in circumstances. The people who get on in this world are they who get up and look for the circumstances they want, and, if they can't find them, make them.

—George Bernard Shaw

clear through the round. We can then begin to survey the territory into which we've ventured, noting what it looks like, feeling how it feels. Having premised the possibility of peace in a given circumstance, we find our minds and hearts liberated to engage in the practical consideration of how to find our way back to the present from that premised future.

This approach is not to be mistaken for daydreaming or fantasy. On the contrary, once the radical assumption has been made that peace is indeed possible, we must demonstrate an exceptional rigor in evaluating the most plausible means of reaching that state. All that we know of current trends and past history, all that we know of the personalities and predilections of the powers and peoples involved, must come into play in figuring practical means of moving between here and there. We thus simultaneously exercise those two faculties most often at odds with one another, imagination and intellect. The imagination stretches the boundaries prescribed by the intellect while the intellect disciplines the otherwise anarchic character of the imagination.

It is no small irony that this technique has thus far found its most extensive development not in planning for peace but in planning for war. The late Herman Kahn, longtime dean of defense intellectuals, devoted his considerable intellect and curious imagination to the exploration of "unthinkable" nuclear war scenarios. He called his method "Gedanken" (thought) experiments, hypothetical inquiries into the likely consequences of undertaking various strategies in a pro-

Let me exhort everyone to do their utmost to think outside and beyond our present circle of ideas. For every idea gained is a hundred years of slavery remitted.

—Richard Jefferies

305

longed but limited nuclear war. While we may justifiably differ with Kahn's use or abuse of intellect and imagination to test assumptions which are themselves too utterly repugnant to contemplate, we may also respect the rigor of his method and the sometimes startling objectivity of his observations.

As a means of considering policy options in the midst of a prolonged nuclear exchange, Kahn would set up a hypothetical circumstance, place his actors where he wanted them in order to evaluate the effects of his policy choice, then set the scene in motion and observe how they moved, given his knowledge of their past behavior and present tendencies. In Kahn's method, one's speculations move only forward, from a hypothetical future towards a still more distant future. But in the case of a peace scenario, one would premise a future, then work back towards the present moment and thrash one's way through the thicket of obstacles from "here" to "there."

I would like to propose that specialists in peace work consider developing and using peace scenarios as one tool for the construction of alternatives to nuclear deterrence. It is an approach ideally suited to group work. Scenarios may be invented either by the individual or the group, but a group process, involving as it does the mingling of diverse perspectives, might be especially well suited to testing the validity of scenarios. Through collective critical analysis, the group may jointly appraise what is likely to happen and what is simply not. As an integral step in the exercise, the "price of admission to the game,"

To make no mistakes is not in the power of man; but from their errors and mistakes the wise and good learn wisdom for the future.

—Plutarch

the group would be responsible for providing more plausible versions of those events it does not find credible. The group would thus undertake a collective invention, guiding itself in equal measure by the faculties of intellect and imagination.

How does this approach differ from techniques of research and analysis already in use? In a few essential respects, it employs techniques that have already proven successful in other contexts. Elise Boulding's and Warren Ziegler's imaging workshops, designed for use with the general public, have elicited much interest in the limited community in which they've been tried. But the technique has never, to my knowledge, been applied to a group of specialists with the expertise to evaluate the plausibility of scenarios. In addition, the method has not been applied as a problem-solving technique for specific cases of conflict but rather as a general proposition: How did peace come to us by the year X?

The more traditional mode of analysis and policy proposal has always been a work of the intellect. World order studies, which have projected "preferred worlds" and "relevant utopias," have been characterized by a high degree of abstraction which, despite their merit, renders them difficult both to evaluate and to penetrate. Adding imagination to intellect gives us tangible imagery to clothe otherwise barren policy options. But much more significantly, imagination adds an unpredictable and highly creative element to the mix, a lateral mode of thinking to complement the linear mode of critical policy analysis.

Apathy can only be overcome by enthusiasm, and enthusiasm can only be aroused by two things: first, an ideal which takes the imagination by storm, and second, a definite intelligible plan for carrying that ideal into practice.

—Arnold Toynbee

307

Jumping Ahead and Looking Back at the Future

Every breeze wafts intelligence from country to country, every wave rolls it and gives it forth, and all in turn receive it. There is a vast commerce of ideas, there are marts and exchanges for intellectual discoveries, and a wonderful fellowship of those individual intelligences which make up the minds and opinions of the age.

—Daniel Webster

There are two ways of spreading light: to be the candle or the mirror that reflects it.

—Edith Wharton

What I am suggesting is that we create a kind of political science fiction—that is, that we unite the three disciplines of politics, science, and the imaginative arts to evoke and evaluate the various possible routes to a sustainable peace. From politics we take a sober recognition of the primacy of self-interest and a shrewd strategy for making the highest use of that lowly motivation; from science, an objective evaluation of the risks and benefits of each choice; and from the arts, their animating quality, their capacity to evoke illuminating imagery and resonant feeling. Like science fiction, political science fiction would concern the future, but not a narrowly technical one; unlike science fiction, it would be specifically designed as a problem-solving technique, a conscious instrument of social invention.

William Faulkner once confided to an interviewer that he did not always feel immediately at home with the figures he invented in his novels. He would start by willing his characters and scenes into existence by a highly deliberate and admittedly artificial process of appointment. But at a certain juncture in each novel ("right about page 357," he testified), he would watch in astonishment while his characters rose up and claimed the story from him. Then he knew he had one—a live possibility. We may likewise find it necessary to conjure up a good many peace scenarios before we evolve even just a few with a passing chance of making history. But the process of invention will reward us richly in insights. And maybe also in making a few of those histories real.

"Jumping ahead and looking back at the future," the title for this section, describes the workshops on social imaging led by Elise Boulding, one of the deans of peace studies. Here she not only describes how the workshops proceed, but also the benefits and limitations of them and the range of specific images generated in them. Alongside the chapter run a series of excerpts from writing by Chellis Glendinning, a San Francisco psychologist who has led many similar workshops. The chapter is illustrated with details from the "Peace Trek" image created by Diane and Joel Schatz, who asked many respondents for their visions of a peaceful world—visions that Diane juxtaposed graphically, thus complementing the verbal accounts of Boulding and Glendinning.

Enlivening Our Social Imagination

Elise Boulding

IN FOCUSSED SOCIAL IMAGING, A person is being asked to engage with a group of colleagues in work on behalf of normatively defined social goals. They begin with agreement on shared social concerns such as reducing community violence, improving community health services or finding new economic opportunities for unemployed youth. Each person is then asked to step into a future time, say twenty years from the present, in which those concerns have been dealt with. There is a powerful contradiction between the invitation to enter into the free-flowing inner world of mental imagery with its evanescent material that can hardly be handled with hammer and nails and the instruction to *see*

You know, there's one fundamental finding that is more or less neglected in contemporary science because it really doesn't fit in very well. It would fit much better with a different scientific paradigm. It's not neglected in the business world, however, and the world of sports and various other places, and that is the power of the image that is held and the power of the belief that is asserted inwardly. This is the sort of thing that is used in training athletes by having them image perfect performance. It's the sort of thing that business executives learn to do—to hold the positive image—not being too wedded to it that you're going to be crushed if it doesn't come about, but recognizing that when you create a vision you have already set in motion the factors and the forces that will contribute to bringing that vision into fruition.

—Willis Harman
on audio cassette, "A Better Game Than War"

a community in which previously stated goals have been realized. Yet it can be done. The interaction between individual imaging and small group discussion in which each person describes her own imagery and addresses questions to others about their images gradually brings out more and more details about what this future world is like. Further details emerge from the same inner sensory world that the original image came from. Certain features of this reality begin to take on a compelling character as the imager examines them further. Eventually a working group develops shared imagery, and more and more details are built up. The future has not in any way been *determined* by this activity. Rather, participants have discovered that they can visualize an alternative possibility for the future in regard to a pressing social problem.

Imaging a World Without Weapons

Since the arms races of the twentieth century, including the present nuclear arms race, present one of the most urgent crises humanity is now facing, it seems appropriate to try to activate the social imaging through the imaging process in relation to this problem. Experimental workshops have been held in the U.S. over a twelve-month period from September, 1981, to September, 1982. People concerned over the nuclear arms race have come together for sessions varying in length from two hours to two and a half days to try to construct in imagination a viable social order functioning without weapons as conventionally defined. The problem is far more complex than imaging the realization of a simpler type of social goal in one's own community, since it involves accounting for national and international phenomena as well as one's own local scene. Participants have been all ages from the late teens to the eighties. Most have had some college education; a few have completed advanced degrees. Occupations have included farmers, housewives, research scientists, teachers, ministers, artists, community workers.

Detail of "Peace Trek" image created by Diane and Joel Schatz   311

Professional expertise about international relations, arms races and security issues is not called for in these workshops. Those who come with professional expertise as physical or social scientists are asked to set that knowledge to one side—to the degree that they can—since it may evoke a kind of reasoning that will block the imagery of the totally other. When Fred Polak first conceived his ideas about imaging a future, he made a careful distinction between social planning, blueprints, next-stepism, and other types of near-term thinking, and imaging the totally other. As a planner himself for the postwar Dutch government, facing the ruins of destroyed cities, he felt that social despair could not be dealt with only by means of blueprints for factories. There had to be a vision of a new social order for Europe, something to aspire to, something to work for. The human mind had to make a breach in time, Polak said, and envision what might lie on the far side of the breach. Blueprints would come later.

The concept of a breach in time is not only a poetic flight of fancy but an absolute necessity if one is to free the imagination to do its work. If one tries to work toward the future from the present, the known realities cling like tendrils to every new idea, smothering it with awareness of what won't work because of the way things are. This is particularly true in the case of visualizing a weapon-free world, because the world is so highly armed at present that it is almost impossible to imagine that things could be different. The breach in time enables the mind to overleap

In the Nuclear Age we live with no conscious picture of what life might be like in ten or twenty years, or even next month, and we live with the pent-up frustration and fear that such uncertainty elicits. It is as if we exist each moment in the line of fire—with no discernible meaning and no positive end in sight. This vacuum of vision protects us from what we suspect in our deepest selves: that there will be no future, no life in ten or twenty years, or maybe even next month. The purpose of the workshops I give is to restore our future visions—with our feelings, our imaginations, and our actions. We begin by conjuring up the pictures that already inhabit our minds and hearts. We share aloud what many of us have never even admitted to ourselves, and we share our feelings about these visions. Our denial.

312

those local impossibilities that loom so large in the present. There, in the new time-space, the mind can look around and see and hear with the inward eye and ear how things are in a world that we know, by declaration (there must be a willing suspension of disbelief), has no weapons. A thirty-year leap into the future is mandated to allow enough elapsed time for some social change to take place.

This exercise comes only after participants have released the processes of their own mental imagery through recalling childhood scenes and memories. A substantial effort is made to help people visualize stepping physically into the "future present moment" through a gate or doorway so they are *there*. There are no instructions about what to see. The raw materials for that imagery which presents itself comes from many sources, including past experience. The "processing space" inside each individual where imagery is generated remains for us a black box. We know very little about the contents and less about the processes that go on within that box. Because of a deliberate emphasis on personal physical location in the future, the initial imagery tends to be of local community scenes. In the course of a few hours, through repeated consultations and mutual questioning in small groups, the implications for what is witnessed in terms of the character of the larger social order are gradually spelled out: education, political and economic structures, communication patterns, arrangements for the management of conflict and violence. People are encouraged to draw and write about the

Despair. Rage. Terror. Sadness. Our longing for better times. Over and over again, in diverse settings across the country among Americans of different backgrounds, I have found that it is only when we divest ourselves of the visions our world logically leads us to believe—visions of disaster, pollution, and war—that we can invent new, more positive ones.

—Chellis Glendinning

future they see on large sheets of newsprint which are placed on the walls of the meeting room. Groups are formed as soon as commonalities are perceived. Merging different perceptions into a common scenario is a difficult and challenging task but also acts as a testing of the social validity of the images. Can one individual's images make sense to colleagues? Can an image stand up under critical questioning by others?

If we cannot envision the world we would like to live in, we cannot work towards its creation. If we cannot place ourselves in it in our imagination, we will not believe it is possible. As participants in my workshops pass down an imaginary corridor, I ask: What strengths do you bring to this new world? Where is your power? How can you make it possible? A biologist says he is carrying a box of tools. A psychotherapist tells us she brings her understanding of human suffering. A retired naval officer says he offers his experience of working for years close to the danger— on nuclear submarines. A landscaper tells us he brings a soft side: his love of delicate living things, and a hard side: his outrage at injustice.

When this exercise is brought to a close, participants are requested to become historians. They go off individually to record historical happenings from the "future present moment" they have been describing back to the original present. They are encouraged to feel their way from the future back to the present in five-year time spans. Events, in fact, are juggled around chronologically to "make sense." The blend of eidetic imagery and intellectual inquiry which has characterized the work of constructing the future also continues in the tracing of social process back to the present. For many people, process concepts emerge in relation to disarmament that had not been thought of before. If there is time, group future histories are constructed in the same way that group future scenarios were constructed.

How the World of 2012 Looks

What do these essentially middleclass United States citizens of assorted ages see when they enter the world of 2012 in their imaginations? In the description that follows, I have taken materials from the work of several hundred individuals and woven them into a scenario. The result is a composite tapestry of the future, not representing the imagery of any one individual participant in the workshop.

Generally, workshop participants see a very localist world imbued with a strong sense of planetary consciousness, an earth-sense, a Gaia-sense. Often the first image will be of walking about looking relaxed, secure and free from fear. Another image will be of children as visible everywhere in the community and old people as well. What emerges from the descriptions is a composite image of an active local community, more towards the rural end of the rural-urban continuum, consisting of households not unlike the preindustrial French *communautés* or *frèrèches*, or the Eastern European *zadruga*. The emphasis is nearly always on extended family households, whether the households consist of unrelated families living together or a kin-based extended family. Households are often characterized by occupational specialization, and specializations run the gamut from high-technology, computer-based occupations to low-technology craft work. The bulk of work involves human services and social facilitation of various kinds, with a great emphasis on life-long training in conflict resolution skills and the maintenance of community conflict resolution centers. The theme of food is an important one in 2012. Everyone grows some food, whether they live in rural, small-town or urban settings. In cities, shopping malls, garages and roofs of buildings have become vegetable gardens. There is much attention to reclamation of exhausted or polluted soils.

A businessman says he brings his many contacts and his knowledge of organizational development. What is the threshold like? I ask. How do you feel standing before the door to a better world? A scientist tells of an inviting wooden door set into a stone wall, opened just a crack. A construction worker reports a high-tech entrance way with digital numbers, beepers, and flashing lights. To enter he need only punch in the correct code. A teenager reports a teepee flap, portal to a sacred ceremonial ground. Everyone reports feeling excited, expectant, afraid, unprepared, hesitant, grief-stricken, or ecstatic—all feelings natural to personal transition.

—Chellis Glendinning

There is an audible, gentle hum of activity in these communities. People are visible to one another, weave in and out of each other's lives, alternate work and play (a maypole at the center of town is one symbol used) and see education as a life-long activity accompanying their work and play life. Everyone does some teaching, which is why children are seen everywhere, at work places as well as community centers. (Women actually bear few children, because of worldwide population pressures.) There are no age-segregated school buildings. What can't be taught at work is taught at community centers. Men and women share work roles and parenting roles equally but with a yin-yang consciousness of male-female differentiation. Individuality is highly prized in women and men and children and the elderly. The concept of balance between physical, or *bread labor*, and mental, or *spirit labor*, common to traditions as diverse as the Hindu-based Gandhian teachings and the Christian-based Benedictine teachings has reappeared. Everyone does some type of work with their hands (hence the importance of local growing of food) as well as using computers and electronic technology. Many old school, hospital, bank and factory buildings have been turned into multi-use community centers. The arts are used actively in recreation, and there is no spectator-leisure industry.

These are not conflict-free communities, nor are they parochial. Conflict is valued as a source of creativity, growth and development, as an important social resource. Hence, the life-long training, beginning with very

The worlds that participants discover on the other side are remarkably similar. They see rivers, lakes, hills, gardens, windmills, animals. They see people working under clean blue skies; people building, reorganizing, raising food, raising children, teaching, learning, meeting, helping and healing each other; people mediating conflict, dreaming, inventing. Some see

316

young children, in creative management of conflict. There is active awareness of the international community—memories of the conflicts and wars of the twentieth century are still very much alive. Much attention is paid to transnational communication networks of all kinds, with frequent teleconferencing between individuals, special interest groups and sister communities in different parts of the world. Multilinguality is highly valued and emphasized in early childhood training, but computer translation is also available for all international communication. Every university in the world is now an international university, and local communities take pride in the members they have sent to these special international learning centers. Every household is a part of at least one transnational network reflecting the interests of that household. Private transportation is almost nonexistent; but there is much travel between communities by air, sea and land vehicles. All information flows are interactive and two-way, including the mass media.

Governance is slowly emerging at the international level, with much emphasis on regional and local autonomy. The successor structures to the United Nations handle international mediation and arbitration procedures with the help of a consortium of international universities (perhaps successor to the United Nations University?) and administer compliance machinery. Nation states continue to exist; but, with no armies to maintain, they have much smaller budgets. At the national level, as at the international, a great

completely new kinds of buildings and travel ways— domes and earth houses, settlements in circles, cities softened against the planet's curve. To others dwellings and roads look pretty much the same as they are now. What is different is the way people relate to one another, how the government operates, how work is conducted, and how the threat of disaster has disappeared. Such visions are essential. They provide us with psychic containers for our creative energies. They give us guidance as we embark on our journey to make a better future, and healing when we feel bruised by our experiences in a society preparing, or posturing, to fight nuclear war.

—Chellis Glendinning

On the surface our demon was nuclear technology. But it had psychological and social dimensions too. It was our stubbornness. It was our attempts to measure, categorize, name, and tame all of life that is wild, flowing, and unpredictable. It was our life energy denied, displaced, and disembodied. It was our unwillingness to live life with questions. It was our over-emphasis on answers. Our demon, we said, was how we as a society put more weight on national ego than on global survival. It was our myth of material conquest at the expense of the natural balance of nature. It was our society's inability to resolve conflict without violence. It was a system that allowed a few people to determine life and death issues for all people. It was our individual feelings of powerlessness and alienation in the face of the system that created nuclear war.

deal of training in conflict resolution is demanded of all government officials, appointed or elected. Stiff qualifying examinations are given to aspirants to public office. Since self-regulation is the norm at each level within the state, a major function of the national government is to ensure the free flow of information. Secrecy is outlawed, and efforts to hoard information are seen as danger signals for the possibility of the return of physical violence and weaponry. The great emphasis on conflict resolution skills and machinery is not only because of the value of conflict as a developmental resource but because of the need to prevent badly handled conflict from escalating into a temptation to a renewed militarism. International peace brigades, training in nonviolent civilian defense for all citizens of border towns in all countries and special cross-generational conflict resolution teams consisting of the elderly and the young are all devices to help prevent that escalation.

At the international level, new representative bodies have been formed that are part of an emerging new federative world structure. These bodies include in their membership representatives from nongovernmental organizations and special-function groups of various kinds having a transnational nature, as well as nation states.

In short, the world of 2012 is seen as a localist, participatory society with strong links between people on every part of the planet, minimal regulatory systems, and a great emphasis on life-long education, life-long social participation and training in the use of conflict as a resource instead of as a threat.

The imaging workshops have demonstrated that the social imaginations regarding possible futures can be activated in a constructive way in people of different ages and with varying levels of education. These imaging workshops must now be tried with all the varied cultural groups that coexist in North America, with folk from other continents and with intercultural groups, to see what types of imagery emerge. What will be the commonalities and the differences in comparison with the imagery generated by the group I have just described? Differences there will certainly be, but one clue to possible commonalities lies in a recent study of ethnic separatist movements around the world—movements for increased cultural, economic and political autonomy for an ethnic minority located within the borders of another state. Many of the goals and aspirations of these ethnic groups were couched in the language of localism, cross-generational participation in the life of the community, a reassertion of the values of traditional ritual and folk knowledge in maintaining community health and welfare, mutual aid, self-regulation and self-management of conflict, and local power over resource allocation. It could be argued that the Americans in the imaging workshops were simplistically and romantically harking back to the preindustrial era, particularly in invoking *frèrèche*-type households and Benedictine concepts of labor. But the focus on appropriate uses of high technology and on the skills of conflict resolution argue against such an in-

When everyone felt we had named our demon, we planned a ritual for changing this creature from a destructive one into a life-affirming one. As we contemplated what the ritual might include, we felt the weight of world survival on our shoulders and in our hearts. One woman suggested we gather in a circle. Another wanted us to use our voices. Finally we lay on our backs in a circle with our heads in the inner orb and our feet around the periphery. And we chanted. We chanted sad voices, angry voices, powerful voices. We chanted the voices each of us felt in facing our unknown potential for transforming the demon called "no future" and the unpredictable outcome of our efforts.

—Chellis Glendinning

I often wonder why people do not make more of the marvelous power there is in kindness. It is the greatest lever to move the hearts of men that the world has ever known— greater by far than anything that mere ingenuity can devise or subtlety suggest. Kindness is the kingpin of success in life; it is the prime factor in overcoming friction and making the human machinery run smoothly.

—Andrew Chapman

terpretation. What further blends of the old and the new will emerge from third world imagery of the future which will be instructive? Some of this imagery will certainly wear an unfamiliar face to the Western eye.

It is important to remember that workshop participants were asked to visualize the future with no thought of how it was to be achieved. (It was very difficult, incidentally, to free participants from their concern with "how to" during the actual imaging process. One technique was to refuse to allow language that placed them mentally in 1982. They were continually reminded to use the present tense at all times in everything they said regarding 2012.) What they described was the world as they would like it to be, expressed in terms of their own intentions and including their own imagined behavior. For most participants, this was the first time they had ever seriously allowed themselves to think what they wanted the world to be like. Only when they had described the world in some detail did we put to them the question, "how did this happen?"

Futures History: From 2012 Back to 1982

As workshop participants looked backwards in time from their 2012 present moment, they saw many different kinds of events; but all saw some kind of "turning." "The Great Turning" was the term some would use for this phenomenon. Through the eighties and the early nineties, they pictured crescendoing crises. Sometimes these were seen in terms of heightening military threats, nuclear

Detail of "Peace Trek" image created by Diane and Joel Schatz   321

In the history of the world the prize has not gone to those species which specialized in methods of violence, or even in defensive armor. In fact, nature began with producing animals encased in hard shells for defense against the ill of life. But smaller animals, without external armor, warm-blooded, sensitive, alert, have cleared those monsters off the face of the earth.

—Alfred North Whitehead

terrorism and limited and/or accidental nuclear war. Sometimes the crises were seen in terms of food shortages and recurring famines linked with various kinds of humanly induced environmental catastrophes and natural catastrophes such as major earthquakes. Sometimes the crises were seen in terms of economic collapse and a breakdown in the regulatory capabilities of governments. No one pictured all-out nuclear war or total collapse of the social order. The turning itself was seen in part as the development of a new awareness at the grass roots level, in part as the emergence of new leadership. Sometimes the new awareness was primarily political, sometimes psychosocial or involving the development of spiritual sensitivities. The turning had generally started by the mid-nineties. By 2002 the restructuring had begun which made disarmament by 2012 possible.

The turning was generally pictured as people taking more responsibility into their own hands for the world they lived in, by forming new types of groups and developing new skills or redeveloping older folk traditions that were seen as having new relevance. Multinational peace brigades drawing on various traditions (Hindu, Buddhist, Judaic, Islamic, Christian) for training in nonviolence were pictured as having brought about peaceful settlements of disputes in Central America, Northern Ireland, Southern Africa, Southeast Asia and the Middle East. A strong coalition of European and North American activists was seen as bringing new local problem-solving skills to those communities on both sides of the Atlantic suffering from the increasing inability of governmental machinery to handle mounting resource conflicts. The new leadership emerging out of this activist coalition saw weaponry as a set of useless and outdated technologies withdrawing resources from areas of real human need. "Bury the weapons" became the new social theme. Children were often pictured as taking leadership in ending the preoccupation with weaponry in a late twentieth-century version of the medieval children's crusades. Nine- to twelve-year-olds, or teenaged youth, traveled in teams around the world, holding international gatherings (one was pictured in Geneva), refusing to attend school or obey parental commands as a strategy in their struggle for the right to have a world to grow up in.

Many older (pre-1980) transnational, nongovernmental organizations were seen as taking on new life, along with new transnationals, developing new strategies for resource-sharing and conflict management between world regions. Labor unions, churches, and a rash of new professional associations along the lines of "Physicians for Social Responsiblility," for teachers, artists, and scientists all took on new war-prevention roles. They created new cooperative structures, assisted by computer specialists who helped them set up world communication networks. Under the threat of nuclear extinction, an alliance of world cities set up its own network for communication and cooperation, and rural-urban cooperatives developed for food-sharing and mutual aid between country and city. New

All the best things and treasures of this world are not to be produced by each generation for itself, but we are all intended, not to carve our work in snow that will melt, but each and all of us to be continually rolling a great white gathering snowball, higher and higher, larger and larger, along the Alps of human power.

—John Ruskin

323

breeds of "development specialists" with a strong ecological orientation traveled in teams with storytellers who in song, dance, and story shared the peacemaking traditions of every culture in towns and villages around the world. National universities were reconstituted as world universities with multinational faculties and student bodies. A new multidisciplinary field of studies drawing on the sciences and the humanities came into exisence: earth studies.

Disarmament was seen as happening by stages while the new institutions were developing. Different categories of weapons were scrapped for reuse in the new technological toolkits of the twenty-first century in successive five-year periods. The fact that disarmament was complete by 2012 was, of course, an artifact of the instructions given to workshop participants. What the imaging exercise demonstrated for many participants was that it was possible to visualize such a world and have it be a coherent and attractive world. As might be expected, not everyone succeeded in the visualization process. For the majority who did, the type of concession to the 1980s weapons mentality that appeared in their scenarios was an occasional visualization of a small transnational police force, very lightly armed, just in case things got out of hand.

One common theme underlay these imagined historical developments: the more human and peaceful social order that people were trying to account for came about as a result of enormous human effort in every

The precondition for a real solution of the security problem is a certain mutual trust by both parties, a trust which cannot be replaced by any kind of technological measures.

—Albert Einstein

sphere of life, by people of all ages, and would only endure as a result of continued human effort. Since the knowledge to build weapons continued to exist in every society, the only way to keep that knowledge from being activated was the widespread development of social values, skills and institutional structures which would make weapons appear as obsolete tools for achieving either personal or social goals. The rewards of living in a society which protected individuality at the same time that it institutionalized sharing were seen as another powerful factor in the continued viability of the weapon-free social order.

No grand plan for disarmament results from such workshops, but that was not sought. Rather, a group of empowered individuals have breached the future and seen with their own inward eyes a tomorrow that can be more peaceful than today. They have had the experience of constructing a world out of the materials of their own minds and life experiences, seen that it was viable, and have clues about some possible next steps. As one participant said, "We have given form to hope and made it mentally more concrete than fear." Part of the excitement generated by the workshops comes from the fact that participants were being asked to use faculties and parts of their minds that they had not consciously drawn on sometimes for years. These faculties are generally unused in formal education and normal decision settings. Participants found tangible, useful real-world insights and strategies emerging from the exercise of these socially belittled faculties.

When you have to make a choice and don't make it, that in itself is a choice.

—William James

I learned about how to reduce international tensions by observing how our government deliberately escalated tensions in certain circumstances and then by realizing that similar techniques would work in reverse. For example, a strategy of calculated escalation has four salient features: first, the steps are unilaterally initiated (we did not negotiate with the North Vietnamese about increasing the tempo of our bombing or moving it closer to Hanoi; we just did it unilaterally); second, each step propels the opponent into reciprocating if he can, with more aggressive steps of his own (our development of multiple nuclear warheads propels the Soviets into analogous developments); third; such steps are necessarily graduated in nature—by the unpredictability of technological breakthroughs, by the limitations imposed by logistics, and by the oscillating level of perceived threat. Fourth, calculated escalation is obviously a tension-increasing process, the termination of which is a military resolution—

The Limits of Imaging

Imaging workshops are not "the answer" to the world's problems, only another framework for dealing with them. The imagery and the purposive action visualized by those workshop participants who were able to enter fully into the exercise have just been summarized for the reader. While it is true that most of the participants were able to generate such imagery, in every workshop there were several participants who either felt that the whole affair was an enterprise in self-deception and preferred to stay with intellectual analysis or who could not evoke imagery of any kind. Indeed, the sense of the excitement which the majority of participants felt as their own imagery began to come clear could lead to self-deception. Every effort was made during workshops to introduce the strongest critical judgment about the images—*after* the images had been produced.

Workshops are physically exhausting to the participants. This is because the two approaches of allowing a free (yet focussed) flow of imagery and then directing the powers of the intellect to that imagery are very difficult to harness together in the same enterprise. There is always the danger that in other, less disciplined settings people will indulge in fantasy-type imagery and persuade themselves they are thereby creating the future or that charismatic leaders will "sell" fantasy images to people longing for instant social transformation.

The test of the validity of imaging the future as an activity is the oldest of tests: "By their fruits ye shall know them." The history-writing back to the present is as important as the visualization of the future itself because, in imaging how that future came to be, the mind is drawn to consider a variety of social roles and possible institutional structures, a variety of individual and group activities that do not now exist. In the course of inventing a general history, people come to see something which they could do, which they find themselves wanting to do. They have been energized and empowered by their own mental constructions to a course of action in the present. Sometimes it is a completely new course of action they have never thought of; sometimes familiar activity takes on new dimensions.

In order for this action-enhancing effect to have its fullest play, imaging groups optimally continue meeting together from time to time over a period of months or even years, continually refining their imaged social goals and critiquing their real-life actions. The concrete record of social invention for organizations and community groups which have worked together in this way on common problems for several years exists in a series of case histories and in the historical memory of these groups. The full story has yet to be compiled. With regard to that hardest of all human problems, the historical tendency to seek military solutions to social problems, any local imaging group of necessity can only arrive at very incomplete action plans. Therefore, not very much can be said at this time about the usefulness of this approach to the attainment of

victory, defeat, or (in our time) even mutual annihilation. Now, if we change this last feature of calculated escalation—shift it from tension-induction to tension-reduction—we have the essence of a calculated de-escalation strategy in conflict situations. Nation A devises patterns of small steps, well within its own limits of security, designed to reduce tensions and induce reciprocating steps from nation B. If such unilateral initiatives are persistently applied, and reciprocation is obtained, then the margin for risk-taking is widened and somewhat larger steps can be taken. Both sides, in effect, begin edging down the tension ladder, and both are moving—within what they perceive as reasonable limits of national security—toward a political rather than a military resolution.

—Charles E. Osgood, "The Way GRIT Works," in *Securing Our Planet*

Not one of us knows what effect his life produces, and what he gives to others; that is hidden from us and must remain so, though we are often allowed to see some little fraction of it, so that we may not lose courage. The way in which power works is a mystery.

—Albert Schweitzer

a more peaceful world. However, if transnational groups can be formed to work together on this type of imaging over time, then the full richness of local tradition and wisdom around the world can at least be brought to bear on the problem of planetary violence.

The concept of bringing endogenous creativity from around the world to bear on the future of our planetary society underlies this symposium series. It is a stirring concept, corresponding to our deepest understandings about the creative process at work in the body social. It invites the use of every kind of mental faculty, of all the "multiple intelligence" that can be identified in order to survey what humans have known how to do, and what they could aspire to learn to do. It also invites an active effort, particularly on the part of the West, to examine every type of knowledge in order to place the achievements of science and technology in the context of a broader array of human possibilities. Finally, it is a challenge to rediscover the *joys of effort* as we use our faculties to turn knowledge into wisdom and vision into social reality.

328

When Richard Lamm wrote this essay he was governor of Colorado. There are not many elected officials who refer to Woody Allen, the War of Jenkins' Ear, Sri Lanka, the Bhagavad Gita, Aeschylus, and a Vietnamese proverb, or who publicly imagine details of a nuclear war, albeit it a limited one involving a mere twenty detonations. In Lamm's fantasy, the time of peace comes only after sudden enormous destruction. Fortunately for Americans, it occurs on somebody else's continent. Athough Lamm concludes that "in the end reality was the only effective teacher," clearly he himself can envision a horrible situation vividly enough so that he can draw conclusions without waiting for it actually to occur. Let's hope that enough of us can do the same.

Against Our Will Comes Wisdom

Richard D. Lamm

When we released the energy from the atom, everything changed except our way of thinking. Because of that, we drift toward unparalleled disaster. We shall require a substantially new manner of thinking if mankind is to survive.
—Albert Einstein

ALBERT EINSTEIN'S PROPHETIC WORDS foreshadowed The Time of Peace; 1994 was the year of the ultimate war and the year that a lasting peace finally arrived on earth.

History shows periods of peace to be the exception rather than the rule. Since the dawn of history, neighbor has fought neighbor; tribe has fought tribe; religion has fought religion; nation has fought nation. The history of man is partially written in blood: construction giving way to destruction; peace and stability turning into war and chaos. Wars have

329

Whoever does not understand that when it comes to nuclear weapons the whole concept of relative advantage is illusory—whoever does not understand that when you are talking about absurd and preposterous quantities of overkill the relative sizes of arsenals have no serious meaning—whoever does not understand that the danger lies, not in the possibility that someone else might have more missiles and warheads than we do, but in the very existence of these unconscionable quantities of highly poisonous explosives, and their existence, above all, in hands as weak and shaky and undependable as those of ourselves or our adversaries or any other mere human beings: whoever does not understand these things is never going to guide us out of this increasingly dark and menacing forest of bewilderments into which we have all wandered.

—George F. Kennan, "Deep Cuts," in *Securing Our Planet*

been as inevitable to history as storms are to weather.

Violence and terrorism increased dramatically as the twentieth century, already history's most destructive century, lurched to a close. In the 1970s and 1980s, violence seemed to reach a crescendo. By the late 1980s, Russia and the United States both instituted "launch on warning" nuclear systems. A myriad of local wars, revolutions, incidents of religious and sectarian strife, terrorism, and random acts of violence were made even more frightening by the rapid growth of the nuclear club. Peace was a stranger. Man seemed to have lost his capacity for shock, inundated as he was—wherever he lived—by daily news bulletins and TV reports of wars, terrorism, and violence.

One American wit, Woody Allen, seemed to sum up the dilemma: "More than any other time in history, mankind faces the crossroads. . . . One path leads to despair and utter hopelessness, the other to total extinction. I pray we have the wisdom to choose wisely."

The flash point came, with history's usual irony, in the least expected place. Although India and Pakistan had fought three wars (1947, 1965, and 1971), an uneasy truce had existed between them. Despite their legacy of hate and distrust, no significant increase in tensions is known to have preceded the devastating nuclear exchange. None of history's usual causations seemed to trigger the conflagration: no jihad, no territorial dispute, no recent reason for revenge. History's most bloody war was apparently caused by some minor miscalculation. Like the War of Jenkins' Ear, the cause, while lost in the radiated ashes, was so insignificant as to conjure up Hannah Arendt's phrase, "The banality of evil." No international threat or declaration from either country harbingered the holocaust. It just happened.

The morning of November 29, 1994, dawned clear and cool over the Indian subcontinent. The harvests had been sparse but adequate. The border between India and Pakistan, long filled with minor incidents, had been exceptionally quiet.

Granted, the religious differences were as strong as ever, but no known incident or aggravation was present. November 29 was like so many similar days—alive with pungent smells, buzzing women on the way to market, mischievous children, men sweating in the fields. True, the Hindus worshipped a myriad of gods, while the Muslims worshipped one; the Muslims eschewed pork and were quiet in their worship, while the Hindus proscribed beef and had music in their worship. Both shared a legacy of religious strife and conflict that defied even a peacemaker such as Gandhi and resulted in the partition of a continent. But nothing in the mind or imagination of man could have justified or explained a spasm of hate equal to "The Great Annihilation."

Simply put, one moment tens of millions of people were going about their daily routines and the next moment they were ashes. For historical accuracy, it must be pointed out that satellite pictures confirm that India was attacked first, but American satellites monitor-

"Peace" in military mouths today is a synonym for "war expected." The word has become a pure provocative, and no government wishing peace sincerely should allow it ever to be printed in a newspaper. Every up-to-date dictionary should say that "peace" and "war" mean the same thing, now in posse [potentially], now in actu [actually]. It may even reasonably be said that the intensely sharp competitive preparation for war by the nations is the real war, permanent, unceasing; and that the battles are only a sort of public verification of the mastery gained during the "peace"-interval.

—William James, "The Moral Equivalent of War," in *Securing Our Planet*

When anger rises, think of the consequences.

—Confucius

331

ing radio traffic over the Indian subcontinent recorded that the Indians had a sudden, unmanageable fear that the Pakistanis had mobilized and were prepared to launch their recently acquired, supposedly obsolete, American-purchased cruise missiles. So India sent its rockets, just purchased from Russia, on a preemptive strike. Analysts later agreed that there must have been a computer failure in New Delhi. But in the end, it is impossible to assign "blame"; even the concept seems irrelevant to the horror that followed.

What is important to note is the unpredictability of events and how easily one minor event led to another, with increasing speed and significance, until a human chain reaction caused a nuclear chain reaction. The twentieth century had seen a world of isolated, independent events become an interdependent global village. Just as assassination in Sarajevo started a chain of events, one following inevitably after another, it is likely that on the Indian subcontinent some slight error led to an insult; an insult to an incident; an incident to an outrage; and an outrage to a holocaust. Events soon passed beyond all human control. The "Guns of August" became the "Missiles of November."

"If the iron dice must roll, may God help us," anguished Theobald von Bethmann-Hollweg on August 1, 1914. Eighty years later the nuclear dice rolled—on a scale that eclipsed even the destruction of two world wars. But the rolling dice did something else, more important: it made absurd such concepts as "winners" or "losers" in modern warfare. President Dole, in her characteristic way, put

I would...like to see a United Nations Spying Organization which would spy on everybody and publish the results immediately. Secrecy in the international system is a very important cause in itself of strain. It produces extraordinary misapprehensions and illusions. Indeed, there is no segment of the social system in which the images of the world in the minds of the powerful decision makers are more deliberately formed by biased and inaccurate information. Even if one could not have a United Nations Spying Organization in the present state of mythology of the international system, one could at least have a United Nations Intelli-

Jumping Ahead and Looking Back at the Future

it succinctly: "Winning a nuclear war is like saying, 'Your end of the boat is sinking!'"

The total devastation of modern weapons is seen in the absence of reports from either Pakistan or India. Few were left to carry the word. The first news came from U.S. and Russian satellites that reported a nuclear exchange involving at least twenty detonations. There were no "stop the presses" telegrams from Sarajevo, no cacophony of reports from Pearl Harbor. The first sound of this war was silence.

Chilling, eerie silence.

When reports did come, they were of "multiple blinding flashes seen to the northwest," as radioed from Colombo, Sri Lanka. A radio operator in Bangalore, India reported "large mushroom clouds rising from Bangalore and Madras." Seismic recorders around the world registered multiple shocks in both India and Pakistan.

If one could pinpoint the beginning of The Time of Peace, it would be December 1, 1994, when the first television reports burst upon a world that had thought itself beyond shock. The initial images were pictures taken from the air by American network news organizations in leased airplanes hurriedly flown to India from Sri Lanka and Thailand. The first images were sweeping panoramas of a moonlike landscape. Nothing stood but charred rubble. News reports repeated Robert Oppenheimer's observation at the first successful atomic test five decades earlier, when he recalled the Bhagavad-Gita: "I have become Death/Destroyer of Worlds!" Here was a world destroyed.

gence Organization for the study and publication of social indicators of strain on the system and, with more difficulty, its strength. With present techniques of the analysis of events data and content analysis, a great deal could be done to present the current picture of the international system as it moves from day to day in terms which are relatively free from bias and which are based on objective sampling. This, one hopes, would supplement and perhaps eventually supplant the vast apparatus of biased information collected and processed through spies, diplomats, state departments, and foreign offices.

—Kenneth Boulding, "Seven Planks for a Platform," in *Securing Our Planet*

Nine-tenths of wisdom consists in being wise in time.

—Theodore Roosevelt

333

Jumping Ahead and Looking Back at the Future

While it is difficult to believe that anyone would dare to assume responsibility for initiating the appalling slaughter and destruction that war would bring in its wake, there is no denying that the conflagration could be started by some chance and unforeseen circumstance.... Hence justice, right reason, and the recognition of man's dignity cry out insistently for a cessation to the arms race. The stockpiles of armaments which have been built up in various countries must be reduced all round and simultaneously by the parties concerned. Nuclear weapons must be banned....

In those moments—with a horrified world glued to its television sets in homes or in windows of stores with TV sets—came the horror of modern weapons. Craters where cities once stood. A myriad of people struck blind whose only mistake had been to look at the fireball. Into every world capital, country town, village, barrio, ghetto, fravello, and most huts, the universality of suffering was dramatically played out before shocked eyes. Nuclear war, like Medusa, consumed all who looked it in the face.

Thus wisdom came not through treaty but through tragedy. The goal of peace was no longer something left to politicians, but became the demand of every citizen. If "war was too important to be left to generals," in Clemenceau's famous phrase, peace became a groundswell that swept over politicians and nationalities. The demonic horror of the Indian subcontinent brought home to everyone the universality not of brotherhood, but of the vulnerability of man. Man looked into the abyss and he was horrified beyond words. No religious or national goals could justify destruction and desolation on this scale. War was mutual suicide. The message went not only to the head but to the heart. As Aeschylus had said:

> Even in our sleep
> Pain that we cannot forget
> Falls drop by drop upon the heart
> Until in our own despair
> Against our will
> Comes wisdom
> Through the awful grace of God.

Jumping Ahead and Looking Back at the Future

One is cynically tempted to cite Tacitus: "When they made a desert, they called it Peace." The aphorism would seem appropriate if restricted to the survivors of India and Pakistan. Those two countries were left with a desert, their people too exhausted and traumatized to fight. They could only suffer. Hundreds of millions of refugees in both countries rushed to escape the fallout. Survival was determined by the caprice of the winds.

But this "desert" aphorism misses the symbolic value of the horror. It ignores the vividness of the pictures sent around the world. Unlike Carthage, whose destruction was witnessed by a few, the Great Annihilation was witnessed by all. Grim pictures of the widespread suffering were transmitted to the end of the globe. Children died who were guilty of no sins. . . . The whole world could clearly see that in a nuclear war, the survivors would envy the dead. In a thousand languages and dialects, people of different faiths recognized, "There, but for the grace of God, go I."

As if to drive the point home came The Years Without Summer. The nuclear explosions and resulting fires put large quantities of fine dust and soot into the atmosphere and changed the climate of the entire Northern Hemisphere. Actually, everyone outside the Indian subcontinent was fortunate, even though all suffered through three successive summers that were ten to fifteen degrees below normal, with resulting crop losses that were barely overcome by emptying America's gigantic grain storage bins. But if it had been fifty bombs instead of twenty, the "nuclear

We are hopeful that, by establishing contact with one another and by a policy of negotiation, nations will come to a better recognition of the natural ties that bind them together as men. We are hopeful, too, that they will come to a fairer realization of one of the cardinal duties deriving from our common nature: namely, that love, not fear, must dominate the relationships between individuals and between nations. It is principally characteristic of love that it draws men together in all sorts of ways, sincerely united in the bonds of mind and matter; and this is a union from which countless blessings can flow.

—Pope John XXIII, "Pacem in Terris," 1963

335

winter" would have destroyed all life on earth.

Tests showed that, in addition, the atmosphere's ozone, which shields man from the carcinogenic ultraviolet radiation, had been permanently damaged. Man learned unequivocally that a depletion in the stratospheric ozone by nuclear explosions would dangerously increase solar ultraviolet radiation. Nuclear war was hydra-headed: first the catastrophe of the blast; then the devastation of the fallout; then the climatic disaster of a nuclear winter; and, finally, after the soot and dust had settled out, the continuing curse of ultraviolet radiation.

No formal arms control agreement followed the holocaust. Politicians continued to find barriers to treaties. As always, technical problems and difficulties of ensuring compliance were solemnly cited. But peace is neither the absence of war nor the presence of a disarmament agreement. Peace is a change of heart. Both the U.S.S.R. and the U.S. simply stopped building new weapons and missiles. These were not weapons but suicide devices. Man had at last invented a doomsday machine.

The revulsion came in many forms and in many languages. The nations of the world clearly shared too small a star to allow this to happen again. Peace was not negotiated: it burst on a stunned mankind. Multiple Messiahs preached the common theme of Peace on Earth. "Blessed are the peacemakers," urged Christian ministers. "Never in the world can hatred be stilled by hatred; it will be stilled only by non-hatred—this is the law eternal," quoted the followers of Buddha. A

When I read Carl Sagan's remarks about a nuclear winter it's true I'm frightened, but if that's all that happens, it really goes nowhere, so I think that while it's enormously important to get people's attention, we as a nation and we as individuals must go beyond simply the fear issues.

—Don Carlson on audio cassette, "Beyond the Boundaries"

religious leader from China, quoting an old Vietnamese proverb, "If we take vengeance on vengeance, vengeance will never end," gained millions of converts. The ancient simple truths of love and charity were reinforced by the terror of example.

In the words of Shelley:

> Most wretched men are cradled into
>   poetry by wrong,
> They learn in suffering what they teach
>   in song.

A tidal wave of peace swept the world.

Other factors supplemented the change of heart. Both the U.S. and Russia were increasingly frustrated by the pouring of resources into the arms race. Each had to match the other, but the cost was high. Both had built the twenty-first-century equivalent of the Maginot line: an awesomely expensive but unusable defense system. This system gave little military security, and that at the expense of economic security. Both nations suffered domestically because of the resources put into arms. Both had lost the economic race while struggling to win the arms race.

By 1994, the U.S. was allocating 40 percent of its scientists and 9 percent of its gross national product to the military. Its previous role as world economic leader was suffering severely. Once having had the highest per capita income, by 1994 it was down to seventh in per capita income. Once the world-leading exporter, it had become the world's leading importer, with a devastating negative balance of trade. Once the financier of the world, since

It is fanciful in the extreme to suppose that the prospect of any new American deployment which could undermine the effectiveness of Soviet missile forces will not be met by a most determined and sustained response. This inevitable Soviet reaction is studiously neglected by Secretary Weinberger when he argues in defense of Star Wars that today's skeptics are as wrong as those who said we could never get to the moon. The effort to get to the moon was not complicated by the presence of an adversary. A platoon of hostile moon-men with axes could have made it a disaster.

—McGeorge Bundy, George F. Kennan, Robert S. McNamara, Gerard Smith, "The President's Choice: Star Wars or Arms Control," in *Securing Our Planet*

337

If the United States were to lead the way, would the Soviet Union follow us? There is growing evidence that Soviet leadership desires serious negotiations to reduce the growing threat of annihilation and the crushing burden of the arms race. The Soviet economy, far less efficient and productive than that of the United States, has a host of economic problems—including failing agriculture, a shrinking work force, shortages of consumer goods, and backward technology—that plague the Soviet system. Increasing trouble with Russia's ethnic minorities, unrest in Poland, and a continuing war in Afghanistan add to the problems the Soviet leadership cannot ignore. Reducing the drain of the arms race on their economy would enable the U.S.S.R. to focus on serious domestic problems and perhaps curb its appetite for international adventurism. As is the case with any competitor, it is unrealistic to expect the Soviets to act in our

1987 it had been a debtor nation. America was an economic giant crippled by the costs of defense and an economy that had lost its magic.

The Soviet Union was similarly beset. Its expensive nuclear arsenal was no help for its real problems. The Russian Bear was beset by multiple problems: a billion Chinese on one border who hated Soviets; an unwinnable war in Afghanistan; a military machine that drained 20 percent of its gross national product; restive national minorities and rebellious satellites; a history of bad harvests; and the highest alcoholism rate in the world.

Like two clumsy, muscle-bound fighters eyeing each other suspiciously, the two superpowers added useless missile upon useless missile while other sectors of their economies suffered and while living standards started to decline. The peace process, once started, also became an economic issue. The wisdom came because the costs of war in economic as well as human terms became manifest.

One additional result completes the picture: the "Adopt a Refugee" program. So many children were orphaned, so many needed extraordinary care, that the developed world agreed to take in these children for treatment and adoption. The one international conference that did succeed was the "Save the Children" conference, organized by Switzerland. At that conference, Russia made a dramatic announcement that it would accept the same number of children that the U.S. did. All nations took in some of the injured, and as these children spread across the world, they served as a grim reminder of the human costs of breaking the peace.

John Locke observed, "Hell is truth seen too late." In our time, peace was hell seen just in time. Peace came not from the efforts of the actors on the world stage who had failed so often, but through a preview of coming events.

The front line of nuclear war was everyman's backyard. It was neither idealism nor love of mankind that brought peace, but the reality therapy of war. It was not the abstract odds of war, but the recognition of the devastating stakes. Man looked into the abyss and saw an irradiated hell and recoiled in horror. Both heads and hearts came to realize that war was mutual suicide that would destroy not only nations but species.

The cost was high but, in the end, reality was the only effective teacher.

interest. But it is perfectly realistic to expect them to act in their own self-interest, if given the opportunity. Reversing the nuclear arms race is as much in their interest as it is in ours.

—Harold Willens, "Taking the Next Steps," in *Securing Our Planet*

Some would say that in the nuclear age national governments have not been doing badly at keeping the peace. Between the end of WW I and the start of WW II there were only twenty years of something called peace; but since Hiroshima we've had a run of over forty years without a world war, even though "local" conflicts have created millions of casualties. Thankful as we are for the respite from general war, some of us see no reason to believe that the present system of hair-trigger "deterrence" can persist forever, or that anybody will succeed in creating an adequate defense against the "delivery" of nuclear devices. Neither superpower is dealing with these realities. Their devotion to theories of nuclear-warfighting and to fantasies of creating a "Star Wars" defense to protect people have led some thinkers to look for other political levels at which to act. A while ago much hope was placed in organizations that would unite, or somehow stand above, nation-states. In view of what some regard as the disappointing history of the U.N. as a peace-keeper, speculation now centers around methods that, instead of trying to bring nations together, cut across national lines. One example of a transnational method is citizen diplomacy. Another is Michael Shuman's idea for a Global Union of Municipalities. If the national governments are stuck, he says, work through units closer to home, and let these units form a network.

Acting Globally Through Your Locality

Michael H. Shuman

HIROSHIMA—IT WAS EXACTLY SIXTY-five years ago here that the first nuclear weapon incinerated one hundred thousand human beings. But today Hiroshima has become a symbol of humanity's hope. Next to the twisted lattice of melted iron now stand the recently completed Global Assembly buildings, where representatives of the world's people will soon begin to debate, formulate, and interpret international law. By erecting a new center of world politics in the ruins of Hiroshima, we have sought to remind ourselves of why we must never fail.

Today it is official: every nation on the planet has ratified the World Constitution, and a new era of what Immanual Kant once called "perpetual peace" can begin. As we prepare to celebrate, it is worth reflecting on our new Constitution—what it contains, and how we achieved it—for as early as 1985, today would have seemed a complete impossibility.

The Four Great Principles

It was only fifteen years ago that the party leaders of the Global Union of Municipalities began constructing the World Constitution. The drafters sought to answer one basic question: What minimal principles can prevent global warfare? By searching for "minimal principles," the drafters deliberately tried to avoid creating a centralized, omnipotent world government. Instead, they tried to specify the most basic international institutions with the fewest powers that could support perpetual peace. After five years of debate, they settled on four principles: noninterventiontionism, disarmament, mobility, and law.

Principle #1: Noninterventionism

The framers fashioned the first principle to prevent what they viewed as the most persistent cause of war—the quest for territory. It directs every nation not to place its troops, weapons, or military advisors on any territory

The inescapable reality is that there is literally no hope that Star Wars can make nuclear weapons obsolete. Perhaps the first and most important political task for those who wish to save the country from the expensive and dangerous pursuit of a mirage is to make this basic proposition clear. As long as the American people believe that Star Wars offers real hope of reaching the President's asserted goal, it will have a level of political support unrelated to reality. The American people, properly and sensibly, would like nothing better than to make nuclear weapons "impotent and obsolete," but the last thing they want or need is to pay an astronomic bill for a vastly intensified nuclear competition sold to them under a false label. Yet that is what Star Wars will bring us.

—McGeorge Bundy, George F. Kennan, Robert S. McNamara, Gerard Smith, "The President's Choice: Star Wars or Arms Control," in *Securing Our Planet*

341

Within ten years perhaps thirty nations will command this power of death for mankind. By that time the weapons of total annihilation will be so cheap that criminal elements may obtain this power to hold mankind for ransom. Breakthroughs in chemical and biological and nuclear warfare will magnify and compound the forces of destruction. This is a new historic time of dread. In this new age no nation ever again will find positive national security and political independence by use of its power to destroy human life. In this new age an attempt to destroy an enemy can destroy mankind. All nations have moved into a common chamber of danger. The world is like a room filled with gas, in which men who strike matches endanger the lives of everyone in the room. We must create new history. It is no longer safe merely to relive old history. There will always be war and aggression between nations until there is created a global safety authority of some kind, with the strength and the authority

but its own. To enable nations to abandon their alliances and power blocs, the framers designed a Global Peacekeeping Authority (GPA), comprised of every nation's troops, weapons, and military advisors. Under the Constitution, any nation finding itself threatened by actual or imminent aggression will receive upon request immediate defense assistance from the GPA. Once called, the GPA will restore borders to the *status quo ante.*

With regard to internal struggles and civil wars, the framers decided that the GPA should remain completely neutral, with two exceptions. First, to enforce the principle of nonintervention, the GPA will have the power to embargo all international shipments of arms to the embroiled nation. Second, the GPA can enter that nation to ensure that both sides continue complying with the world's new rules on disarmament.

Principle #2: Disarmament

The drafters of the Constitution were deeply committed to preventing the biggest threat to the planet's survival—nuclear war. To achieve this, the Constitution bans not only nuclear weapons, but also *offensive* non-nuclear weapons through which a regional conventional war could escalate into a global nuclear war. The only weapons the Constitution now allows nations to possess are those with zero-range or short-range capabilities—that is, weapons unusable for offensive purposes. Thus, nations can now have bazookas but not tanks, surface-to-air missiles but not bombers, and short-range precision-guided munitions but not long-range cruise missiles.

Jumping Ahead and Looking Back at the Future

To ensure compliance with these rules, the Constitution empowers a World Disarmament Authority (WDA) to have broad powers of on-site inspection within every nation. For the past twenty years, an early version of the WDA has monitored treaty compliance through its satellite system and its widely respected weekly reports of global military activity. With a track record of thoroughness and fairness, the WDA seems well-equipped to expand its activities to on-site searches for illicit uranium mines, fuel cycle facilities, or weapons deployments.

Should the WDA find any cheating, it is empowered to go to the World Court and get a "cease and desist" order. If the cheating nation does not comply, the GPA will then enforce the order with the minimum level of force necessary.

Principle #3: Mobility

The drafters of the Constitution recognized that wars were not always just about territory or weapons, but also about injustice. Yet they were unable to arrive at any workable definition of justice. Western democracies pressed for freedoms of speech, press, voting, and religions, while socialist nations demanded enforceable minimum standards of nutrition, education, health care, and housing. To resolve this issue, the drafters reformulated the concept of justice to fit the one point on which they all could agree: All peoples should evaluate the justice of their own positions, and they should have the right to escape perceived injustices with their feet. If people deem their country hopelessly un-

to maintain the common good of national security and political independence for all nations. Historians and political scientists find no precedent for such a Global Safety Authority. But before 1940 there was no precedent for atomic bombs, as before recent times there was no precedent for many of the miracles of modern medical science. We live in an age that breaks precedents. We need not be enslaved by historical precedents of war and catastrophe.

—Howard G. Kurtz, "Proposed Speech in Search of a Statesman Capable of Delivering It," in *Securing Our Planet*

just, the Constitution set up mechanisms for them to leave instead of revolt.

The Constitution thus made migration a fundamental human right that will be promoted by a World Migration Bureau (WMB). It binds all nations to give the WMB permission to enter their nation, to inform people of their right to leave, and to offer financial assistance to those who decide to exercise that right. It further binds nations to accept a number of immigrants each year up to one per cent of its total population. Finally, the Constitution sets up procedures by which the WMB will work with recipient nations to ensure an equitable distribution of immigrants. Even though the framers recognized that the costs of relocating millions of dissatisfied human beings each year would be billions of dollars, they further recognized that these costs were lower than the alternative costs—both national and international—of revolution and civil war.

Principle #4: Law

The framers were united in their fears that uncontrolled international institutions could easily become tyrants and new sources of global warfare. They therefore made the fourth principle of the Constitution legal due process. Every act by the various institutions is to be governed strictly by laws enunciated by a two-house Global Assembly and interpreted by A World Court System (open to all citizens' complaints).

The Constitution empowers the Global Assembly to begin implementing the details of these principles. It specifies that the GPA, WDA and WMB must all be set up and oper-

If there is righteousness in the heart there will be beauty in the character. If there be beauty in the character, there will be harmony in the home. If there is harmony in the home, there will be order in the nation. When there is order in the nation, there will be peace in the world.

—Chinese proverb

344

ating for a period of five years before the final steps of disarmament occur. But it also specifies that the Assembly must complete the disarmament process by the year 2020.

That the world's leaders have now agreed to even these minimal principles would have shocked observers from the past. Yet all of this has happened. And the one dynamic, more than any other, that made this all possible was a sudden burst of activity by people to take control of their own destiny

Early Roots

As early as the 1980s, the publics of the world were terrified by the threat of nuclear annihilation but were also overwhelmed by a sense of hopelessness. The early history of the twentieth century had shown that, even when leaders arose with a deep sincere determination to effect global peace, they inevitably became tangled in old habits of building monstrous new weapons, controlling marginal ones, and jealously protecting national interests. The turning point came when popular movements arose demanding stronger international norms, laws, and institutions.

Throughout the twentieth century, people seeking the Four Great Principles were politically ineffective. So-called "world order activists" tried educating people and lobbying national leaders, but they found themselves with insufficient money and legitimacy to wield much influence. What finally transformed them into a powerful global movement was a political unit long overlooked—local government.

The big ideas in this world cannot survive unless they come to life in the individual citizen. It is what each man does in responding to his convictions that provides the forward thrust for any great movement.

—Norman Cousins

Jumping Ahead and Looking Back at the Future

Real peace in the world requires something more than the documents which we sign to terminate wars. Peace requires unremitting, courageous campaigns, laid with strategy and carried on successfully on a hundred fronts and sustained in the spirit and from the hearts of every individual in every town and village of our country.

—Herbert Hoover

Local governments turned out to be especially well-tuned for world order activism for three reasons:

First, localities wanted disarmament because they had a unique appreciation of the consequences of war. While to the national security planners a limited nuclear war meant many megadeaths on paper, to civic officials it meant the destruction of *their* buildings and people. This appreciation led the Greater City Council of London in 1984, for example, to hire a dozen internationally renowned scientists to publicize the various kinds of nuclear threats the city faced.

Second, localities wanted to prune world expenditures on weapons because they, more than national governments, had to cope with the economic consequences of military spending in the form of unemployment, poverty, crime, and alienation. Even for communities that benefitted from military spending, this understanding led to the establishment of local "conversion councils" that sought to minimize the boom-and-bust impacts of military spending.

Finally, as the principal administrators of police, courts, arbitration, and social services, municipal governments had better expertise than national governments with the nonviolent conflict resolution techniques necessary for a stronger world order.

Municipal activism began in democracies like the United States, where local leaders had the freedom to dissent from national leaders. In the early 1980s, literally hundreds of state legislatures and city councils had endorsed an initiative to "freeze" the nuclear arms race. A smaller number of cities created "nuclear free zones" that banned the transportation, manufacture, and deployment of nuclear weapons within their jurisdiction. Gradually, cities turned to a broader agenda of world order issues.

Local government entered into "contracts" with other nations and their localities on such innocuous issues as trade and cultural exchange, effecting some important political changes. Ohio's trade pact with China's Wu Wei Province, signed in 1983, led to the establishment of the Joint Ohio-China Peace Research Institute by 1989. San Francisco's 1984 trade pact with Shanghai opened channels for a human rights dialogue that resulted in dramatic revisions in Chinese civil rights laws in 1990.

Each new local initiative spawned even more daring, more effective initiatives elsewhere. Between 1985 and 1990, the United States, for example, witnessed the following activities:

Cities, including Oakland, undertook campaigns granting trade preferences to favored nations, such as Argentina, and closing its harbors to disfavored nations, particularly South Africa;

The U.S. Conference of Mayors organized efforts to ship food, tools, dollars, or credit to friends of the community abroad; and

Hundreds of cities established a small corps of individuals to lobby decision-makers in Congress and the United Nations on foreign affairs issues important to the community.

And is not peace, in the last analysis, basically a matter of human rights— the right to live out our lives without fear of devastation, the right to breathe air as nature provided it, the right of future generations to a healthy existence?

—John F. Kennedy

347

The message of citizen diplomacy is that individual people acting on their own beliefs and in their own ways can alter the curve of global politics and it's the kind of democratization of foreign policy that I think Thomas Jefferson would have liked to have seen. Had he been around right now and seen the way that decisions are made about the fate of the earth, he would have thought it was authoritarian. So democratizing the foreign policy-making process by making it possible for individual, ordinary people to participate in this complex game that goes on in Geneva and Moscow and Washington is really encouraging.

—Gordon Feller on audio cassette, "Beyond the Boundaries"

As these activities multiplied, communities found it expedient to consolidate them all under one roof in "municipal state departments." Some communities then began electing the heads of these programs, which educated voters, increased public support, and attracted media attention.

Of course, not all towns believed in these activities. But those that did acted and began searching for allies throughout the world. Unlike the world order organizations of the 1970s, local governments had a strong financial backbone and a modicum of popular legitimacy; their "official" undertakings were taken more seriously, drew more ongoing press attention, and involved more—and more diverse—community members. By 1990, the democracies witnessed a veritable explosion of locally undertaken world order activism.

National governments mounted legal challenges to these activities, but by 1990 public support for them was too strong to overcome. Even though some new laws prohibited certain transnational exchanges of money, ideas, messages, and people, they were either loose enough to be evaded or so stringent that they were ultimately rejected as strangling highly valued democratic rights of speech, travel, and assembly.

A Global Union of Municipalities

As more and more municipalities participated in foreign affairs, they began seeking better ways to cooperate with one another to lower the cost of their programs while increasing their effectiveness. Networks formed and multiplied, and eventually there arose a need for an interconnecting "super-network" to improve communication between, for example, the food relief networks and human rights networks; to share common problems like national prosecutions of activist municipalities; and to lobby for common agenda items like stronger diplomatic immunities for local diplomats.

To meet this need for a "super-network," two hundred local governments from twenty-seven nations came together in 1993 and formed the Global Union of Municipalities. It urged any community of any size to join, providing it met two requirements. First, a community's representative had to be chosen through the most democratic means available. Thus, communities in democratic nations had to elect their representatives, and communities in communist nations had to appoint their representatives through the same party procedures used to appoint other officials. Second, each municipality had to pay a small per capita tithe to support the Union's activities.

At first, the Union focused its efforts on increasing membership to have greater financial strength and political clout. It turned out, however, that the Union received so much publicity that thousands of localities wanted to "get in on the ground floor." For many municipalities, the Union provided the *raison d'etre* to begin involving themselves, since it provided, for the first time ever, an organization designed specifically to voice their concerns in foreign affairs.

By the mid-1990s, the Union began

It is time to recognize that the escalating arms race is itself our enemy. It saps our strength, is mainly responsible for our huge deficits, pushes aside essential domestic programs, puts pressure on interest rates and inflation. We should be out in front leading the world in our attack on the arms race.

—James Rouse, Chairman, The Rouse Co.

The process of building a U.N. which can truly preserve international security will require two interrelated parts. First, it will require a profound change in the way nations view their place in the world, and a reassessment of what is needed to provide security for their populations in the nuclear age.... Second, building a United Nations worthy of the name will require a series of concrete steps to strengthen the system and gradually transform it into a true alternative security system. Without the existence of such an alternative system, our efforts at arms control are doomed to failure. Only when nations see global institutions that work will they be prepared to entrust their security to the world community. There is an ironic circularity to the U.N. dilemma: nations,

developing and proposing new directions for both national foreign policies and international organizations; communicating these new directions directly to the publics of the world; and lobbying communities, nations, and international organizations to adopt these new directions. Even though it only had advisory powers, it became a powerful force for building international loyalties and challenging the power of states.

The Union began with fewer participants, narrower objectives, and less recognition than the world's other main advisory body, the United Nations (U.N.), yet it ultimately became a more effective builder of world order, for three reasons.

First, while the U.N. could only deal with agendas supported by national governments, the Union raised the critical issues all national governments had previously resisted. Thus, by the year 2000, the Union finished preparing the World Constitution, which recommended international infringements on national power which U.N. representatives would have never entertained.

Second, in contrast to the U.N.'s exclusion of citizens from its daily operations, the democratic appointment of many Union representatives invited, encouraged, and magnified grassroots participation. Deriving power and legitimacy from the votes of individuals, the Union's directly elected representatives were able to generate a level of public support for their recommendations that U.N. representatives had never been able to accomplish.

The third advantage of the Union was

that it had at its core a commitment to change global politics. While the U.N. was created by nation-states to improve dialogue between nation-states, the Union was created by communities with an interest in replacing rigid, geographically defined nation-to-nation alliances (e.g., "the West" versus "the East" versus "the South") with fluid, politically defined people-to-people alliances (e.g., "free marketers" versus "socialists"). Making communities a basic building block of international diplomacy unmasked thousands of new alliances the old nation-state cleavages had hidden.

Toward a Global Legislature

By 1995, the Union had municipal representatives from nearly ten thousand states and cities. The size of the Union was getting unmanageable, and everyone knew it. The leaders of the Union's five largest political parties began meeting privately to discuss ways of reforming the Union into a smaller, more effective body. On August 6th, 2000, exactly ten years ago, these leaders unveiled not only a plan for reforming the Union, but also a new World Constitution. A tidal wave of political activity ensued.

The proposals for Union reform were easily accepted. Whereas previously the Union had given a seat to any subnational government, the new Constitution consolidated the world into one thousand carefully drawn electoral districts and required that every representative be subject to recall every two years. The former election rule—that the

not believing it can work effectively in their interest, fail to give the U.N. the support it would need to perform its tasks; then they cite its weakness as a reason for their lack of support. To break out of this cycle of impotence, we propose a strategy of "confidence building" steps in the areas of U.N. peacekeeping and peacemaking— incremental changes that will noticeably improve U.N. functioning and build international support for further development.... In general, the U.N.'s peacekeeping forces have been consistently under-manned, undermandated, underarmed and under-financed. Considering these handicaps it's remarkable what an important role they have played.

—Donald Keys, "Peace-Keeping Forces," in *Securing Our Planet*

Where are we going to obtain the technicians needed to work with the peoples of underdeveloped lands outside the normal diplomatic channels—and by "technicians" I include engineers, doctors, teachers, agricultural experts, specialists in public law, labor, taxation, civil service—all the skills necessary to establish a viable economy, a stable government, and a decent standard of living? ... Think of the wonders skilled American personnel could work, building goodwill, building the peace. There is not enough money in all America to relieve the misery of the underdeveloped world in a giant and endless soup kitchen. But there is enough know-how and enough knowledgeable people to help these nations help themselves. I therefore propose that our inadequate efforts in this area be supplemented by a Peace Corps of talented young men and women, willing and able to serve their country in this fashion for three years as an alternative or as a supplement to

most democratic process available be used—was retained but strengthened. A bipartisan Electoral Review Panel was set up to evaluate every district's electoral process, and if it found serious flaws, it was empowered to decertify that district until the next elections.

The new Constitution, which proposed creating a two-house legislature comprised of the U.N. and the reformed Union, encountered much more resistance. Yet in the ten years that followed, the pressures for nations to join became overwhelming.

The first nations to accede to the Constitution were the democracies. In country after country, the Union's political parties worked with national political parties and municipal state departments to topple unsympathetic national leaders.

Authoritarian and totalitarian governments joined more slowly, but they were persuaded to enter the Union in three ways. First, the spread of photocopying machines, personal computers, and direct-broadcast satellite messages had already brought the peoples of nondemocratic countries in contact with the Union's agenda, and their demands for participation began to grow. Second, as the Union gained more power, many nondemocratic countries saw it in their interest to prevent the Union from becoming strictly a pro-democracy forum that might foment uprisings in their own backyard. Finally, national elites ultimately realized the obvious: that wars were obsolete, weapons expenditures were terrible wastes, and migration impediments fundamentally unjust. Militarily weaker nations endorsed the Constitution to safeguard against invasions by more powerful nations; thus, the fundamentalist Afghanistani dictator signed to prevent a rerun of the 1979 Soviet take-over. And militarily powerful nations endorsed the constitution to shore up their economic and political power.

While only ten nations had ratified the Constitution in 2001, by 2005, 128 nations had ratified, and by 2009, 168 nations had. During this past year, the final twenty hold-outs have ratified. With universal acceptance, the constitution finally goes into effect.

No one expects the next fifty years to be easy. New political conflicts will erupt, new conquests will arise, and the disarmament rules will be violated. But if violence erupts, it will be brief and manageable. If the four principles stand the test of time, it will not be long before the peoples of the world begin demanding a fifth, a sixth, and a hundred more principles to remove, once and for all, violence from the planet.

The past twenty-five years have arguably been the most important in the maturity of our species. From a position of utter despair, we have built new political institutions for world peace and justice. We have begun to transform international conflict into a globally integrated politics in which we debate and resolve our differences through party alliances, legislative decisions, and predictable enforcement procedures.

The Union built institutions that idealists had talked about for centuries. What gave the idealists' visions new life was a concrete

peacetime selective service—well-qualified through rigorous standards; well-trained in the language, skills, and customs they will need to know; and directed and paid for by [U.S. government foreign aid] agencies. We cannot discontinue training our young men as soldiers of war—but we also want them as "ambassadors of peace."

—John F. Kennedy, "All the Skills Necessary," in *Securing Our Planet*

It was a thought that built this whole portentous war establishment, and a thought shall melt it away.

—Ralph Waldo Emerson

353

Trust men and they will be true to you; treat them greatly and they will show themselves great.

— *Ralph Waldo Emerson*

political task that everybody, everywhere could undertake. By joining hands with their neighbors to harness their local governments, people had enough legitimacy and funding to create an unprecedented lobby for a new world order.

Today, children from throughout the world have gathered on the steps of the Union's chambers to recite the following words from Lao-Tse, written 2,500 years ago: "Leaders are best when people scarcely know they exist, not so when people obey and acclaim them, worst when people despise them. Fail to honor people, they fail to honor you. But of good leaders who talk little, when their work is done, their aim fulfilled, the people will all say: 'We did this ourselves.'"

354

In *Securing Our Planet,* a companion to this book, we reprint "The Moral Equivalent of War," an essay by William James that is often referred to but, in spite of its clarity, wit, and relevance, seldom studied. In the spirit of this classic essay, Thomas Fehsenfeld understands that our goal is not peace. As he says, "Peace has very little to do with life, which is full of conflict." Instead, in the tradition of Gandhi, who was inspired by Tolstoy, who was inspired by Emerson and Thoreau, he seeks to detach conflict from violence. In the India of the 1940s this effort involved salt marches, spinning wheels, and hunger fasts; in the 1990s, says Fehsenfeld, owner of an oil products service business, it will involve computer networks. (In effect, he outlines part of the *modus operandi* of the Ark Communications Institute.) Believing that workable ideas emerge through exchange, Fehsenfeld casts his proposals in the form of a dialogue, as Fuller also does. Part of this approach is a way for the U.S. to improve the superpower relationship by taking many steps without any formal agreement— what Fehsenfeld calls a strategy of "irresistable opportunity."

On-Line with Conflict Management

Thomas Fehsenfeld

THE FOLLOWING IS AN EXCERPT FROM the online conference "Peace in Our Time," which was held on the MacroNet Educational Network, May 17, 2010:

MN: There has been a great transformation in international relations during the past 25 years. During most of the twentieth century, nations looked upon war as a terrible but necessary part of international relations. War and threats of war were their final resort when diplomacy had broken down.

355

Many of the techniques used in building a successful business can be applied productively to issues of national security as well. Executives and entrepreneurs, it is said, are practical, action-oriented, and open-minded. They understand the relationship between costs and benefits; they can relate short-term tactics to long-term goals; and they can move quickly from a plan that doesn't work to one that might. "If a guy is hard-headed enough to run a business," says New Forum co-founder Allan M. Brown, also president of Vance M. Brown and Sons Inc., a building contractor in Palo Alto, "he presumably has a rational, pragmatic approach to life, as opposed to being a total visionary or philosopher. I mean,

In the short span of 25 years, this view has almost disappeared from the world. Military budgets worldwide have dropped to one-tenth their twentieth-century levels (figures adjusted for deflation). The incidence of war has dropped to .25 wars per year from the twentieth-century level of 1.5 per year.

Another measure of this change is that wars, when they do occur, have become less deadly. The last war to claim 100,000 victims was the Iran/Iraq war of the 1980s. Most wars today are settled quickly with the loss of less than 1,000 lives.

To help us understand this great change, we have invited Dr. John McConnell to join our conference. Welcome Dr. McConnell.

McC: Thank you.

MN: You played an important part in the changes that helped establish our current "peace system." Could you explain how the McConnell network was established?

McC: First, I have to disagree with your statement that what we now have is a "peace system." We have as many conflicts as ever between nations—it might be more accurate to say that we have a "conflict management system." Peace, after all, is not something that humanity naturally seeks.

MN: It would seem that everyone seeks peace—statesmen are continually talking about it.

McC: Of course they talk about it, but peace has very little to do with life, which is full of conflict. Nations seek prestige, wealth, power, and security. They look for peace only when the wolf is at the door and usually find that the wolf is not very interested in peace.

MN: Isn't this merely a semantic quibble?

McC: No. Peace is a transitory condition. It is a (usually short) "era of good feelings" between nations. Continual peace is neither possible nor desirable because it is through conflict that ideals are tested and either reaffirmed or changed.

Conflict management, on the other hand, is a very realistic goal. It allows conflicts to develop and find resolution, but directs them away from violence.

Our goal with the so-called McConnell network was to find strategies that would allow for conflicts of national interests, but keep them from erupting into violence. In certain instances, we found that conflicts had to be encouraged in the short run to keep them from festering into total conflicts.

MN: What is the meaning of "total conflict"?

McC: It was a phrase we coined to describe those conflicts in which the only perceived solution is the destruction of the opponent. One of the most famous total conflicts was the series of wars between Rome and Carthage which ended in the total destruction of Carthage. Our conflicts with the Soviets were at one time seen as total.

MN: Returning to the McConnell network, please describe how it was formed, how it functioned, and some of the ideas it developed.

McC: It began during the mid-1980s when there were serious questions about humanity's survival. I had been working for

I have to approach everything in a problem-solving way, what's right and what's wrong. Here it's bricks and mortar, and I have to put one on top of the other every day if the business is going to succeed."

—Lucien Rhodes,
"Being Dead Is Bad for
Business," in *Securing
Our Planet*

The best armor is to keep out of gunshot.

—Francis Bacon

357

several years at the Russian Studies Institute of the University of Michigan and had published an article questioning our approach to relations with the Soviets.

It seemed to me that we were working backward. Our government was working very hard to make agreements with a government we didn't like or trust. This was bound to fail.

MN: This is what you called the "fallacy of legality."

McC: Yes. I had begun to look at the US and the USSR as partners in the survival of the world. When you have a partner you trust and respect, you can carry on your business on a handshake. On the other hand, when two partners have a poor relationship, when they are continually jockeying for advantage, then no contract is sufficient. Any agreement devised by the mind of man can be circumvented by the mind of man.

I suggested that we had to find ways to improve the underlying relationship between us. If we did this, agreements would be much easier to conclude—in fact, such an improvement would make many agreements unnecessary.

MN: How would it make agreements unnecessary?

McC: Well, for instance, we did not need agreements with France to limit their nuclear stockpiles because we were confident that they had no intention of aiming their missiles at us.

Our underlying relationship with France was one of sympathy and respect (although they often frustrated us). War between us was

---

We assume far too easily that everything has to be explicit. A richer and more realistic model of the social and international system would reveal the enormous importance of what is not said, not signed, but quietly taken as a rule of behavior. Without this element in social life, indeed, all societies would fall apart almost overnight. What I am looking for here is an almost half-conscious peace policy, communicated by nods, smiles, and raised eyebrows, and an atmosphere of intercourse which underlies the agreements, treaties, and declarations and often makes all the difference between failure and success.

—Kenneth Boulding, "Seven Planks for a Platform," in *Securing Our Planet*

"unthinkable" in spite of frequent conflicts.

MN: What specific proposals did you make?

McC: The article contained about a dozen low cost steps we could take to improve our underlying relations. I listed them not because they were great ideas, but simply to illustrate that once you focused on the underlying relationship instead of the legalities, it was easy to find ways.

Some of the things suggested were the establishment of a joint US/USSR trade center with a data-base to aid in matching products and markets, a jointly financed and operated space station, diplomatic restraint when we were not directly involved in a problem created by the Soviets. (We had a tendency at the time to take over other nations' problems with the Soviets and make them our own.)

MN: What happened next?

McC: In spite of being a simple idea, the article was a success. It happened to get picked up by a couple of liberal senators looking for a new idea. Liberals were on the run at the time and fresh out of new ideas.

They liked it because it gave them an approach to the USSR which was not belligerent, nor did it suggest sacrificing our national interest just to nail down formal agreements—something the conservatives had accused them of.

As a result of the article, I was asked to testify before the Senate Foreign Relations Committee and got some publicity. This helped me to make contacts which led to the formation of the New Relations Work-

The melting of the freeze at the public policy level cannot be attributed entirely to the ambivalence of the American voting public. Their perplexity reflects their twin concerns that nuclear weapons might kill them but that the Russians might otherwise do so first. While the freeze was intended to be mutual and bilateral, no one has yet come up with a formula the public believes will allow us to escape both fates. The public's reluctance to step into the vast unknown territory beyond nuclear deterrence demonstrates the incompleteness of the freeze as an alternative to the present system of international relations. The freeze says, "Stop right there! Don't move another inch!" It does not, however, say, "Go this way instead. It's much safer." Of course, this one initiative was never intended to answer all questions; it was intended, rather, as a way to begin asking them.

—Gordon Feller and Mark Sommer, "Lessons of the Nuclear Freeze Initiative," in *Securing Our Planet*

ing Group, which the media called the McConnell network.

MN: How was it organized?

McC: I had some initial meetings with members of Congress and people in the administration who were interested in further discussions on our relations with the Soviets, but being busy people, no one had time for meetings so we formed a computer network to exchange views. That was not so common then as it is today.

MN: Did that mode work well for you?

McC: Yes. It was fascinating to watch the ideas develop—it worked almost as a group mind. It turned out that by using the computer network ideas were detached from ego. They were thrown into the data-base without anyone caring if they survived or not.

Ideas would build into theories almost effortlessly. Participants would come and go, adding their perspectives and experience. A kind of natural selection took place until we began to distill an approach to conflict which was unique, and which worked.

MN: Please describe some of your conclusions.

McC: We began with Soviet/American relations because almost every national conflict at that time was cast in the light of the overall East/West conflict.

If Somalia was being armed by the Soviets, we would send arms to Ethiopia—if Ethiopia had a revolution and jumped into the Soviet camp, we would begin arming the Somalis. It was crazy.

Many leaders of third-world nations

In the heady days of the early 1970s, when Nixon and Brezhnev ushered in the era of detente, American policy was based on the assumption that a web of interdependence in the areas of arms control, trade, and cultural, scientific, and technological exchanges would reduce the level and intensity of competition between the two countries. It was at the same time the expectation of Soviet policy that the regularization of this competitive relationship would lead to the modernization of the Soviet economy and the

360

understood this, of course. They played off the superpowers to enrich themselves and were showered with an incredible amount of sophisticated weaponry. Our weapons and the Soviets' fueled every war during the last half of the twentieth century.

Moreover, every strategy tried since World War II to control this mounting conflict had failed. The United Nations failed— it became a forum that created and intensified conflicts; the arms-control process had failed—each new agreement left us with higher levels of armaments; detente had failed—each side was left feeling betrayed because there was never a common understanding of what detente meant. Nothing seemed to work.

MN: And yet, solutions were there.

McC: Yes, they were. But at the time, the people who wanted a better relationship with the Soviets kept pushing the same failed solutions. They wanted a United Nations that "worked," or another arms agreement which would be obsolete with the next breakthrough, or a freeze of nuclear weapons at ridiculously high levels.

Our group took a different tack. A consensus emerged that we should focus on measures that would improve the underlying relationship (as my initial article had). A second point was that America could take many steps without any formal agreement that would improve this relationship. We developed a strategy of "irresistible opportunity."

MN: What did you mean by that?

McC: We looked at actions we could take which would draw the Soviets into the

expansion of its global influence. The political decision for detente led to the expansion of economic interchange. In the course of the 1970s Soviet foreign trade turnover with the West tripled, and the American share of Western exports to the Soviet Union grew from 8 percent in 1974 to 20 percent in 1979. By the early 1980s, however, while Soviet imports from the West remained high, the American share had dropped below 10 percent. The economic downturn has been produced in part by a revised American outlook toward the Soviets in the early 1980s. The American response to the Soviet occupation of Afghanistan and to the imposition of military rule in Poland with Soviet backing led to constraints in the relations between the two countries over a whole range of dimensions, including a political decision to reduce exports to the Soviet Union. Trade is now seen as disproportionately advantageous to the Soviet Union and as contributing significantly to Soviet military capabilities.

world economy and world culture exchange without threatening their identity. Ways were explored in which the ruble could be turned into a hard currency, for instance, to facilitate their entry into world trade on an equal basis with other countries. We thought that this would be an irresistible opportunity for them because their economy was ailing.

We also looked at our own defense policy to find ways of improving our relationship. We suggested many actions which might make our defense posture less threatening to them without endangering our own security. There were a whole range of actions which we called by the name of "minimum assured deterrence." The basic idea was that we should have the minimum amount of force available to protect ourselves. Holding excess force in reserve tends to look threatening from the other side and draws a response which leads to escalation. We sought actions that we could take unilaterally to deescalate the arms race.

Eventually, as some of these proposals were adopted, they created an irresistible opportunity for the Soviets to lower their own spending on arms.

MN: What made your approach different from other groups that were making these types of proposals at the time? Why did your group receive a hearing and eventually have some of its ideas adopted?

McC: There were two ways in which we were different. First, we were an open group in which anyone who had access to a computer terminal could participate. All earlier attempts had been made by narrow, usually elite groups which did not build widespread support.

Secondly, we decided early in our endeavor that it was not enough to think up new ideas and make logical arguments for them. There was a wise old politician who joined our group, George Winslow. He continually asked of each idea, "Who has the power to implement this? How could they be motivated to do so?" It was fine to argue about what should be, but if no one could find an answer to George's questions, the idea was dropped.

MN: Was it Mr. Winslow who came up with the idea of "a program, a constituency, a coalition?"

McC: Yes. After we had answered his questions about who had the power to implement the idea or program, we could ask what groups in our society would benefit by its implementation and what groups could influence the policymaker. We then searched for a way to create a coalition between them to get the job done. This approach worked very well.

We had to carry it one step further, of course, and ask which groups would be opposed to such a change and how their opposition could be dealt with.

MN: Especially the armed forces and their suppliers?

McC: The military-industrial complex is what we called it then. They had to be dealt with. In a pluralistic society such as ours, you could not simply advocate ideas which would put many hundreds of thousands out of a job. New missions had to be found for them. Luckily, there were many missions available

Each of us must accept total responsibility for the earth's survival. We are the curators of life on earth, standing at a crossroads in time. We must awake from our false sense of security and commit ourselves to using democracy constructively to save the human species, or our democratic heritage will atrophy and be lost.

—Helen Caldicott

The care of life and happiness, and not their destruction, is the first and only legitimate object of good government.

—Thomas Jefferson

363

for brave and dedicated people.

When you said that military budgets have dropped to one-tenth their twentieth century level, you were technically correct. But as everyone knows, we still have a very large army. They are simply performing non-military missions. Every school kid knows about President Andrews' West Point speech of 1993 in which he said, "For 200 years, you have defended the Republic and the Constitution. Now you must defend the Earth itself."

The ecological disasters of the late 1980s were the main motivation in this change. And the reforestation of the Sahara by the American Army was one of its finest hours.

Today, the American services are widely respected and welcomed around the world for their contributions to preserving the ecosystem and aiding in the construction of transportation and communications systems. Their scientific work on the seas and in space is providing us with greater understanding of our world and our place in it.

MN: How could a simple computer network gain so much influence?

McC: Numbers. We simply recruited and recruited. At its height in the early 1990s, we had almost 20,000 active members who participated in discussions and the building of a data-base on conflict management. This in itself was a powerful forum for new ideas.

Equally important were the many groups which used the network. Many politicians (both liberals and conservatives) mined our data-base to find ideas and new directions. President Andrews' campaign statement,

If we connect peace and justice it raises questions about the use of violence to achieve social justice and a "lasting" peace. Throughout history, many of the voices for peace and justice have decried the use of physical violence. They argue that the means must be consistent with the ends, that physical violence is unjustified, and that we must find non-violent methods of seeking justice. Yet in many situations it is not always easy to see the moral and practical grounds for non-violence.

364

"The Republicans have thrown money at our security problems, but have not made us more secure," was picked up on one of our online conferences.

Politicians are in the business of winning elections—maximizing their votes. When they joined our network, they had an important resource that they could use to find the facts they needed or test ideas (sometimes anonymously). Quite often they put out appeals for money on the network as well.

It also spawned many businesses. The conflict management industry did not exist 25 years ago. Now, of course, there are thousands of firms offering conflict management services and many of them began with conversations on our network. Now there are many conflict management data-bases available, expert systems programs, consulting groups, conflict resolution centers. They deal with anything from family disputes to labor/management problems, to international relations. Even the socialist countries have established similar institutions.

MN: Didn't the commercial nature of the network cause a split during the 1990s?

McC: Yes. Many of those who were grounded in the old peace movement felt that there was something immoral about making money on conflict management. I and many others argued that it was important for people to be able to earn a living in this line of work. After all, people had been earning a living on war for thousands of years. Why not on peace?

The dominant culture of America is

What types of action were in the best interests of peace and justice for American slaves? How could we peacefully oppose a Hitler aimed and bent on world domination? How can peasants in an oppressive and violent dictatorship peacefully seek to redress their grievances? How can the black people of South Africa act for peace and justice? What is the peaceful way for a woman to face a would-be rapist? These are difficult and complex questions, but all too real. Can we condone violence in certain situations? How can we be sensitive to the reality of suffering and injustice?

—Educators for Social Responsibility

Government is itself an art, one of the subtlest of the arts. It is neither business, nor technology, nor applied science. It is the art of making men live together in peace and with reasonable happiness.

—Felix Frankfurter

business. It has been since the Civil War. We had to turn conflict management into a business or it would have remained forever on the sidelines.

Those who disagreed formed the Satyagraha network which deals mainly with philosophical and religious approaches to peace. They perform a valuable function and most competent conflict managers keep in touch with their ideas.

MN: Where does the conflict management movement go from here?

McC: There is a growing awareness that we must move beyond conflict management. The companies which specialize only in conflict management are facing a shrinking market because their techniques are now so widely known and applied. People are becoming better managers of their own conflicts.

The most progressive companies are developing approaches to emphasize the constructive uses of conflict. After all, once the connection between conflict and violence is broken, it can be a very creative experience....

Like the essays by Lamm and Fehsenfeld, this chapter was originally written for a contest sponsored by the *Christian Science Monitor*, which invited entrants to envision peace in the year 2010. Excerpts from some of the essays appear in *How Peace Came to the World*, edited by Earl W. Foell and Richard A. Nenneman (MIT Press, 1986). Craig Schindler and Toby Herzlich run Project Victory in Santa Cruz, California. Instead of surrendering words such as "victory" to the war-fighters, they demand "victory for all"—just as we might reply, when challenged about national security, "Yes, we insist upon it, for *all* nations." (In today's conditions, if one superpower feels insecure, the other can't sleep easily.) Schindler and Herzlich proceed from the premise that the Soviets are ill-equipped to take the lead in creating a more constructive relationship, that in contrast the U.S. *can* do so, and that the necessary initiatives require a profound healing of our own divisions and a democratizing of foreign policy. In their story, the superpowers ultimately join in what the authors wittily call "mutual assured development"—a satiric allusion to the current policy of deterrence through the threat of mutual assured destruction.

The Great Turning

Craig Schindler
Toby Herzlich

AUGUST 6, 2025—ALAMAGORDO, NEW Mexico. The sky is clearing, the air fresh from a desert rain. Lightning flashes in the distance. The storm has passed. The white sands of New Mexico shimmer in the late afternoon sun. Looking out across this vast expanse, I am struck by its awesome beauty. It seems altogether fitting that this place should be the site for the first World Monument.

Standing at the base of the Monument, I am moved by its grandeur and simple elegance. As in the Jefferson and Lincoln Memorials, the designers have captured some ineffable quality, a living tribute sculpted from the world's finest materials.

I remember being here ten years ago at the dedication ceremony, with 500,000 people from almost every country gathered in celebration and prayer. The inscription carved into stone reads:

Monument for the Recognition of World Leadership

"In appreciation and gratitude to the people and the government of the United States of America for your leadership in establishing a new era of human dignity and peace. Through your initiative we have achieved the greatest victory in human history." (Signed by the leaders of nations worldwide.)

Around the monument, there is a circle of national flags and immense flower gardens. It is a shrine in the midst of the desert, an oasis of life. Thousands of people visit this spot each year. I cannot express the joy and thankfulness that I feel to be here, to have lived through the period in which the threat of nuclear war was overcome.

Alamagordo, New Mexico: the Trinity site. Here, just before dawn on July 16, 1945, several hundred scientists and military personnel watched the explosion of the first atom bomb. It lit up the desert and the surrounding mountains as if it were noon. The thunder from the blast continued to echo through the valley as though it would never stop. A mushroom cloud, glowing brilliantly purple, rose off the desert floor and seemed to hang there

A true weapon is at best something with which you endeavor to affect the behavior of another society by influencing the minds, the calculations, the intentions, of the men that control it; it is not something with which you destroy indiscriminately the lives, the substance, the hopes, the culture, the civilization, of another people. What a confession of intellectual poverty it would be—what a bankruptcy of intelligent statesmanship—if we had to admit that such blind, senseless acts of destruction were the best use we could make of what we have come to view as the forever. As one witness said, "The sun is rising in the wrong direction."

Twenty-three days later, the first atom bomb was dropped on a civilian population at Hiroshima, Japan.

Alamagordo, it was Apache country. But the handful of cattle ranchers and home-steaders who lived here in 1945 called it by the Spanish name, Jornado Del Muerto, the Journey of Death. That was sixty-five years ago, the dawn of the nuclear age.

There was a time when it looked pretty grim. I remember when my son was a small boy, wondering if he would be killed in a nuclear war before he grew up. We were closer to the edge than most of us were willing to admit to ourselves. By the mid-1980s we had accumulated more than 50,000 nuclear war-heads worldwide. Scientists estimated that if only a small percentage of these bombs were used, it would darken the skies for many months and precipitate a new ice age, a nu-clear winter. By 1987, ten nations had nuclear exterminating devices and it was predicted that by the year 2000, there would be thirty. It looked like the Journey of Death. Many were convinced it was inevitable.

The United States and the Soviet Union were embroiled in an arms race which was out of control, each side always trying to get the lead, only to be matched by the other.

We MIRVed our missiles, and the Soviets MIRVed theirs—the result was that everyone was less secure. We deployed Cruise Missiles, giving us the capacity to penetrate behind their radar. They did the same. We began to

leading elements of our military strength! To my mind, the nuclear bomb is the most useless weapon ever invented. It can be employed to no rational purpose. It is not even an effective defense against itself. It is only something with which, in a moment of petulance or panic, you commit such fearful acts of destruction as no sane person would ever wish to have upon his conscience.

—George F. Kennan, "Deep Cuts," in *Securing Our Planets*

369

militarize space and the Soviets quickly followed. Billions of dollars and rubles later, neither superpower had an advantage and the citizens of the world were in increasingly grave danger. Both countries had military plans to fight and win a nuclear war.

By 1985, we Americans were engaged in the most expensive military build-up in history. We were siphoning our money away from our own needs. Schools and hospitals, social services for the poor and the elderly, research and development, even our space program—all had begun to suffer severely. The economic stress of arming ourselves was beginning to tear apart the fabric of our society. Our national debt rose higher than ever before: for the first time the United States owed the world more than we were owed.

In effect, we had created an artificial economy. Having manufactured billions of dollars' worth of arms yearly, we were compelled to find markets for them. To do this, we offered loans to Third World countries to enable them to buy our weapons. Then, as they repeatedly defaulted, the world economy became less and less stable. Rather than promoting real economic development, we were paying the bill to arm vast areas of the globe. Along with the Soviets, the United States was helping to erode and destabilize the world situation. Perhaps the hardest thing for us to grasp was that we could do anything about it. The situation seemed so overwhelming. Like almost everyone, I resisted confronting the threat of nuclear war as a personal issue for many years. I suppose at some level I believed

"When a man's ways please the Lord," the scriptures tell us, "he maketh even his enemies to be at peace with him." And is not peace, in the last analysis, basically a matter of human rights— the right to live out our lives without fear of devastation—the right to breathe air as nature provided it—the right of future generations to a healthy existence? While we proceed to safeguard our national interests, let us also safeguard human interests. And the

370

it was hopeless. Certainly I believed it was beyond my capacity to affect the outcome.

We were on the edge. Little did we know that we were also on the edge of a breakthrough. It began with individuals. Slowly and imperceptibly at first, the number of people who realized what was at stake increased. What appeared to be the Journey of Death became an impetus for us to wake up, to take charge of our destiny.

Albert Einstein is memorialized here, along with other great Americans and world citizens who contributed to the coming of this time. Einstein emphasized that nuclear weapons were not the root of the problem—that the nuclear crisis was fundamentally a crisis of human understanding and communication. Our security was intertwined as never before. We were compelled to acknowledge our interdependence and to seek the highest mutual gain possible for all parties.

Just like any major step, at the time it seemed so far out of reach. But now, historians of the twenty-first century refer to this period as the time of "the Great Turning" (roughly dated from 1980 to 2000 or 2010). It was a period like no other. Just a few years earlier, the events of the next two decades were inconceivable. Historians still debate how it all happened. They generally outline four states of development:

Stage One: Waking Up

Most historians agree that the first stage began at the outset of the 1980s as thousands of people voiced an unprecedented level of

elimination of war and arms is clearly in the interest of both. No treaty, however much it may be to the advantage of all, however tightly it may be worded, can provide absolute security against the risks of deception and evasion. But it can—if it is sufficiently effective in its enforcement and it is sufficiently in the interests of its signers—offer far more security and far fewer risks than an unabated, uncontrolled, unpredictable arms race.

—John F. Kennedy, from a 1963 speech reprinted in *Securing Our Planet*

Can we, in fact, develop another strategy that doesn't involve threatening annihilation, but that can induce changes in Soviet international behavior? I think that's crucial, because I don't think the American people are willing to end the arms race until they know that we can pressure or change or cajole or convert [the Soviets] through other than military means.

—Gordon Feller on audio cassette, "Beyond the Boundaries"

concern about the increasing threat of nuclear war. There were movies, television programs, public school curricula, and the active participation of professional and community groups—all with the purpose of informing ourselves about the factual consequences of nuclear war. The public became increasingly involved in the debate over arms control. There was a massive shift in public opinion. Although nuclear weapons had been around since World War II, it was not until the 1980s that an overwhelming percentage of the American public expressed the clear understanding that a nuclear war was not winnable, was likely to destroy most life on Earth, and hence must not be fought.

At the same time Americans became more concerned about nuclear war, they also became more and more divided about what should be done. By the mid-1980s the debate over nuclear policy was deadlocked in a bitter stalemate between two opposing factions. The Hawks focused on the threat of Soviet expansionism and argued for peace through military strength and arms build-up. The Doves focused on the threat of nuclear annihilation and argued for peace through cooperation and arms reduction. We were divided against ourselves.

The arms control talks of the early 1980s between the United States and the Soviet Union demonstrated little real commitment on the part of either superpower to de-escalate the arms race—except on their own terms. We in the United States did not have a clear vision of our own role and national purpose.

372

The vacillation between American Hawk and Dove factions sent a conflicting signal to the Soviets. What was our intention? Did we intend to regain nuclear superiority, to be able to prevail in a nuclear war? Or, did we intend to acknowledge nuclear parity, and work towards coexistence? And what was their intention toward us? Nothing was clear. It was a quagmire of miscommunication and deception. Both the Americans and the Russians were preparing for World War III. The negotiations were stalemated and the momentum toward nuclear catastrophe continued to accelerate.

Stage Two: National Reconciliation

Stage two began, quietly at first, as small groups of people from different points of view recognized that it was up to the United States to take the leadership toward world peace. We were the only nation with both the strength and the freedom to initiate a new direction. Yet, we were split as to what to do. Our vacillations helped to undermine whatever Soviet incentive there was to negotiate in earnest. As long as the Russians perceived they could exploit our divisions, they continued to do so.

Realistically, it became evident to more and more of us that we needed a new national consensus in order to send a clear, unambiguous signal to the Soviet Union. So long as we were divided as to our national purpose, this was impossible. Only by healing the divisions within the United States could we send an unwavering message to the Soviets and sus-

We've been assuming all along that failure was certain, that our universe was running down and it was strictly you or me, kill or be killed as long as it lasted. But now, in our century, we've discovered that man can be a success on his planet and this is the great change that has come over our thinking.

—R. Buckminster Fuller

373

tain a steady course toward lasting peace.

Warily at first, people from opposing camps began to step across our narrow partisan boundaries to listen to each other and to understand each other's perspective. Soon, there were discussion groups and house meetings around the country, bringing Hawks and Doves together in a common search for the way out of our predicament. We began to talk with each other about our fears and what to do. Doves came to understand that in their fear of nuclear annihilation, they had been blinded to the threat of Soviet domination. Hawks came to understand that in their fear of totalitarian repression, they had been blinded to the global consequences of nuclear war. Both Hawks and Doves acknowledged that in focusing narrowly on the nuclear weapons debate, they had neglected the broader discussion of how to transform the underlying conditions that threaten peace.

Previous interactions between camps had been bitter and adversarial. Now, there was a growing recognition that the next step had to emerge from constructive dialogue. Each camp learned from the other and thereby increased our shared insight and options about how to proceed. It was a time of national reconciliation. Thus, we recognized the need for an undivided national purpose to address the twin threat of totalitarianism and nuclear catastrophe.

The message spread from person to person, through friendship circles, neighborhoods and professional associations. There was no stopping it. And what was the message? Hard to put in words. We were called to participate in changing the course of human history. The essence was for each of us to take personal responsibility to contribute our piece of the puzzle.

All manner of folks started to participate in the renewal of our democratic life, dedicating their talents and skills to overcoming the common danger. Business executives, civic organizations and universities sponsored all points of view forums. Military leaders and officials of the War Colleges put together a regular publication entitled *The New Warrior*. It was aimed at generating dialogue within military circles about how to deal with the twin threat of Soviet expansion and nuclear war. The bitter divisions from the Vietnam era were increasingly healed as more and more people from the "Baby-Boom Generation" became involved. Many who had been alienated from American life during the turmoil of the sixties returned. Blacks, Chicanos, and other minority groups voiced impassioned concern over the decay of urban society in the wake of rising military expenditures.

Professional associations—doctors, lawyers, psychologists, architects—played a major part in facilitating dialogue within their ranks. Christians, Jews, and people of all faiths renewed their commitment to the sanctity of life. A quiet movement began to "pass the peace" from person to person, group to group, across all denominations and points of view. Finally, the impact of women—assuming leadership within groups throughout the society—cannot be overstated.

The word citizen diplomacy, which Mr. Reagan used in his post-Geneva [Summit] remarks, has been a way of life for businesspeople for centuries. It's accelerated in recent years as trade crossed boundaries more rapidly and as we as businesspeople moved into a world market. In a sense any businessperson who is doing business in other countries by definition has become a citizen diplomat.

—Don Carlson on audio cassette, "Beyond the Boundaries"

There were neighborhood gatherings, town meetings, and conferences which focused on discovering the elements of a new national consensus. Television and media played a critical role, enabling us to conduct national discussions via satellite and to communicate with each other in creative new ways. Network news teams made a concerted effort to report the discussion on nuclear policy in a way that was more informational and less adversarial. Satellite television, coupled with personal computer systems, became a vehicle for a new level of electronically facilitated interactive democracy.

You could really see when the tide was beginning to turn. Though it manifested as an impression of national unity, the pivotal change, the fulcrum, was the individual. I don't remember exactly what the first pledge of personal responsibility said or where it came from. It was translated into so many different languages in so many different places. And everybody had a different way of saying it. My pledge goes:

I pledge to take personal responsibility to prevent nuclear war. I will make it a priority in my life to reach out to other people so that they will take personal responsibility starting with my circle of friends and associates.

I will work for peace through strength and compassion, both in my personal life and in the world around me. And I will continue until we have attained victory for everyone.

The efforts of committed individuals and groups began to be expressed in our national life. There was a National Day of Listening

376

Jumping Ahead and Looking Back at the Future

which involved people from all walks of life, in the process of dialogue with someone holding an opposing point of view. By facilitating better listening and understanding, we discovered new options for national action. The following year, July 4 was dedicated to a celebration of our shared intention to prevent nuclear war. Cities across the nation sponsored free concerts featuring artists and musicians from a wide spectrum of American life. Starting from Los Angeles—the site of the 1984 Olympics—a torch was carried from person to person, some running, some walking, some in wheel chairs. It traveled from city to city across the country. In each community, the torch kindled a permanent flame to commemorate the 200th Anniversary of the United States Constitution and renew our dedication to the task of taking leadership for global peace. It symbolized both the commitment of the individual carrying the torch, and the commitment of our nation.

The pattern of events and level of responsiveness of this time reminds me of vitality around the first American movement for independence. It reaffirmed the original ideas upon which our country was founded. People began to appreciate and exercise the freedoms of our democracy, directed toward choosing our future. After twenty years of movies about the inevitable apocalypse (coming soon to your local theater), the movies changed—telling the adventure stories of how the human race took charge in the latter part of the twentieth century to overcome the forces of death and destruction. There were rallies and gatherings.

The freeze was supported by more than twelve million voters in nine states. It has been described as the largest referendum on a single issue in the history of the United States, and citizen support for its common-sense clarity continues to grow. Six months after the 1982 election results, a national poll showed that 79 percent of Americans favored the freeze. Its bipartisan support was demonstrated by the fact that 72 percent of the Republicans polled favored the freeze. Even the noted conservative columnist James Kilpatrick has stated that "there is nothing in the freeze resolution that a good conservative could not support."

—Harold Willens, "Taking the Next Steps," in *Securing Our Planet*

A new generation of musicians gave us songs of determination and celebration.

What I remember most is a profound sense of purpose. We felt connected to other people—we were engaged in a common endeavor. The more involved and committed we became, the more we felt the joy of knowing we were going to make it. In a sense, we began to celebrate the victory of our common humanity long before it was assured.

By the late 1980s we had reached a new level of undivided national purpose. After nine presidential elections (since 1945) in which the question of nuclear policy was little discussed or noted, the presidential election of 1988 reflected a profound shift in our willingness to take responsibility. The discussion throughout the primaries and the Fall was thoughtful and well-informed. Even before the election, both presidential candidates pledged that, if elected, they would reach out with their opponent to develop a bi-partisan effort to send a clear, unwavering signal to the Soviet Union. Most historians date this as the beginning of stage three.

Stage Three: Pulling Back from the Brink

Our new administration, backed by a broadly based consensus of public opinion, immediately undertook a series of steps to pull us back from the brink. Previous arms-control negotiations between the U.S. and the U.S.S.R. had been primarily empty posturings, each side trying to maximize their advantage without any real intent to negotiate. It was

Let us be clear about this: there are major differences between our two countries. Soviet values are diametrically opposed to ours. Contention between us on a global scale is a fact of life. Suspicion is the keynote of our relations.

But having said that, let me add this: on the evidence, the Soviets do keep agreements provided each side has an interest in the other's keeping the agreement, and provided each side can verify compliance for itself.

—Thomas J. Watson, Jr. former Ambassador to the Soviet Union and President of IBM

378

during Stage Three that we began to establish limits and allowances on weapons systems which were truly in the interests and safety of both superpowers (and the rest of the world).

The old guard in the Kremlin, forged under Stalin, had passed away. The Politbureau was generally younger, less ideological and more pragmatic. They were faced with pressures at home to stabilize the Soviet economy, as well as increasing protests from independently spirited satellite countries. The widespread demand for a more consumer-oriented economy made it expedient for Soviet leaders to seek military controls and cut-backs.

The President of the United States and the Soviet Premier agreed upon a set of procedures designed to increase safety and communication during times of crisis. These included a direct telephone line between the White House and the Kremlin, and a sophisticated monitoring system on both sides to reduce the risk of computer errors. The U.S. proposed the renewal of the Comprehensive Test Ban talks. In the meantime, we pledged ourselves to refrain from the testing of nuclear weapons so long as other nations abided by the moratorium.

Both superpowers agreed to create nuclear free zones in troubled spots around the world. This reduced the risk of a "limited" nuclear exchange which could escalate into global war. Both the United States and the Soviet Union acknowledged it was in their interests to stop the proliferation of nuclear weapons to other countries. Supported by the

Nations ought to form amongst themselves a special alliance which might be termed the alliance of peace, and which would differ from an ordinary treaty of peace, inasmuch as it would not merely end one war, but would terminate war altogether.

—Immanuel Kant

business community in the United States, the U.S. and the Soviet Union applied pressure to the other nuclear countries to halt all sales of nuclear-related technologies. After prolonged discussions both at home and abroad, the U.S. and the U.S.S.R. reached an agreement to prohibit all nuclear weapons in space.

Stage Four: Lasting Peace

Looking back, I can see the antecedents of the Great Turning. At the beginning of the twentieth century, the American philosopher William James said, "What we must discover is the moral equivalent of war." It was President John F. Kennedy who first suggested in 1961 that we could redirect the energies of war toward the dual frontier of global development and outer space.

By the early 1990s, having pulled back from the brink, the United States took the initiative to address the social, economic, and environmental conditions which underlie lasting peace. We saw that the threat of global suicide was present in many forms: biological and chemical warfare, environmental pollution, the extinction of species, the greenhouse effect, resource depletion, overpopulation, vast famine, and poverty. As the world's strongest democracy, we took responsibility to articulate and implement a policy which came to be called "mutually assured development"—the establishment of economic and cultural relations between countries in which all parties achieve the highest mutual gain.

We began by proposing increased avenues of mutual trade with the Soviet Union,

America also needs to revive the promising economic initiatives that Richard Nixon undertook a decade ago when he encouraged U.S. trade with the Soviets. Because of its population decline, the Soviet Union expects labor shortages in the future, which means it is desperate to rebuild its industrial facilities with high-tech automation. Our allies in Japan and Western Europe are already developing this vast market; they're delighted that Cold War hysteria in the U.S. keeps

380

offering goods and services desired by the Soviets, but which in no way threatened our national security. Of course there were still significant ideological differences, but we found that the most effective "weapon" we had against the spread of totalitarianism was to exercise the real strengths of our democracy and market economy. We engaged the Soviet Union in a peaceful competition, drawing upon our economic ingenuity. Similarly, we took the initiative in suggesting various cultural programs between the U.S.S.R. and the U.S.A.: student exchange programs, increased scientific and artistic conferences and collaborations. By creating trade and cultural incentives, we reinforced those elements of Soviet society which were committed to development and increased flexibility. Once again, the historical insight that persecution builds faith proved true. The gradual deepening of religious life in the Soviet Union began to affect Soviet national culture by the mid-1990s. No longer could the Soviet government afford to openly suppress or persecute religious Jews and Christians. Indeed, the spirit of reconciliation happening in the West between groups of different denominations and points of view helped to inspire increased support among differing elements of the religious community in the Soviet Union. The strength of religion, combined with advances in cultural and scientific flexibility, contributed to the gradual development of a less repressive and more tolerant Soviet society.

It became irrevocably clear that the United States and the Soviet Union could not

American businesses from competing with them. The common-sense solution to this situation—American business plunging full steam into the Soviet marketplace—may not be as remote as it sounds. The Commerce Department recently reopened trade talks with the Soviets, focusing on some of the same projects abandoned in the mid-1970s when détente collapsed. American companies have the best technology in the world for mineral extraction and production—coal, oil, natural gas—and the Russians want to buy it.

—William Greider, "The Economics of Security," in *Securing Our Planet*

Jumping Ahead and Looking Back at the Future

So far, war has been the only force that can discipline a whole community, and until an equivalent discipline is organized, I believe that war must have its way. But I have no serious doubt that the ordinary prides and shames of social man, once developed to a certain intensity, are capable of organizing...a moral equivalent.

—William James, "The Moral Equivalent of War," in *Securing Our Planet*

continue massive military expenditures and at the same time undertake the challenge of the next step of human development. We could not afford to journey to the stars, nor to eradicate hunger and poverty, if we devoted most of our resources and best talents to arming the planet. Thus, the President of the United States, speaking before a joint session of Congress, challenged the Soviets to a peaceful, all-out competition to explore the outer recesses of our solar system, to eliminate starvation on Earth and to restore the quality of our global environment. Soon the race was in full swing. Instead of trying to destabilize and arm the world, we began to offer the tools of true development to less developed countries. I remember vividly when the last pocket of starving people were fed and taught the skills for their own self-sufficient development.

A Final Word:
Dance Your Troubles Away

6

One afternoon with a couple of friends I was flying over Silicon Valley, thinking what a bull's-eye it undoubtedly is for Soviet missiles, and what a source of components for our own weaponry. At that time I was bemused, along with my media-conscious friends, by the success of the Live-Aid benefit-concerts that had just been broadcast by space-satellite all over the world. And I was pondering the notion that it's impossible to "save humanity," because humanity doesn't yet exist; it isn't fully conscious of itself.

As we gained altitude, I began to think about a worldwide celebration. Instead of showing only rock stars, this celebration would also feature ordinary people dancing to their local music and becoming conscious of one another, in their joy, through the magic of "uplinks" and "downlinks." (In fact, this satellite jargon began to sound to me like the names of new dances—as in "let's do the uplink.") The whole world would take the day off and everybody would link with one another. For the first time, in a single day, humanity would see itself.

But what could possibly justify, or even motivate, such a global occasion?

As I looked west to the Pacific, an image came to me of UN technicians, in front of the whole world, dismantling two thermonuclear weapons. Since these cannot be obtained on the open market, yet, they would have to be donated to the celebration by the U.S. and the Soviet Union, who would be listed as "sustaining patrons" of the party. After the radioactive material was removed, it would be rendered harmless and then stored in such a way as to be inaccessible. Such a spectacle would be worth a mass celebration.

As tribes once gathered around settlement fires, humanity would gather around TV, but instead of viewing the usual melodramas about greed, malice, jealousy and violence, they would watch one another watching the start of disarmament. If "nuclear winter" calculations are accurate, the start of disarmament would be as much a cause for celebration in Rio, Lagos, Cairo, New Delhi, and Tokyo, as in the military superpowers. And there are some wonderful dancers in each of those places.

Of course the dismantling of two bombs, in itself, would have zero military significance. Who would miss a couple of thermonuclear warheads when so many thousands would remain?

But the event would make people aware of a simple fact about these city-busters and flesh-burners, these air-poisoners, these gene-twisters, these sky-darkeners and crop-killers—just as they have been deliberately manufactured, they can be deliberately taken apart. Then the question would arise, "Why not take apart some more?"

What Live-Aid did for the famine of Ethiopia, drawing attention to it and raising money for relief and long-term development, this new show could do for weapons capable of bringing famine, not to mention more immediate effects, to the entire northern hemisphere. During the disarmament party, weapons built and deployed in secret would be dismantled under a billion eyes.

In the Pacific Northwest natives used to conduct "potlatches," celebrations at which people would compete to offer the biggest gift. Prestige was based upon ability and willingness to let go of property. In modern times our biggest treasures appear to be missiles, submarines, bombers, and warheads. It's as if we've been preparing for a nuclear potlatch. Why not start it?

Of course this vision is crazy. I know that. Years ago at a physics conference, I am told, somebody read a theoretical paper that cut against everyone's ways of thinking. Respondents called it crazy. Niels Bohr stood up and said: I agree the paper is crazy—the question is, is it crazy enough to be true?

Reviewing the disappointing record of "arms control," I keep asking about new ideas: are they crazy enough to have a chance of working? The point of a global disarmament party would be less to "control arms" than to display a positive spirit between the superpowers.

The show could have a couple of simple themes—starting with whole earth security. People would grasp that in the nuclear age no single nation can possibly assure its own security. That among the superpowers one side can never be more secure than the other.

Another theme would be planetary citizenship, based upon a sense of caring for our little earth in the vastness of space, and of helping each culture enrich itself by learning from what is now strange to it.

A thinker once said that all truly challenging thoughts pass through a reception of three stages. At first people say, "That's the silliest thing I've ever heard, it's harmless romanticism, it will never work." If it begins to take effect, they say, "This idea will destroy civilization, we've got to stop it." And as it begins to triumph, they say, "Well, of course, I thought of this myself years ago. . . . "

In some cases, however, there are people who say, "That would be wonderful if it could work; let's act *as if* it could, and see what happens."

What matters here is not the specific idea for a day of celebration in response to the start of disarmament, during which humanity would see itself at its best. (And if such an idea turns out to be useful, it's because a hundred other people have already been half-thinking it.) The work will take thousands of forms. Think of one yourself. Share it with other people, be part of doing it.

—Craig Comstock

Prevailing in Spite of It All

After it became clear that nobody could "win" a nuclear war, military planners began to talk about "prevailing" in one. Presumably this means our country would terrify the other side into backing down the "ladder of escalation" or, at any rate, would somehow suffer less damage in the "exchange."

In his Nobel Prize address, William Faulkner responded to a widespread covert acceptance, in many circles, of the end of man. His credo was otherwise:

"I believe that man will not merely endure: he will prevail. He is immortal, not because he alone among creatures has an inexhaustible voice, but because he has a soul, a spirit capable of compassion and sacrifice and endurance. The poet's, the writer's duty is to write about these things. It is his privilege to help man endure by lifting his heart, by reminding him of the courage and honor and hope and pride and compassion and pity and sacrifice which have been the glory of his past."

When Faulkner says that man will prevail, he has something less radioactive in mind than the military planners. We believe it is the duty not only of poets and editors to write about the qualities that Faulker praises, but of all of us, as citizens, to reclaim this heritage. In this book we have simply tried to mark out a few of the many pathways up to the summits of the human spirit, summits that we could share with adversaries.

—The Editors

Acknowledgements

It was Don Carlson who, despite the pressures of an intense business life, noticed that most "peace books" have actually been anti-war books, often dependent upon arousing fear rather than encouraging hope. He asked the crucial question, "What's being done or proposed that's productive but not yet widely known or fully employed?" He imagined a positive book that would include and stimulate images of a peaceful world. While Carlson provided financial support to the project through the Ark Communications Institute, his more remarkable contribution has been asking the right questions. He also came up with the idea of running quotations alongside the text of *Citizen Summitry*, gathered hundreds of brief passages from his reading, and worked closely with me in the final editing.

It was my role to develop this approach into the particulars of a book project by creating an editorial structure that would express our vision, exploring available material (both published and newly written) and selecting the best of it, commissioning other papers, finding people to help with the project, editing the texts, and writing the introductions to the various sections and chapters.

What started as a single book grew and eventually became two—*Citizen Summitry* and *Securing Our Planet*. Of this pair, the first deals with communication, people-to-people exchanges, self-transformation, and the envisioning of alternative futures; the second, with particular steps that can be taken to create a less dangerous, more satisfying world. Both volumes are published in the U.S. by Jeremy P. Tarcher, Inc. of Los Angeles and distributed to the book trade by St. Martin's Press of New York.

In editing the two books, Carlson and I received advice from friends, colleagues, and experts too numerous to list, including many of the contributors and others active in the field, whether in government, academic life, business, the media, or public interest organizations. To give only a single example, both of us have benefited by involvement in Business Executives for National Security (BENS), a bipartisan organization with an appeal to conservatives disturbed by

Federal deficits attributable to military spending, liberals worried about the arms race that is sustained by that spending, and military reformers (such as Gary Hart) who believe there's nothing more dangerous than a "defense" establishment that's not only costly and provocative but arguably ineffective.

For advice and specific leads, Carlson and I turned above all to Gordon Feller, an Ark colleague who is well-informed about the field. (Some of his knowledge is now available in *Taking the Next Steps*, a succinct guide to resources, described below in "Other Ark Products.") In obtaining the Soviet contribution to *Citizen Summitry*, we had the assistance of Joel Schatz, a citizen diplomat who created an experimental computer network between the U.S. and the Soviet Union. (Schatz has a chapter in *Citizen Summitry*, and Feller in *Securing Our Planet*.) At the start of this project Elaine Ratner assisted with research, and at the end Matt Chanoff edited the introductions and Mary Dresser helped with the flow of material. Linda Lazarre made a number of contributions, including the Ark logo. Dick Schuettge supervised production. Type was set by Classic Typography of Ukiah, California, under the eye of Stan Shoptaugh. Quickly grasping our intent in editing these books, Jeremy Tarcher offered his full support in publishing them.

For illustrations, we thank Dave Bohn for the photograph of a tree that opens section 4, NASA for the photograph of the Apollo-Soyuz hookup, Tobey Sanford for the photograph of Soviet and American fishermen, Diane Schatz for her ink drawing of a space-bridge which opens section 3, Diane and Joel Schatz for the "Peace Trek" image, details of which are shown in section 5, Joel Schatz for the photographs of Soviet people which appear in his chapter, "Through the Eyes of a Citizen Diplomat," and one of which opens section 2, and Norman Ung for his design which opens section 1.

Thanks to all of you for your commitment and your articulate energy.

—*Craig Comstock*

388

The editors gratefully acknowledge the following publishers and authors for permission to reprint the following material:

GOING BEYOND WAR

"What Is It About?" by Thomas Powers: from *Atlantic Monthly*, January 1984. By permission of the author.

"A Longing for Something Better" by Norman Cousins: excerpted from *Human Options*, published by W. W. Norton & Co., Inc. © 1981. By permission of the author.

"A Better Game Than War" by Robert Fuller: adapted from *Evolutionary Blues*, volume 2, published by Ten Directions Foundation. © 1983. By permission of the author.

GETTING TO KNOW THE OTHER SIDE

"Letter to a Russian" by Larry Levinger: from *New Age Journal*, July 1984. Reprinted by permission of *New Age Journal* and the author. © 1984. All rights reserved (*NAJ*, 342 Western Ave., Brighton, MA 02135).

"Meeting the Soviets Face-to-face" by Craig Staats and Jennifer Donovan: adapted from "To Russia with an Open Mind" by Craig Staats, *Oakland Tribune*, January 23, 1984. By permission of *Oakland Tribune*. "Meeting the Soviets Face to Face" by Jennifer Donovan, *San Francisco Chronicle*, February 19, 1985. Reprinted by permission of the publishers.

TRANSFORMING OUR CONSCIOUSNESS

"A Positive Vision in a Cynical Age" by Michael Nagler: originally published as "Redefining Peace" in *The Bulletin of the Atomic Scientists*, November 1984. Reprinted by permission of *The Bulletin of the Atomic Scientists*, a magazine of science and world affairs. Copyright © 1984 by the Educational Foundation for Nuclear Science.

"Switching on the Light" by Marilyn Ferguson: from *The Aquarian Conspiracy* by Marilyn Ferguson. Copyright © 1980. Reprinted by permission of the publisher, Jeremy P. Tarcher, Inc.

"Nuclear Weapons and the Expansion of Consciousness" by Willis W. Harman: adapted from "Consciousness Research and Nuclear War," *Institute of Noetic Sciences Newsletter*, Spring 1984. By permission of the author.

JUMPING AHEAD AND LOOKING BACK AT THE FUTURE

The following chapters were written for (or appear as a whole for the first time in) *Citizen Summitry*:

"Danger and Opportunity" by Don Carlson

"Through the Eyes of a Citizen Diplomat" by Joel Schatz

"Effectiveness of the New Diplomats" by Michael H. Shuman and Gale Warner

"Space-Bridge Pioneers" by Jim Garrison, David Landau, and Ralph Macdonald

"Building a Space-Bridge: a Soviet Contribution" (the entire section consisting of six chapters and several brief comments)

"As in Health, So in Peace" by Fritjof Capra

"Spinning Peace Scenarios" by Mark Sommer

"Acting Globally Through Your Locality" by Michael H. Shuman

"The Great Turning" by Craig Schindler and Toby Herzlich

creating an ark
as big as the earth

A Word About Ark

When the flood came, Noah was able to save a remnant of life by taking it aboard his ark. Today, facing the possibility of nuclear war, we need to create an imaginary ark as big as the earth itself. Safety lies not in trying to find a refuge, but only in preventing a general catastrophe. In order to avoid war, we need to become global citizens— not in place of our loyalties to an organization, an ethnic group, a religion, or a homeland, but in addition to them. To the extent that we build in our minds an ark to encompass the earth, we can not only prevent disaster but enlarge the possibilities of life.

In this spirit, Don Carlson, a successful entrepreneur, founded Ark Communications Institute in 1985 as a non-profit operating foundation. Ark shares the goal of some "anti-war" groups, but differs in at least two ways from most of them. While respecting the need to oppose evils, we put most of our energy into developing positive alternatives. And while treasuring much of what is usually meant by "peace," we accept conflict as part of being alive, believing that, like anything else, it can be handled destructively or creatively. We see the energies that are sometimes expressed in conflict as a resource, like fire, to be employed. Society does not try to "ban" fire or put it out wherever it's found; we put it to work in furnaces, stoves, boilers, and engines.

In dealing with conflict between two sides, Ark tries to look for common ground, not in the sense of a lowest common denominator, but of a third way, perhaps in the form of a shared task. While aware of the prolonged attempts to deal with many destructive conflicts, we also often feel that almost nothing has been tried.

As Einstein once observed, many problems can be dealt with only by shifting to a new level. On this new level, people can often communicate in ways that were formerly blocked. To us, communication has many senses. We have begun using high technology to link people in the two superpowers and to link Americans working for a better world. In addition to books, we are interested in using mass media to show visions of enemies becoming adversaries—a word that President Kennedy was careful to use—adversaries becoming rivals, rivals becoming competitors, and competitors possibly becoming partners.

We are developing methods to help people think and communicate on more levels than they ordinarily do. We take a deep interest in the connection between inner growth and political change, believing that neither can reach its full potential without the other. For this reason, we are exploring methods for each of us to find inner peace by getting in touch with neglected or formerly inaccessible parts of ourselves.

Our research thus ranges from inner development to international relations. One day we are creating a "game" in which widely diverse and quarreling participants imagine a positive future; on the next, investigating alpha wave biofeedback equipment, and on the third day, planning a trip for citizen diplomats to the Soviet Union.

In our first year, Ark has sponsored this book and a companion volume, edited by two of the principals in the institute; helped to create a computer link and the potential for slow-scan TV space-bridges between the U.S. and the Soviet Union; produced a series of radio documentaries starting with "Beyond the Boundaries" and "A Better Game Than War"; served as creative consultants for a major TV show; set up meetings between government officials and influential citizens in the area of arms control; consulted with think-tanks on public policy; helped to create "Peace Net," a data base and electronic mail system; and sent our staff to speak at a wide variety of conferences and forums.

As a non-profit operating foundation, we sponsor our own programs rather than giving grants to others. These programs include products such as this book, the sale of which helps sustain our broader work. An affiliated entity, the Ark Foundation, makes small grants to related programs conducted by outside organizations and individuals.

One way to keep in touch with the range of activities in which we take an interest is through *Global Partners*, our newsletter. To receive a free sample copy, please send us a stamped business-size envelope addressed to you, or simply request a copy when ordering any of Ark's products described below. Our address is Ark Communications Institute, 250 Lafayette Circle, Lafayette, CA 94549.

Other Ark Products

In addition to this book, *Citizen Summitry* (price, $10.95), the following items are available through the Ark Communications Institute:

1. *Securing Our Planet: How to Succeed When Threats Are Too Risky and There's Really No Defense*, a companion to this volume, also edited by Don Carlson and Craig Comstock and published in the U.S. by Jeremy P. Tarcher, Inc./St. Martin's Press, 1986 (price, $10.95). A complete table of contents for this book appears below.* Order SECURING OUR PLANET.

2. A 60-minute audio cassette containing two professionally produced half-hour radio programs, "Beyond the Boundaries" and "A Better Game Than War," both of which consist of further thoughts from contributors to *Citizen Summitry* and *Securing Our Planet* (price of the cassette together with a transcript of it, $9.95). Order AUDIO CASSETTE.

3. *Taking the Next Steps*, by Gordon Feller: a succinct guide to the most useful resources for readers who want to explore further (and to act upon) ideas contained in the Ark Communications Institute books (price, $2.95). Order TAKING NEXT STEPS.

4. *Peace Trek*, a "family coloring book," 42 pages in large format, answering the question, "What would the world look like if peace broke out?" (price, $5.95). Details from the art appear in *Citizen Summitry* as illustrations to the chapter by Elise Boulding. *Peace Trek* has been called "interesting, beautiful and effective" (Linus Pauling, Nobel Laureate), and "a wonderful tool to help families explore practical options for waging peace" (Gerald G. Jampolsky, M.D.). Order PEACE TREK.

Citizen Summitry and Securing Our Planet are available from your bookseller, and Peace Trek from selected stores that sell items for children. Or you may order any of the books, as well as the audio cassette, direct from:

Ark Communications Institute
250 Lafayette Circle
Lafayette, California 94549

Please specify the items you want and the quantity for each, print your address, and enclose a check or money order for the total price (with appropriate sales tax for California residents), plus $1 per order for handling. Allow 4–8 weeks for delivery.

*Table of contents for the companion volume:

Securing Our Planet:

Breaking the Trance—*Don Carlson*

Section 1: Setting Positive Mutual Examples

The Way GRIT Works—*Charles Osgood*
A Strategy of Peace—*John F. Kennedy*
The Kennedy Experiment—*Amatai Etzioni*
The Next Initiatives—*Harold Willens*
Getting to Yes—*Roger Fisher, William Ury*

Section 2: Developing Institutions That Favor Peace

The Moral Equivalent of War—*William James*
All the Skills Necessary—*John F. Kennedy*
Proposal for a World Peace Corps—*Robert Fuller*
The First Earth Battalion—*Jim Channon*
Peace-Keeping Forces—*Donald Keys*

Section 3: Redefining the Role of Business

Farewell Address—*Dwight D. Eisenhower*
Eisenhower's Legacy—*Thomas J. Watson, Jr.*
Technology and Freedom—*Regis McKenna*
The Trimtab Factor—*Harold Willens*
Security and the Bottom Line—*Don Carlson*
Being Dead Is Bad for Business—*Lucien Rhodes*

Section 4: Shifting to a Global Peacetime Economy

The Economics of Security—*William Greider*

The Impact of Trade on Soviet Society—
Cyril E. Black, Robbin F. Laird

Joint Ventures with the Eastern Bloc—*William C. Norris*

Section 5: Cooperating in Outer Space

The President's Choice—
*McGeorge Bundy, George F. Kennan,
Robert S. McNamara, Gerard Smith*

Star Wars and the State of Our Souls—
Patricia M. Mische

Speech in Search of a Statesman Capable of Delivering It—
Howard Kurtz

Everybody's Satellites—*Arthur C. Clarke*

The Age of Transparency—*Kevin Sanders*

Unlocking Space—*Daniel Deudney*

Section 6: Finding Effective Lower-Risk Means of Defense

The Delhi Declaration—*Five Continent Peace Initiative*

Deep Cuts—*George F. Kennan*

I Cut, You Choose—*Stephen H. Salter*

David and Goliath—*Freeman Dyson*

Alternative Security Systems—*Mark Sommer*

Non-Military Means of Defense—*Gene Sharp*

Section 7: Moving Toward the World We Want

Lessons of the Nuclear Freeze Initiative—
Gordon Feller, Mark Sommer

A Step-by-Step Approach—*Randall Forsberg*

Seven Planks for a Platform—*Kenneth Boulding*

To Gain a Peace in the Nuclear Age—*Roger Fisher*

All introductions are by Craig Comstock